D0498601

The Zeronauts

A world of nine billion people by mid-century will demand fundamental changes in our mindsets, behaviors, cultures, and overarching paradigm. Just as our species broke the Sound Barrier during the 1940s and 1950s, a new breed of innovator, entrepreneur, and investor is lining up to break the Sustainability Barrier.

In this book, John Elkington introduces the Zeronauts – a new breed of innovator, determined to drive problems such as carbon, waste, toxics, and poverty to zero – as well as creating the first Zeronaut Roll of Honor, spotlighting 50 pioneers in the field of zero. Zeronauts are innovating in an astonishing range of areas, tackling hugely diverse economic, social, environmental, and governance challenges. To give a sense of progress to date, we zero in on five key challenges (the 5Ps): population growth, pandemics, poverty, pollution, and proliferation.

The power of zero has been trumpeted, notably in relation to zero defects. This book spotlights key lessons learned in the field of total quality management – and introduces a five-stage "Pathways to Zero" model, running through from the Eureka! discovery moment to the point where a new way of doing things becomes endemic in the economy.

In order to move from incremental to transformative change, we must embrace wider framings, deeper insights, higher targets, and longer time scales. This book investigates some ways in which leading Zeronauts are pushing change in relevant directions, with cases drawn from a spectrum of human activity – from water profligacy to human genital mutilation. If we learn from these pioneers, the twenty-first century could be our best yet.

John Elkington has been a leader in the environmental and sustainability movements since the early 1970s. He has cofounded three companies: Environmental Data Services (ENDS) in 1978, SustainAbility in 1987, and Volans in 2008. All three still push the boundaries. He has published 17 previous books, including the number one bestseller *The Green Consumer Guide*.

The Zeronauts
Breaking the Sustainability Barrier

John Elkington

Routledge
Taylor & Francis Group

LONDON AND NEW YORK

First published 2012
by Routledge
2 Park Square, Milton Park, Abingdon, Oxon OX14 4RN

Simultaneously published in the USA and Canada
by Routledge
711 Third Avenue, New York, NY 10017

Routledge is an imprint of the Taylor & Francis Group, an informa business

British Library Cataloguing in Publication Data
A catalogue record for this book is available from the British Library

Library of Congress Cataloging in Publication Data
Elkington, John, 1949–
The zeronauts : breaking the sustainability barrier/ John Elkington.
p. cm.
Includes bibliographical references and index.
1. Technological innovations–Environmental aspects. 2. Sustainable development.
3. Entrepreneurship. I. Title.
HD30.255.E453 2012
338.9′27–dc23
2011043778

ISBN: 978-1-84971-397-9 (hbk)
ISBN: 978-0-203-12135-1 (ebk)

Typeset in 10pt on 13pt Frutiger LT Std
by Saxon Graphics Ltd, Derby

Printed and bound in Great Britain by the MPG Books Group

In memory of Ray Anderson (01934–02011)[1]
Radical Industrialist, Early Zeronaut

零
LING

In the end, beginnings

An old order is ending, new ones beginning. What follows is a thought experiment. In arguing that zero is our future, Zeronauts act in the same way as the Zen masters who use a <u>koan</u> to jolt other people into a different state of awareness, to open their minds to new possibilities. A case in point: the Long Now Foundation sticks a zero in front of the year — e.g. 02012 — to help us expand our time horizons.

"If you look at zero you see nothing", Robert Kaplan wrote in <u>The Nothing that Is</u>, subtitled "A natural history of zero". "But look through it", he continued, "and you see the world".[2]

And the Chinese character above? LING. Another mind expander. Its meaning is context specific, evolving over time; but it stands for "zero". Serendipitously, other possible meanings include "an end" and "a beginning", "starting from scratch" and "new horizons".

Link this with the immense potential impact of China upon our common future, for good or ill, and <u>ling</u> looks like a useful starting point for a global conversation on how we can radically shrink our environmental footprints — and help a better future take flight.[3]

To track — and support — our work, please visit www.zeronauts.com.

零
LING

Contents

Executive Summary

the future. We introduce the first Zeronaut Roll of Honor, spotlighting 50 pioneers – referring out to coverage elsewhere in the book.

II   CRACKING THE 1-EARTH CODE

4   Turbulent Teens: Our Detox Decade

The decade to 2020 is set to be our Detox Decade, in which we are forced to abandon unsustainable mindsets, behaviors, and valuation models. Three scenarios are presented: breakdown, change as usual, and breakthrough. We dig into five key domains (the 5Cs) where innovation is taking place: citizens, corporations, cities, countries, and, ultimately, our civilization.

III   BREAKING THROUGH

5   The Race to Zero

The power of zero has been trumpeted in various areas of business, notably in relation to zero defects. Here we look at lessons learned in the field of total quality management – and introduce a five-stage "Pathways to Zero" model, running through from the Eureka! discovery moment to the point where a new way of doing things becomes endemic in the economy.

6   Zeronautics 101

Five stepping-stones take transformative change agents from their breakthrough insight to the point where their impact is so evident that it is increasingly taken for granted. Introducing the emerging discipline of Zeronautics, we move through the five stages (the 5Es): Eureka!, experimentation, enterprise, ecosystems, and economy.

7   It's the System that's Stupid

Zeronauts are innovating in an astonishing range of areas, tackling hugely diverse economic, social, environmental, and governance challenges. To give a sense of progress to date, we zero in on five key challenges (the 5Ps): population growth, pandemics, poverty, pollution, and WMD proliferation.

IV   BEYOND ZERO

8   Ambassadors from the Future

In order to move from incremental to transformative change, we must embrace wider framings, deeper insights, higher targets, and longer time scales. We investigate some ways in which leading Zeronauts are pushing change in relevant directions, with cases drawn from a spectrum of human activity – from water profligacy to human genital mutilation. If we learn from these pioneers, the twenty-first century could be our best yet.

9   The Zero Countdown – and Beyond

So, to cut to the chase, what should your board, C-suite, or senior management group do to manage risks – and seize opportunities – created by the Zeronaut agenda? Here are some starter questions that you can pose to your team or wider organization.

List of Figures, Tables, and Boxes

Figures

Tables

Boxes

ZERONAUT, *n.* 1. An inventor, innovator, entrepreneur, intrapreneur, investor, manager, or educator who promotes wealth creation while driving adverse environmental, social, and economic impacts toward zero. 2. Someone who finds, investigates, and develops breakthrough, footprint-shrinking solutions for the growing tensions between demography, consumerist lifestyles, and sustainability. 3. Political leader or policy-maker who helps to create the regulatory frameworks and incentives needed to drive related "1-Earth" solutions to scale. 4. For some current examples, see Box 3.1 (pp.44–6) for the first "Zeronaut 50" Roll of Honor.

Foreword

The genesis of the book

It's not every day that a genius, in the shape of your country's poet laureate, writes a poem based on your latest book[4] – and then publishes said poem in one of the nation's main newspapers. But that's what happened to me in 01987, when Ted Hughes wrote a poem for *The Times* called "Lobby from Under the Carpet". His muse, he said, had just read my book *The Poisoned Womb*, republished as a Pelican paperback the previous year – "I thought her heart would break", he reported. So the man of letters had swung into action: "I sent a copy to Maggie: 'O Maggie, Read Elkington, and awake!'"

God only knows what Margaret Thatcher made of it all, particularly the poet laureate's deliberate dropping of a full stop and a comma at one point in the poem to symbolize the threatened extinction of human egg and sperm.

I only met Mrs. T once – she was having one of those days where she was in Louis XIV ("Sun King") mode. Her perfume clung around for so long on the hand with which I had shaken hers that I wondered if that handshake alone had cost the natural world several pods of spermaceti-rich whales.

But while the encounter underscored the perpetual challenge of engaging our leaders on issues they see as marginal to the task of winning the next election, or keeping shareholders happy, this exchange between poet laureate and prime minister spotlights some of the unlikely channels through which culture change can sometimes flow.

And the basic point had been made. Politicians, governments, and what used to be called the "captains of industry" ignore what we would now call the sustainability agenda at their peril, and ours. To be honest, even at the time I didn't think that this was one of Hughes's great poems. But it had a certain muscular, edgy energy. Its last verse ended:

Outside the door of Number Ten,
While the whole building's a-quake,
With every bankrupt Industry
Bawling: "Awake! Awake!"

Looking back, my own awakening, my personal road to zero, has been long, winding, and often instinctively followed rather than planned. It began when I found myself in a pitch-dark field in Northern Ireland in the mid-01950s, as a child of six or seven, with no moon, as a vast, invisible sheet of elvers – young eels – squirmed every which way around my ankles. After a moment of panic, I experienced a sense of intense connection (I knew about the distant Sargasso Sea where these creatures were eventually headed) that has never left me.

The process continued in fits and starts as the family uprooted to Cyprus. Then when I was 11, and away at prep school in England, I found myself one day standing in front of all the boys and asking for – and getting – their pocket money for two weeks as a contribution to the infant World Wide Fund for Nature (WWF), founded that year.

For years, I had no idea of what had come over me, a shy child with no appetite whatever for public speaking. Then one day, in the late 01970s, I was driving down to WWF's Godalming headquarters with one of the organization's founders, the late, great Max Nicholson, with whom I had recently cofounded Environmental Data Services (ENDS). He asked me how I had got started in the field and I told him the story, commenting that I had no idea how it had happened. He promptly said he did know.

How could he possibly, I wondered? He recalled WWF had got a major splash in a major newspaper to announce their launch – and as soon as he said that I recalled walking into the school library, devouring the newspaper on a reading stand, and impetuously deciding I had to do something.

Later, over many decades, I have somehow found myself repeatedly in more or less the right place at more or less the right time as the environmental and sustainability movements evolved. As an entrepreneur, for example, I have been immensely privileged to be involved in cofounding three companies, all still advancing the cause at the time of writing.

The first two were ENDS, which we launched with the late David Layton in 01978, which helped to open up business to wider discussions around safety, health, environment, and, later, sustainability, and then SustainAbility itself, launched in 01987, which has helped to open up corporate boards and C-suites worldwide to the sustainable development agenda. In 02008, I went on to cofound Volans Ventures, to help disruptive innovators and entrepreneurs to do more, better, faster.

As to where zero first came in, I had been aware of the world of people like Ray Anderson and Gunter Pauli for a long time. Next, in 02000, a good friend and colleague, Andrea Spencer-Cooke, wrote a profile of Paul Tebo, then at DuPont, for the now defunct *Tomorrow* magazine, entitled "Hero of Zero".[5] And in 02004, I had been involved in the Zero Waste initiative (see p.248) launched by the Royal Society of Arts (RSA) as part of its 250th anniversary celebrations.[6]

But the first time that zero really seized control of my mind was when the newly formed Volans team was brainstorming for a proposal to an embryonic global foundation, which in the end lost its ability to fund as the Great Recession bit into the finances of its Dubai-based backers. At a fairly late stage in the day, working onto enormous blank panels under the direction of David Christie of the Value Web and Innovation Arts, I wrote – graffiti style and tongue in cheek – **I ♥ ZERO**.

These days, that ♥ symbol is wildly over-commercialized; but I knew that the symbolism of the other component – zero – has also been extremely powerful through history. In Mayan culture, for example, the symbol for zero was a spiral. And that resonated: for many years I had been besotted with spirals, even integrating one into a long-running SustainAbility logo, which counterpointed a trigram (representing balance across multiple dimensions of value) with a spiral (creativity, imagination, innovation, and evolution).

Definitions

ZE•RO/'zi(ə)rō/

Verb: Adjust or drive to ZERO.

Number: No quantity or number; naught/nought; the figure 0.

Targets: These can be expressed as "zero carbon", "zero waste", or "zero whatever", but may also appear in different forms – for example, "100 percent" renewables (means zero fossil fuels, zero nuclear) or "nuclear free". In some cases, zero may be misleading, as in "zero emissions" for an electric vehicle, which ignores the emissions produced in generating the electricity used by the vehicle. At worst, this can involve "zero-washing", in which zero-based targets are used to mask poor performance in other areas.

Zeronauts: See pp.249–51 for definitions – and Box 3.1, pp.44–6, for a listing of 50 pioneers in the field.

If you want to get a sense of the history of the evolution of zero, track down a copy of Charles Seife's wonderful book *Zero: The Biography of a Dangerous Idea*.[7] Zero and infinity turn out to be intimately linked. It is fascinating to learn, too, that the West fought hard to deny zero for two millennia – even burning people at the stake for daring to promote its use.

These days there is no need to take your life in your hands to argue the case for zero, though there are those who energetically argue that it is a fool's errand. Several years back, I co-authored *The Power of Unreasonable People*, with Pamela Hartigan,[8] and it strikes me that the Zeronauts introduced in the following pages are about as unreasonable as innovators and entrepreneurs come. They are calling for a new economic order that is virtually inconceivable for today's business leaders, even those who have publicly embraced the sustainability agenda.

My growing interest in what my Zero Hub colleague Ralph Thurm has dubbed "zero impact growth" does not reflect a desire to bring the global economy to a halt, though it sometimes seems that it will achieve that trick on its own (for more on the Zero Hub, see pp.12–13). Instead, it flows from a deeply felt need to help spur the sort of breakthrough innovation now needed to help us break what I have dubbed the Sustainability Barrier.

There has been much discussion of the possibility of decoupling our economies from their adverse environmental impacts; but there has also been a growing sense that the prospects for decoupling are overrated. As we will see in the Introduction, some respected analysts argue that we will need an almost inconceivable 130-fold reduction in our environmental footprints to achieve anything like sustainability during this century.

When I trailed this message in Singapore, at events organized by the Singapore International Foundation, the Family Business Network and the National University of Singapore, I used a slide I had been given a week or so earlier by Peter Boyd, COO of the Carbon War Room. This spotlighted the need, if we are to stabilize our climate, to go in the coming decades from 768 grams of carbon per dollar of economic output to just six grams. There were gasps of astonishment from the audiences.

But, some argue, and I will come back to this in Chapter 9, written on the same trip to Hong Kong and Singapore, that we need to go beyond zero, to technologies and business models that are regenerative – that, for example, actively suck carbon out of the atmosphere.

And my role in all of this? Routinely, I am asked to explain what exactly it is that I do? I find the question almost impossible to answer. Sometimes I deflect the interrogator by saying that I am the modern version of the Fool, whose job it was to speak truth to power in medieval courts. In the Tarot deck, I now discover, the Fool was the only unnumbered card. Indeed, it was sometimes numbered as "0" (zero, nought) and could play high or low. Also known as the Jester, this character displayed "crazy wisdom" – and could get away with saying things others could not.

The appearance of the Fool, standing on the lip of the precipice, seemingly unconcerned about stepping out into the void, was taken as a signal that significant change was coming. And that is often where I seem to operate – as recently when I helped facilitate a three-day session in which a number of international sportswear brands and Greenpeace came together to discuss the potential for driving toxics in supply chains, particularly in China, to zero (see pp.227–8).

Some people got zero – but a fair few didn't.

The aim of what follows is to grow the size of the first group (which in the sportswear case began to talk of launching a "Race to Zero") and shrink the size of the second. That's what we set up Volans to do – and I warmly thank my colleagues both there and at SustainAbility for their support during the genesis and development of *The Zeronauts*. As the book has evolved, it has shown every sign of switching from a project to a program. For details, please visit www.zeronauts.com.

Soon, I believe, the skeptics will have little choice in the matter. A new reality is pressing in. We are moving into a new geological era, the so-called Anthropocene, increasingly defined by what we do as a species. True, most geologists still think that we are living in the Holocene era; but in 2000 Paul Crutzen, an eminent atmospheric chemist, realized he no longer believed that. As *The Economist* has put it: "He was living in some other age, one shaped primarily by people. From their trawlers scraping the floors of the seas to their dams impounding sediment by the gigatonne, from their stripping of forests to their irrigation of farms, from their mile-deep mines to their melting of glaciers, humans were bringing about an age of planetary change. With a colleague, Eugene Stoermer, Dr Crutzen suggested this age be called the Anthropocene – 'the recent age of man'."[9]

In the midst of all of this, I – and the many organizations with which I am associated – have worked with a fair number of the companies mentioned in the following pages, in one way or another. Rather than calling out the associations in each case, except where it fits in with the story, I encourage anyone interested in testing for potential conflicts of interest to visit our websites. See also the Acknowledgements section, which spotlights some of my debts to those who have helped in this stage of my journey – notable among them the Rockefeller Foundation, for the Bellagio Fellowship that enabled me to write a couple of key sections of the book.

That said, both SustainAbility and Volans have been unusually transparent in this area – and, on occasion, we have publicly resigned clients when we judged progress too slow. In future, one key criterion I aim to apply to companies I work with is whether they are at least prepared to play with the idea of zero impact (or zero footprint) growth. Any of us who recalls being a child knows that we can learn a lot from play. Over time, however, that criterion must harden, increasingly requiring the business and public-sector leaders with whom we work to embrace – and then effectively deliver against – the Zeronaut agenda.

Acknowledgements

When was I infected by the Zero Meme? To be honest, I can't remember – but I do recall that in 02002 *Godert van Hardenbroek* – cofounder of Formula Zero in 02003 – handed me an image he had developed of a hydrogen-fueled Formula 1 racing car, dressed up in Greenpeace colors and emblazoned with "Formula Zero". It was imaginary, but I used it for several years afterwards in slide presentations. Godert's subsequent adventures are described on pp.135–41.

Even earlier, a 02000 article by my friend and colleague *Andrea Spencer-Cooke* was also definitely part of the process. She wrote about *Paul Tebo* of DuPont as a "Hero of Zero". But while I can't pin down when the idea took root, I do know when it started to blossom, or at least bud: during a Volans brainstorming session facilitated by Innovation Arts and the Value Web, in August 02009.[10] And for that I thank *David Christie*, together with *Patrick Frick*, who first introduced me to him.

The zero line of thought was further nurtured during an extended brunch with *Paul Hawken* early in 02011. His work has long been a beacon for those of us lost in thick fog and ferocious counter-currents. The thought train was clearly accelerated decades earlier by the work of some early Zeronauts whom I was lucky enough to meet, among them *Buckminster Fuller* and *Ray Anderson*, both now sadly gone – but both of whom had a considerable influence on my thinking.

Science fiction author *Frank Herbert*, whom I met several years before he died, also had an important impact, through his *Dune* series of novels and his environmentalism. But zero shot to the surface again when *Nick Bellorini*, then with Earthscan, asked me in 02010 whether I had any ideas for a new book? *The Zeronauts* started to gel – and I thank Nick, *Gudrun Freese* and *Veruschka Selbach* of Earthscan, and *Louisa Earls*, *Emma Hudson*, *Charlotte Russell*, *Christine James*, and *Andrea Service* of Taylor & Francis for taking on the book.

Thanks, too, to my agents in New York, *Doris Michaels* and *Delia Berrigan Fakis*, and to my long-standing friend and colleague *Rupert Bassett* – who helped me to think through the design side of the book and linked website (www.zeronauts.com) as well as producing the book's illustrations.

At Volans, founded as what some would call a Serendipity Engine,[11] I simply cannot say how much I have appreciated the company and support of our growing band of Volanders, notably *Tim Barrow-Williams*, *Amy Birchall*, *Amanda Feldman*, *Pamela Hartigan*, *Elliot Jackson*, *Sam Lakha*, *Jacqueline Lim*, *Alejandro Litovsky* (who played a critical role in evolving the "Pathways to Scale" model while at Volans; then went on to found the Earth Security Initiative), *Charmian Love*, *Geoff Lye*, *Nadine Mendelbaum*, *Jonny Mallinson*, *Rafael Morais Chiaravalloti* (and *Claudio Padua* who sent Rafael our way), *Rosie Reeve*, *Astrid Sandoval*, *Smita Sircar*, *Allen Tan*, *Kevin Teo*, *Soushiant Zanganehpour* (who helped substantially with the research for the 5Ps sections), and *Zheng Jieying*. Particular thanks here go to Sam and Geoff (who facilitated the latest phase of my learning journey) and to Charmian, as CEO, for helping Volans hold its course through the turbulent early stages of our evolution.

At our sister company, SustainAbility, which I cofounded in 01987, I spotlight and thank my "Zero Scouts": *Jennifer Biringer*, *Kyra Choucroun*, *Jeff Erikson*, *Aaron Jaffe*, *Geoff Kendall*, *Geoff Lye* (again), *Michael Sadowski*, *Mo al-Shawaf* and *Patrin Watanatada*. I also offer my heartfelt thanks to my cofounder, and friend, *Julia Hailes*, and everyone else who has worked with the organization over its first 25 years.

Having written for *The Guardian* since 01978, I particularly appreciate the ongoing partnership with their Sustainable Business team, where I thank *Jo Confino*, *Caroline Holtum*, and *Jenny Purt*. I have drawn on some of the weekly blogs there in *The Zeronauts* – though the flow often went the other way, too.

In retrospect, an absolutely critical stage in the evolution of my own thinking was the award of a three-year grant in 02006 by the Skoll Foundation – and I am eternally grateful to *Sally Osberg* and *Jeff Skoll* for their support, and more broadly for what they have done to drive the development of the crucial fields of social innovation and entrepreneurship.

A key stepping-stone in that direction was the seven-year period I spent working alongside the Schwab Foundation and World Economic Forum, for which I warmly thank *Klaus Schwab* and *Pamela Hartigan*. And I would also like to thank *Jonathan Kua* and his team at Singapore's Economic Development Board (EDB) for their invaluable support in the early days of Volans.

A further huge surprise came in the form of a Bellagio Fellowship from the Rockefeller Foundation, which provided an unbelievably timely opportunity to write a key section of the book during April and May of 02011 at the sublime Bellagio Centre on Lake Como, Italy. I thank *Jane Nelson* hugely for the nomination, *Robert Garris* (managing director, Bellagio Programs) for his support, and *Pilar Palaciá* (managing director, Bellagio Center) and her team for their extraordinary hospitality in Bellagio.

It was also an immense privilege in 02008 to find myself alongside pioneers such as Herman Miller, Seventh Generation and Shorebank (a pioneer now sadly no longer with us) when receiving a Social Capitalist Award from one of my favorite magazines: *Fast Company*.[12] This award, however, underscored the fact that all of the organizations I have cofounded have been for-profit, social mission businesses, which has made the support from foundations such as Skoll, Rockefeller and Tellus Mater (where I thank *James Arbib*, *Kelly Clark*, and *Jessica Brown*) so remarkable.

Once the book was under way, I heard that I had been awarded the American Society for Quality's Spencer Hutchens Medal in 02010, for social responsibility and innovation, which spurred the development of Chapters 4 and 5. At ASQ, I thank *Dorothy Bowers* for the original nomination, together with *Paul Borawski*, *Ron Kingen*, *John Knappenberger*, and *Michelle Mason*. Someone whom I met during the ASQ event in San Francisco early in 02011 was *Daniel Aronson* of Deloitte Innovation, whom I thank (alongside *Ron Kingen*) for very helpful inputs on drafts of Chapters 4 and 5.

Various projects were cranking through at the same time that I was writing *The Zeronauts*, with sometimes fairly intense feedback between the parallel and braiding streams of thinking and work. In this area I thank *Ralph Thurm* and his colleagues at Deloitte Innovation in The Netherlands for their partnership in developing the Zero Hub initiative; *Alastair Morton* of JWT; *Elspeth Finch* and *Nick Roberts* of Atkins; *Neil Hawkins* and *Mark Weick* of The Dow Chemical Company; *Chris West* and *Clare Woodcraft* of the Shell Foundation; and *John Furey* of MindTime Technologies for their support on our latest report, *The Future Quotient*; and, at Nike, *John Frazier*, *Santiago Gowland*, *Sarah Severn*, and *Hannah Jones* for our evolving partnership around the Race to Zero/Zero Discharge of Toxic Chemicals Initiative.

In addition to those already mentioned, I have drawn in infinitely various ways on an immense network of colleagues and friends. I am particularly grateful here to: *David Blood*, *Colin Le Duc*, and *Al Gore*, Generation Investment Management; *Peter Boyd*, Carbon War Room; *Robert C. (Bob) Buck*, DuPont; *Ron Dembo*, Zerofootprint; *Stephanie Draper*, Forum for the Future; *Maria Eitel*, Nike Foundation; *Karin Ekberg*, adidas; *Linda Fisher*, DuPont; *Gil Friend*, Natural Logic; *Claude Fussler*; *Paul Gilding*; *Tony Gourlay*, Global Initiatives; *David Grayson*, Doughty Centre for Social Responsibility, Cranfield University; *Ellen Gustafson*, 30 Project; *Felicity Hartnett*, London Olympic & Paralympics Games; *Peter Head*, Arup and Ecological Sequestration Trust; *David Hodgson*, IdeaHive; *Alex Johnson*, Clownfish; *Georg Kell* and *Gavin Power*, United Nations Global Compact; *Kevin Kelly*; *John Kim*, Herman Miller; *Hugh Knowles*, Forum for the Future; *Roland Kupers*; *Francis Kyle*; *Julia Lalla-Maharajh*, Orchid Project; *Shawn Lester*, Sustainable World Capital; *Hunter Lovins*, Natural Capital Solutions; *Joel Makower*, GreenBiz; *Erin Meezan*, Interface; *Doug Miller* and *Chris Coulter*, GlobeScan; *Keith Miller*, 3M; *Ian Morris*, Stanford University; *Kumi Naidoo*, Greenpeace International; *Yasunori Naito*, *Zhanna Serdyukova*, and *Olivier Vriesendorp* of Ricoh-Europe; *Jean Oelwang*, Virgin Unite; *Nick Parker*, formerly of the Cleantech Group; *Tom Rand*, MaRS; *Jørgen Randers*, BI and Club of

Rome; *Sue Riddlestone* and *Pooran Desai*, BioRegional; *Dawn Rittenhouse*, DuPont; *Karl-Henrik Robèrt*, The Natural Step; *William Rosenzweig*, Physic Ventures; *Heerad Sabeti*, Fourth Sector; *Samer Salty*, zouk ventures; *Allan Savory*, Savory Institute; *Professor Friedrich Schmidt-Bleek*, Factor 10 Institute; *Robyn Scott*, One Leap; *Nick Sharp*, Beyond Zero Emissions; *Andrea Spencer-Cooke/Henman*, One Stone; *David Stubbs*, London Olympic & Paralympic Games; *Pavan Sukhdev*, The Economics of Ecosystems and Biodiversity (TEEB); *James Swanston*, Carbon Voyage; *Nigel Topping*, Carbon Disclosure Project; *Francesca van Dijk*, One Stone; *Mathis Wackernagel* and *Susan Burns*, Global Footprint Network; *Jan-Olaf Willums*, Inspire Invest; *Matthew Wright*, Beyond Zero Emissions; and *Jochen Zeitz*, Puma – the last of whom made some enormously helpful suggestions.

Most of the quotations and facts in the book were cross-checked with sources, but inevitably there will be errors. I would enormously appreciate comments – any unwitting errors can be changed both in later editions and, where appropriate, on our websites.

Finally, there are debts you can never repay, such as those I owe to people who helped me in the early stages of my career, among them *John Roberts* of TEST and *Max Nicholson* and *David Layton* of Environmental Data Services (ENDS), all three sadly now long gone.

But still very much here, despite my lamentable failure over decades to achieve any sort of work–life balance, are my nuclear family of *Elaine*, *Gaia* and *Hania*, plus the extended family that has swirled around Hill House, Little Rissington, since 01959, and particularly around my parents, *Pat* and *Tim*. I'm not sure that one more damned book will make any difference to their assessments of me as father, husband, son, sibling, cousin, or in-law; but it is offered as a token of respect and love, and as an illustration of the wider allegiances I have formed since my epiphany, where it really all started, in a field of eels in Northern Ireland, in the mid-01950s.

It has been a long journey, but the truly weird thing is that it feels as if it is only just beginning. Find out more at www.volans.com or at www.zeronauts.com.

List of Acronyms and Abbreviations

AIDS	acquired immune deficiency syndrome
ASEAN	Association of Southeast Asian Nations
ASQ	American Society for Quality
BCE	before common era
BEAFI	Better Environment Awards for Industry
BoP	base (or bottom) of the pyramid
BPA	bisphenol A
BRICS	Brazil, Russia, India, China, and South Africa
BZE	Beyond Zero Emissions
°C	degrees Celsius
5Cs	citizens, corporations, cities, countries, civilizations
C2C	Cradle to Cradle approach
CCI	Clinton Climate Initiative
CCS	carbon capture and storage
CDC	US Centers for Disease Control
CE	common era
CEO	chief executive officer
CFC	chlorofluorocarbon
CIA	Central Intelligence Agency
CO_2	carbon dioxide
CO_2e	carbon dioxide equivalent
COO	chief operating officer
COP	Conference of the Parties
CSR	corporate social responsibility
CTBT	Comprehensive Nuclear Test Ban Treaty
CZO	chief zero officer
DCF	discounted cash flow
DDT	dichlorodiphenyltrichloroethane
DI	Confederation of Danish Industries
DNA	deoxyribonucleic acid

5Es	Eureka!, experimentation, enterprise, ecosystem, economy
EBC	Environment Business Center
Eco-Q	ecological quotient
EDB	Economic Development Board (Singapore)
ENDS	Environmental Data Services
EPA	US Environmental Protection Agency
EPI	Environmental Performance Index
EQ	emotional quotient
EU	European Union
EV	electric vehicle
FGC	female genital cutting
FIA	Federation Internationale Automobile
FQ	future quotient
FTSE	Financial Times Stock Exchange
FZ	Formula Zero
G20	Group of Twenty
GDP	gross domestic product
GEMI	Global Environmental Management Initiative
GFN	Global Footprint Network
GHG	greenhouse gas
GPEI	Global Polio Eradication Initiative
GSA	US General Services Administration
HFC	hydrofluorocarbon
HIV	human immunodeficiency virus
ICLEI	Local Governments for Sustainability (formerly International Council for Local Environmental Initiatives)
IED	improvised explosive device
IIED	International Institute for Environment and Development
IMF	International Monetary Fund
IMO	International Maritime Organization
IOC	International Olympic Committee
InVEST	Integrated Valuation of Ecosystem Services and Trade-Offs
IQ	intelligence quotient
ISO	International Organization for Standardization
LEED	Leadership in Energy and Environmental Design
LNG	liquefied natural gas
LOCOG	London Organising Committee of the Olympic and Paralympic Games
LOHAS	lifestyles of health and sustainability
MAD	Mutually Assured Destruction strategy
MDG	Millennium Development Goal
MoD	UK Ministry of Defence
MP	member of parliament (UK)

MSW	municipal solid waste
NAFTA	North American Free Trade Agreement
NASA	National Aeronautics and Space Administration
NATO	North Atlantic Treaty Organization
NGO	non-governmental organization
NPT	Nuclear Non-Proliferation Treaty
NPV	net present value
NREL	National Renewable Energy Laboratory (USA)
OECD	Organisation for Economic Co-operation and Development
OPEC	Organization of the Petroleum Exporting Countries
3P	Pollution Prevention Pays program
5Ps	population growth, pandemics, poverty, pollution, proliferation
PBB	polybrominated biphenyl
PC	personal computer
PCB	polychlorinated biphenyl
PDA	Population and Community Development Association
PFOA	perfluorooctanoic acid
PR	public relations
PVC	polyvinyl chloride
4Rs	waste reduction, reuse, recycling, and recovery
R&D	research and development
RAF	Royal Air Force
ROIC	return on invested capital
RSA	Royal Society of Arts
SARS	severe acute respiratory syndrome
SERI	Solar Energy Research Institute
SETI	Search for Extraterrestrial Intelligence
SO_2	sulfur dioxide
SUV	sport utility vehicle
TB	tuberculosis
TBL	triple bottom line
TED	Technology Entertainment and Design conferences
TEEB	The Economics of Ecosystems and Biodiversity
Tepco	Tokyo Electric Power Company
TQEM	total quality environmental management
TQM	total quality management
UCL	University College London
UN	United Nations
VOC	volatile organic compound
WEC	World Environment Center
WEF	World Economic Forum
WHA	World Health Assembly

WHO	World Health Organization
WMD	weapons of mass destruction
WTE	waste to energy
WTO	World Trade Organization
WWF	World Wide Fund for Nature (*formerly* World Wildlife Fund)
ZD	zero defects
ZEF	Zero Environmental Footprint initiative
ZERI	Zero Emissions Research Initiative
ZPG	zero population growth

Introduction
Helping the Future Take Flight

> The Zeronauts are a new breed of innovator, determined to drive problems such as carbon, waste, toxics, and poverty to zero. On the climate front, leading sustainability champions argue the need to cut the carbon intensity of every dollar or euro earned by at least 130 times, suggesting that our economic and business models must be turned upside down, inside out.

Zero is a huge subject – and it's growing all the time. So where to begin? Here's as good a place as any. Paul Tebo didn't just take it as a sign, he took the sign. Around 01995,[1] he was looking for ways to move the giant chemical company DuPont toward a zero waste mindset. Then he stumbled upon a sign at a nearby manufacturing site that stated that **The Goal is "0"**. He took it with him when he left.[2]

Dubbed a "Hero of Zero" in 02000, as previously mentioned, he told me: "I started carrying the sign around the company to talk about the need and business value in moving toward zero injuries, illnesses, incidents (fire, explosions, accidental releases to the environment), waste and emissions, and eventually we added zero new net energy while the company grew." Tebo was an early corporate version of an extraordinary new breed of innovators, entrepreneurs, intrapreneurs, investors, and policy-makers: the Zeronauts. Later, I list him among the 50 pioneers in the first Zeronaut Roll of Honor[3] and interview him on that stage of his career.

Like the Argonauts of legend, and the Astronauts and Cosmonauts of more recent times, these people push the boundaries of the possible. In this case, they see their mission as one of driving the negative environmental and social footprints of our species toward, to, or – in a few telling cases – beyond zero. This is their story, told against the backdrop of epoch-making shifts in demography, resources, economics, and, inevitably (but not always productively), politics.

And speaking of politics, Obama, the embattled president, finally got Osama, the walled-in fugitive, literally as I was drafting this page. Then, a few days after the teetering-on-the-edge-of-chaos raid that sealed the fate of the al-Qaeda leader, a former commando commented starkly on the nature of such missions: "There's only two ways to go in these operations – zero or hero."[4]

As you might suspect by now, the message of *The Zeronauts* is exactly the opposite. The people portrayed here are heroes precisely because they pursue zero – in areas as diverse as population control, poverty alleviation, pollution, and the proliferation of weapons of mass destruction. As they teeter on the edge of a different sort of chaos, they hold zero in their minds as a compass point, guiding light, North Star. They are at the cutting, and often bleeding, edge of the global sustainability movement.

We will dig into the question of who these zero-chasing pioneers are and why they do what they do in Chapter 3. They are market revolutionaries who aim to create wealth while driving adverse environmental, social, and economic impacts toward zero.

Whether or not this is what they intend, they are developing and spreading new *memes*: the psychological, social, and cultural equivalents of genes. The idea behind the "Zero Meme" (see Box 0.1) is that it potentially triggers a cascade of new thinking in those exposed to it – helping them see possibilities (and risks) to which they would otherwise have been blind.

Typically these pioneers admit early on in the conversation that they have made mistakes along the way. This essentially is a process of trial and error. In that spirit, one of the worst professional mistakes I ever made involved getting Bill Ford to admit in an interview we did more than a decade ago that the gas-guzzling sport utility vehicles from which the Ford Motor Company then made a huge slice of its profits were unsustainable.

True, but sometimes you can be too honest too early. It was a candid – and extremely brave – admission from an extraordinary man, illustrating his personal commitment to protecting the environment. But when the interview appeared in Ford's first sustainability report it didn't play at all well in some parts of the business press, particularly the *Wall Street Journal*.

Box 0.1

The Zero Meme

NOUN /mēm

memes, plural

An element of a culture or system of behavior that may be passed from one individual to another by non-genetic means, especially imitation.
                                    Wikipedia (11 August 02011, edited)

See page 57 for some examples

So let me start here with a very public health warning: some people may suffer allergic reactions to the ideas advanced here, particularly some of Bill Ford's compatriots. The warning signs have been there for decades. The late Dixie Lee Ray, a marine biologist, a Democrat, and the first female governor of Washington State, had this to say on the subject: "The reality is that zero defects in products plus zero pollution plus zero risk on the job is equivalent to maximum growth of government plus zero economic growth plus runaway inflation."

She was right, if all this were taken to extremes in short order by idiots. But she was also profoundly mistaken, like too many politicians who find themselves trapped in precariously short electoral terms. She was part of the world's most powerful economy, which – with no intention of doing so – has helped to put the rest of the world on a course to crash much of the planet's biosphere. Interestingly, her college thesis had investigated the lives of burrowing animals – and she inhabited a world where most consumers, most of the time, were happy to burrow into materialism and, in the process, turn a blind eye to longer-term consequences.

That isn't true of the pioneers profiled here. But, at the same time, none of these people wants to set all of the global economy's dials back to zero. They do not believe in Zero Growth[5] – and nor do I, though I cheerfully admit that I was part of a Friends of the Earth-hosted working group called Planners Against Growth in the early 01970s. It is worth noting that even zero impact or net zero impact strategies at the level of the sector, value chain, or company can end up with growing system impacts if the overall rate of economic growth continues. Pretty much all the Zeronauts featured here are focusing their efforts on products, technologies, companies, or sectors – whereas wider system dynamics will become increasingly important over time. Longer term, my hope is to focus future rounds of the Zeronaut Roll of Honor (see Box 3.1, pp.44–6) on people and institutions who drive system change, including politicians, policy-makers, and regulators.

The Zeronauts aim to get our competitive juices flowing with a "Race to Zero" framing[6] of their initiatives – whether it applies to toxics, greenhouse gases, or poverty. They start from the assumption that there is a fundamental design fault in capitalism – both in its prevailing paradigm and in the linked mindsets, behaviors, cultures, economic formulae, business models, and technologies.

Sure, a Zeronaut might say, it's possible that someone, somewhere, will crack the central problem of our times: how most people on the planet can achieve their consumerist dreams, living ever-bigger-ecological-footprint lives, eating increasing quantities of meat, driving SUVs, and living to over 100, while the global population hits – and passes – the nine billion mark. But don't count on it. Instead, we will need to insert zero ahead of more and more of our targets. That's why, for example, people such as Tim Flannery (see p.239) argue for zero-till and zero-kill agriculture.

But Zeronauts do not believe in miracles. I read, for example, that artist Karen Green had constructed what was billed as a "recreating-a-pig-from-bacon" machine.[7] No chance of the world being overrun by resurrected pigs, however: this was a thought experiment – and the book you hold in your hands (another thought experiment) assumes that we won't produce any sort of reverse-Doomsday machine that will allow us to restore the biosphere, oceans, and climate to the state in which our distant ancestors found them.

Instead, the Zeronauts are innovators who have concluded that we must now knuckle down to the hard intergenerational task of building tomorrow's businesses, cities, cultures, and even civilizations around the Race to Zero. Failure risks our very survival, whereas success could open out unparalleled horizons of opportunity.

Not all of the people whom I would dub Zeronauts would totally support the central idea. "I get it that zero footprint is a thought experiment", Mathis Wackernagel, president of the Global Footprint Network, told me, "but it is also – strictly speaking – impossible. Zero carbon is possible. Zero waste is possible, if you adjust your definitions. But in the end there is a budget of nature – and the key question is how to stay within that budget, and what the consequences will be of overdrawing."

Two other people I brand as Zeronauts – although they may not thank me for it – have argued against the misuse of zero language. In their book *Cradle to Cradle*, Michael Braungart and Bill McDonough pull no punches: "If the assumption is that human beings are bad for the planet, surely the best thing is for us not to be here at all. Zero emissions, zero footprint, reduction, avoidance, minimalization – the guilt language is very popular."[8] What we need, they argue, is not "less bad" but "more good".

By contrast, I have talked to many people who have been powerfully inspired by zero. "Zero can be a powerful mind-opener and frame-shifter", Gil Friend of San Francisco-based Natural Logic told me, "especially when I ask CEOs if they know their product-to-non-product ratio for their enterprise.[9] They never do, and they're always horrified when we tell them. They understand the new value proposition in a heartbeat."

But this is something of a fault-line in the sustainability movement, no question. When I asked Jochen Zeitz, chairman of Puma, what he made of it all – he was in the midst of a Braungart–McDonough session in Iceland – he said: "Cradle to cradle is a creative design and innovation approach. We need solutions that don't just reduce a footprint, but that are positive or circular – nature never does zero. But the C2C approach is largely qualitative, and needs to be based in quantitative approaches that target ultimate reductions. That's what we have been doing at Puma with our environmental profit and loss approach. We have had heated but constructive discussions – and there have to be ways to merge the two approaches."[10]

Jochen also pointed me to a quite extraordinary short video from 01972 of psychiatrist and Holocaust survivor Viktor Frankl talking about our search for meaning.[11] Well worth tracking down. The pursuit for zero impact may not yet be the sort of thing that grabs people's souls, but the quest for ways of making life livable for 9 billion people on a small blue planet must in the decades ahead.

We will return to the question of how we can get to – and then go beyond – zero in the final chapter. Like Jochen Zeitz, various people have said, as Gil Friend put it to me, that zero on its own "is not a terribly compelling goal, certainly not as creatively potent as restoration, regeneration, or resilience". But for the moment let's push ahead with the thought experiment. The way Paul Tebo explained it was as follows: "The quicker we get to zero waste, the quicker we'll have 100 percent product. The quicker we get to zero downtime, the quicker we'll be at 100 percent uptime."

A Zeronaut of even longer standing is Gunter Pauli of the Zero Emissions Research Initiative (ZERI), originally launched as a think tank at the United Nations University, based in Japan with the support of the Japanese government – later evolving into a network of foundations, NGOs, and social enterprises scattered across four continents. He told me that zero-based targets are effective precisely because "managers like very clear-cut objectives. Whether it is zero defects or zero stock, such uncompromising objectives set the stage in unequivocal terms."[12]

Pauli recalled that he wrote the first article on "zero emissions" and "zero waste" in 01991 – "too early, of course, but in 01992 we put the concepts into practice at the Ecover factory, which ended up taking the world by storm thanks to CNN Prime Time News and ABC Evening News". Faced by such giant incumbent competitors as Procter & Gamble and Unilever, Ecover decided that its best chance was to develop a completely different business model, with zero footprint at its core. "We achieved zero water waste", Pauli says, "but failed with zero packaging waste – though we were the first to have returnable bottles and filling systems at the point of distribution."

These days, Pauli has moved on to what he calls the "Blue Economy", focusing on solutions that solve sustainability problems, at a profit. But he notes that one place the zero concept really took root was Japan, where it helped to influence the thinking behind the United Nations Kyoto Protocol and where some 2800 companies adopted the concept during the 01990s, thanks to support from the ministries of education and trade and industry. A key reason Japan embraced zero so fervently, he believes, was the history of *kaizen* (or continuous improvement) and total quality management, to which we return in Chapters 5 and 6.

Kaizen can achieve major advances over time, but many of the pioneers whose work we will spotlight feel that only transformative change will do. The Zeronauts profiled below are among the most extraordinary people I have met in a lifetime of meeting extraordinary people. They really do think long term. Pauli, for example, explains that he and his team are focusing on the rising generation of students in engineering and similar disciplines. "It will take a generation, but we have to do it. We can achieve a lot in two decades, a quick generation!"

What follows is not an attempt to pre-empt what others are doing, but to signpost their thinking and ventures – and sketch an agenda for mainstream leaders. So, for example, one group that I have tracked with interest for a long time is the Factor 10 Club, founded by Professor Friedrich Schmidt Bleek.[13] "Factor 4 is the goal of dematerializing the material design of human well-being on average by a factor of four, as an interim step on the way to sustainability", he explained in 02008. In effect, this is a vision of a world in which wealth is doubled and resource use halved.

Pushing the envelope further, toward 90 percent improvements, "Factor 10 is a metaphor for the strategic economic goal of approaching sustainability by increasing the overall resource productivity tenfold on the average in industrialized countries. It has been suggested that by 02050 the worldwide per capita consumption of non-renewable resources should not exceed 5–6 tonnes annually", he noted. "Accordingly, Germany should dematerialize its economy by a factor of 10, Japan by a factor of 6, while the US would need to reach a factor of 15 and Finland a factor 19, based on present per capita consumption of natural resources."

These are immense challenges. When I spoke to one of the pioneers in the field, Claude Fussler, a long-time colleague and friend, he noted that the Factor 4 to 10 movement had been frustrated in its attempts to decouple the economy from environmental impacts by "a combination of perverse subsidies, free riders and public policy fixes to encourage growth and consumption".[14] Some also feel that the approach should have done more to directly address the challenges of poverty, covered in Chapter 7.

Making matters worse, as is so often true with emerging fields, the outlines of the new opportunities, risks and disciplines that these pioneers address often remain blurry. But if you tried to distil the message of this book into a 140-character tweet, you might get:

> Think sustainability is just about corporate citizenship? Think again. It's about driving our adverse footprints to zero. And system change.

Or at least that's my version. In what follows, my aim is to present a business case not just for corporate responsibility or even sustainability as many CEOs define it, but for a fundamental transformation of capitalism. I acknowledge the inputs of many of those who helped in the process on pp.xxi–xiv.

Some of the zero story will be told in the first person because for me this has been a voyage of discovery that began half a century ago in 01961, a voyage that has brought me to the shores of extraordinary opportunity spaces, discovered, mapped, and increasingly colonized by the first wave of Zeronauts.

One thing I seem to have done along the way is create new memes, among them *environmental excellence* (01984), the *green consumer* (01986), and the *triple bottom line* (01994). In cofounding SustainAbility in 01987, I helped to evolve and spread the *sustainability* meme, and now here I go again with the *Sustainability Barrier* (explained overleaf and on p.250), the *Zeronauts*, and their emerging discipline of *Zeronautics*.

The goal throughout has been to find ways to create tomorrow's wealth with new forms of "One Planet" (which I will here render as 1-Earth[15]) capitalism, designed and operated to meet the needs of today's seven billion people without crashing our biosphere, which future generations – including our own children – will depend on to meet their own needs.

One thing capitalism often does spectacularly well is screw up – and I mean that positively. In its efforts to create new forms of wealth, it experiments, makes mistakes, and, at its best, learns and, in time, comes back better, stronger. So times when everything seems to be falling apart may, conversely, be times when a new economic order is beginning to rise, Phoenix-like, from the ashes of the old.[16]

Time and again, however, we become overconfident in the power of the systems we create to ward off wider challenges. For me this was forcefully demonstrated when the 02011 tsunami easily overtopped the massive sea wall designed to protect Taro in Japan, quickly sweeping away much of the town. The survivors noted that the wall, sometimes dubbed Japan's "Great Wall of China", was something residents had "believed" in.[17]

My own belief, by contrast, is that there are many parts of our global economic system that – like the sea wall, and however much we may currently believe in them – are also doomed to fail, potentially catastrophically. Indeed, several years back and frustrated by progress to date, I helped to found a new start-up, Volans Ventures. The purpose of the enterprise is to explore ways to jump our companies, markets, and, ultimately, entire economies to new levels of efficiency and effectiveness in terms of their long-term economic, social, and environmental performance.

The tagline used from the outset was "Helping the future take flight". So there was a powerful moment of surprise and recognition when Alejandro Litovsky and I visited Sir Richard Branson's HQ in London a year or so later and saw a black-on-red mural illustrating the spirit of *Virgin Galactic* (see p.14). It showed six stages in the evolution of flight, from a man with wings (whom at Volans we call *Homo volans*) morphing over time through early flight experiments and the 747 right up to Branson's own Virgin Space Ship at the apex.

For me, the metaphor of flight is a powerful one, informing much of our work at Volans. The name, incidentally, derives from the Latin word for "flying thing", as in the scientific name for the flying fish, *Piscis* (or *Pisces*) *volans*.

In the same way that pilots and technologists struggled to break through the "Sound Barrier" in the late 01940s and early 01950s, our species now faces the challenge of breaking through the "Sustainability Barrier", within a decade or two. The risks are immense. Just as the compression waves encountered by the early aircraft entering transonic flight tore some of them apart, killing a number of pilots, so our next species-level transition will create economic and political compression waves that will shake apart many organizations and value chains that have served us fairly well to date.

But, at the same time, there are enormous opportunities for those who successfully help to shape and drive the new order. Sensing the direction of change, growing numbers of business leaders are embracing the sustainability agenda, at least as they understand it. Having worked for some of the world's best-known companies, though, I confess that something began to break loose in my mind recently.

For seven years, for example, I had been privileged to be part of the faculty for World Economic Forum summits and other events in Davos, Dalian, London, New York, and Palo Alto. In the process, however, I became increasingly disillusioned by the course that much of the corporate social responsibility – or CSR – movement was taking. Corporate citizenship and social responsibility are necessary conditions of progress, no question. But as I wrote in *The Phoenix Economy* in 02008:

> Properly understood, sustainability is not the same as corporate social responsibility (CSR) – nor can it be reduced to achieving an acceptable balance across economic, social and environmental bottom lines. Instead, it is about the fundamental, intergenerational task of winding down the dysfunctional economic and business models of the nineteenth and twentieth centuries, and the evolution of new ones fit for a human population headed towards nine billion people, living on a small planet which is already in "ecological overshoot".[18]

I see zero as akin to the flashing sword of Alexander the Great, helping us to cut through the Gordian complexity of the challenges we now face (see Box 1.2, p.29). A different mindset – ultimately, a different paradigm – is now needed if we are to move from a fundamentally unsustainable path to more sustainable ones. Writing for McKinsey & Company, I explained that: "The uncomfortable truth is that the nature and scale of the economic, social, environmental, and governance challenges we face are unparalleled."[19]

In the end, we didn't breach the Sound Barrier by wishing our way through, but through immense courage and ingenuity, coupled with radical shifts in design and technology. To succeed, we need to massively boost our individual and collective "future quotient" (see Chapter 8). The same will now be true of the Sustainability Barrier that our business models, supply chains, and technologies are increasingly banging into. An interview with Joel Makower, a veteran on what journalists might call the "Zero Beat" – where the world of the media intersects with the world of zero – follows on pp.9–13.

The great paradox of our times, as Tim Jackson has noted, is that we are caught between a rock and a very hard place.[20] If we resist growth on the old models, we risk economic and social collapse. But if we pursue growth, we risk collapsing key parts of the biosphere upon which we – and, even more, future generations – depend. The scale of the decoupling task we must now embrace is immense – and rarely acknowledged. "In a world of 9 billion people all aspiring to western lifestyles", Jackson warns, "the carbon intensity of every dollar of output must be at least 130 times lower in 2050 than it is today. By the end of the century, economic activity will need to be taking carbon out of the atmosphere, not adding to it."

As we work to rein in the sometimes near-exponential worsening in some of the critical challenges we face, so we must now work out how to unleash near-exponential – or even super-exponential – growth in the markets for viable long-term solutions. That is what the Zeronauts are attempting – and what makes their eventual success or failure so fundamentally important to our common future.

Box 0.2

The Zero Beat

Joel Makower is founder of GreenBiz.com, a leader on what the media might call the "Zero Beat" and an expert on what he calls VERGE technologies.[21]

JOHN ELKINGTON (JE): So, Joel, where are we on zero?

JOEL MAKOWER (JM): From a journalist's perspective, a company that has committed to or achieved zero waste is now a "dog bites man" story – that is, non-news. (The same happened seven or eight years ago with companies achieving LEED certification of a building: it became just too commonplace to be seen as newsworthy.)

At the same time, we know that the number of companies that are engaging in "zero" remains relatively small. So, it's a glass-half-full quandary: do you cheer on or ignore the leaders committing to such worthy goals, beat up or ignore the companies that haven't yet engaged, or some combination thereof?

However, that's just about zero waste, which refers to solid waste. The larger question of zero – net water use, net fossil fuel energy, net carbon emissions, etcetera – seems largely unexplored by most companies. Only one US company that I know of – Frito-Lay – has opened what they call a "near net zero" factory, in Casa Grande, Arizona [see p.209]. The company has designed it to operate "almost entirely" on renewable energy sources and recycle approximately 80 percent of its water. That's revolutionary, at least in the United States.

JE: So zero is just getting going?

JM: Waste, as I said, has been the most prevalent focus in the US, though "zero (net) carbon" trended highly a few years ago, then went quiet. Some companies have made specific "zero" goals. For example, Nike at one point had a goal of zero VOCs [volatile organic compounds] used in manufacturing its products. Several companies have zero deforestation goals, others have zero HFC [hydrofluorocarbon] goals. Coke has a zero-net-water goal. It's a mixed bag of goals and commitments.

JE: How deep does this go in companies announcing zero targets?

JM: Any company setting a zero target or commitment has by necessity made a deep dive into its overall footprint. The targets generally reflect a significant component of their footprint – or, if not, a significant component of their reputational footprint. Either way, it's hard to achieve a zero goal without tackling several other aspects of a company's operations. Therefore, I suspect there's relatively little use of zero as a smokescreen or diversionary tactic to avoid tackling other bigger issues – which is not to say that all zero-targeted companies are saints, not by a long shot.

JE: And your new initiative, VERGE?

JM: VERGE is our label for the accelerating convergence of energy, information, buildings, and vehicle technologies, and the economic, environmental, and social benefits this process brings to business and society. VERGE technologies radically improve efficiencies of transportation systems, buildings, cities, factories, and other energy- and resource-intensive activities, and will lead to new products and services, even new industries, much as information technologies – the internet, broadband, smart phones – have done in recent years. VERGE also offers the potential for gigaton reductions in carbon emissions, along with reductions in other pollutants, all the while reducing congestion, improving health and safety, and raising standards of living.

JE: Where are the most dramatic areas for towards-zero improvements?

JM: Water remains one of the untapped opportunities. Many of the world's beverage companies have set ambitious net-zero or near-net-zero water targets, largely as a means of protecting their brands; but there are other water-intensive industries that haven't yet set significant targets.

Zero toxics – whether in the form of carcinogens, teratogens, mutagens, or endocrine disrupters – is also ripe for companies. As chemicals gain unfavorable publicity, such as BPA [bisphenol A] did over the past year or so, some brand-conscious companies have phased them out; but such activities are limited to a very small percentage of chemical-using companies. There's a lot of room for improvement.

JE: And what do you see as the most likely barriers?

JM: The biggest barriers are the same for zero as for most other sustainability activities: the lack of a clear-cut business case, resistance to change, supply-chain pushback, insufficient commitment both at the top of an organization and through the rank and file – and, most of all, underpriced resources that make it cheap to waste.

Most of the media world, however, is blind to all of this – and, as a result, so are most business and government leaders. To begin the process of opening their eyes and minds, Volans has been working with Deloitte Innovation to develop a Zero Hub. As Box 0.3 explains, this aims to take participants through a process where they go into orbit, investigate the emerging discipline of Zeronautics, agree their organizational priorities for zeroing, learn from existing Zeronauts, and then re-enter today's reality with an agreed vision and adaptation plan.

Box 0.3

The Zero Hub

Erasmus Darwin, James Watt, Matthew Boulton, Josiah Wedgwood, and Joseph Priestley were all involved in the Lunar Society, formed during the late eighteenth century. This played a critical role in cross-fertilizing the emerging sciences of chemistry, mineralogy, meteorology, astronomy, and physics.[22] And some of the key pioneers in the information technology and New Economy revolutions, including the cofounders of Apple, were part of Silicon Valley's Home Brew Computing Club during the 01970s and 01980s.[23] Today's equivalents would include convenings around natural capitalism, environmental footprinting, Cradle to Cradle© solutions, biomimicry, and social innovation, enterprise, and investment.

But what about zero impact growth? When I trailed some of the early messages of The Zeronauts at a conference in Rome late in 02010, there was an immediate response from Ralph Thurm, director of sustainability and innovation at Deloitte. Previously the first head of sustainability at Siemens and a leading figure at the Global Reporting Initiative, he spotted the opportunity to create a Home Brew Club for what he promptly dubbed zero impact growth. The current growth paradigm, he had concluded, "puts us on the slow death path".

The learning process for participants in the Zero Hub is modeled on the adventures of the early Astronauts and Cosmonauts, including preparation, blast-off, orbiting, observation, re-entry, debriefing, and the application of the new perspectives, knowledge, and tools. The response from business was enormously positive, and reiterated time and again as we visited companies in Europe.

> The protracted economic downturn and Eurozone crisis didn't help, of course; but many of the business leaders we have spoken to are increasingly aware that capitalism is in real crisis – and that the new order will necessarily be very different. They see a growing need to expose their key people to the new trajectories, innovators, and potential business models.
>
> As the collective download of experience, ambitions, and ideas for next steps continues, we intend to develop multiple cycles of the Zero Hub – and, longer term, the idea is that we will spawn similar initiatives in other parts of the world. Further information can be found at www.zeronauts.com.

So here's how the rest of the book runs.

- *Part I: Zero: The New Black* looks at the way in which our species is routinely blindsided by emerging Earth-security challenges. The evolution of the aerospace industry is used as a parallel to what we are now going through in 1-Earth science, technology, and business. Then we look at the emergence of a new breed of innovators: the Zeronauts.
- *Part II: Cracking the 1-Earth Code* considers how these new challenges present themselves at five levels: those of citizens, the corporation, the city, the country, and, ultimately, an entire civilization. These are the 5Cs.
- *Part III: Breaking Through* introduces a five-stage model (the 5Es) that maps pathways to scale in the Zero Footprint Economy – plus some early lessons about replicating and scaling new solutions. Then we investigate how all of this is playing out in five key areas: population growth, pandemics, poverty, pollution, and the proliferation of weapons of mass destruction (the 5Ps).
- *Part IV: Beyond Zero* pulls the threads together. We also explain why it is that all leaders – wherever they operate – now need to go wider, deeper, higher, and longer to make sense of the new order, in the process measuring and improving their individual and collective future quotients. And we begin to outline some of the basic questions that teams and organizations need to ask themselves as we move into the new era.

Figure 0.1 *The future takes flight*
Source: *Virgin Galactic*

I

ZERO: THE NEW BLACK

I think we have a language problem. Our biggest mistake in outlining the sustainability agenda was to focus it on future generations. It's not going to be the next generation that has the problem – it's going to be us.

Lester Brown,
Earth Policy Institute[1]

LING

1

Breaking the Sustainability Barrier

The evidence suggests that most CEOs and other members of the global C-suite so far fail to grasp the nature and scale of what's coming at them. A world of 9 billion people by mid-century will demand fundamental changes in our mindsets, behaviors, cultures, and paradigms. Happily, just as our species broke the Sound Barrier during the 01940s and 01950s, a new breed of innovator, entrepreneur, and investor is lining up to break the Sustainability Barrier.

Outside it was freezing, the traffic-ridged snow and ice stretching away under a low, leaden sky. But inside the Malmö football stadium's adjoining conference complex all was friendly and warm. Even better, there was the smell of real grass in the purpose-designed space where I was waiting to talk to four separate batches of around 40 top executives of the packaging company Tetra Pak.

They had flown in from all around the world; but wherever they had arrived from, many – and all of them were wearing suits – showed real delight in encountering the freshly laid turf covering the floor as they settled down on what looked rather like the caps of toadstools laid out in lines across the grass. One even wondered aloud whether he could take his socks off.

On the walls around them, three giant screens already showed the first of my images, including a huge blue head of one of the Na'vi people from James Cameron's hit 3D film *Avatar*. I had their attention. But I kicked off by saying that even though the venue might look like something out of the more romantic side of *Avatar* or *The Hobbit*, we were about to focus in on some of the most critical market drivers in the coming decade.

For such competitive companies it is not enough to say we want you to be nicer, gentler with the world around you, more sustainable. The inevitable pushback tends to run like this: where is the business case? What should be our priorities? What targets should we adopt? What are the downside risks? How do we build this into the DNA of the business? How will we know if we are making progress? And how will we be rewarded for success?

Let's take a look at how that might crosscut the worlds of those 150 top executives from Tetra Pak. The main reason I was in Malmö was to help the company celebrate the launch of their fourth corporate strategic objective, focusing on "environmental excellence", though they had no clue that this was a term I had coined way back in 01984, while working for the United Nations Environment Programme.

Each year, Tetra Pak – founded in 01952 – recycles something like 27 billion individual packages. Astonishing. But probe a little and you find that even this massive number accounts for a fairly small proportion of the packages they actually sold each year. In 02009, for example, that figure had accounted for just under one fifth (18.7 percent) of the total produced worldwide. Now, spurred by the new strategic objective, they were proud of the fact that they planned to double their recycling rate to 40 percent by 02020.

I very much liked what I had seen of the company – and their people were clearly intelligent and engaged. But the age-old question for me was whether I was there to celebrate their progress to date, or to provoke their thinking about future market challenges? With the encouragement of Tetra Pak's sustainability team, I ended up doing both.

On the upside, few of us would deny that modern forms of packaging have massively improved our lives. I, for one, am glad that I don't have to eat food out of cans sealed with lead solder. But, on the downside, I reminded them that reclaiming mixed-material packaging (Tetra Pak uses a mix of paper, plastic, and aluminum) is typically a bit of a nightmare. And that was where I began to push the envelope. Being told that the recycling rate would improve to 40 percent over the next decade, I said, was a bit like being told that Tetra Pak was happy to be moving from being 80 percent unsustainable to 60 percent unsustainable over the same period.

Taking an early leaf from *The Zeronauts*, which I was already beginning to sketch out, I argued that zero really was not an option – though not in the sense that they might have assumed. The objective now has to be zero, I insisted: zero waste, zero emissions, zero adverse impact. By 02020, for example, their ambition ought to be that Tetra Pak would no longer sell any packaging without a recycling guarantee.

I confess that I had expected to be challenged fairly energetically; instead I found a considerable degree of interest in at least trying the "thought experiment" I was proposing.

Thought experiments

From Schrödinger's Cat to Maxwell's Demon, scientists have long used thought experiments to test the possible consequences of new principles or operations. Used in the right way, they can stretch our imaginations and understanding. This is key because one of our central problems, as Heerad Sabeti suggested to me after we had done a session for Virgin Unite in Switzerland, is that "our species may not be biologically wired up to live in the world we have created".[2]

He went on:

Imagine a dozen apes sitting around the table in Geneva, with their mobile phones and laptops, dressed in suits, contemplating the negative and unsustainable impact of their species on the planet and future generations – and plotting a strategy to reorganize the behavior of apes all over the world. It would be comical, but that's where we've come to.

Box 1.1

Tackling our demons

There was a demon that lived in the air. They said whoever challenged him would die. Their controls would freeze up, their planes would buffet wildly, and they would disintegrate. The demon lived at Mach 1 on the meter, 750 miles an hour, where the air could no longer move out of the way. He lived behind a barrier through which they said no man could ever pass. They called it the sound barrier.[3]

The Right Stuff, film, 01983

So, what demons lurk ahead of – and behind – the Sustainability Barrier? Like alcoholics plagued by the "demon drink" or addicts by hard drugs, consumerist societies now face a "Detox Decade" (see Chapter 4). One key question: how can we improve our collective "future quotient" (see Chapter 8) to help navigate these challenging times?

The central challenge, he argued, is to change our social, political, economic, and technological systems so that they enable us to make the right decision, every time, "without each of us having to process something as complex as the impact of a coffee cup on the future of the planet and its inhabitants".

One of my favorite recent thought experiments is the Clock of the Long Now, designed to tell time over a 10,000-year time period.[4] With the Zeronauts and the Race to Zero, the idea is to explore the feasibility and potential outcomes of a company's, city's, or country's push for zero adverse impact – in effect, a decision to push a particular organization, business model, or technology through the Sustainability Barrier.

When it came to introducing the concept at Tetra Pak, I clicked the remote control and one wall was suddenly covered with a massive image of an F/A-18 jet punching its way through the Sound Barrier, a cone of white vapor angling back from its fuselage. The great thing was that there was no need to explain the idea: people seemed to get it immediately.

Equally, there is no need here to know the specifics of early attempts to break through the Sound Barrier – of aircraft like the *Mitsubishi Zero* suffering from a deadly tendency to fall out of the sky when in deep dives, of Nazi Germany's Me262 jets possibly achieving breakthrough without realizing it, of the fatal breaking up of all three prototype versions of the de Havilland *Swallow*, or of the eventual success of American Chuck Yeager in his X-1 rocket-plane.

Partly because my own father had been a World War II fighter pilot, these pioneers were my early heroes – and the flight metaphor has been shot through much of the work that I have done in subsequent years. Indeed, for many years a key image I used in presentations was a beautiful black-and-white photo of the Wright Brothers wobbling into the air at Kittyhawk with their *Wright Flyer*. I would note that the sustainability field – far from being established – is now pretty much where the Wright Brothers were in 01903, when they achieved the first elementary controlled, powered, and sustained heavier-than-air human flight.

But I used the image to make another point: that breakthrough innovation often comes from the fringes of the incumbent economic system. Before they took to the air, the Wright Brothers made bicycles. And the interesting thing about bicycles is that their wheels needed wire bracing just like the wings of those early aircraft.

It took just 44 years from Kittyhawk to the first intentional breaking of the Sound Barrier. Once achieved, it seemed to most people that supersonic flight was pretty much inevitable. But that was not at all how things had appeared to those long-ago test pilots as they wrestled with the seriously weird conditions that prevailed close into this invisible barrier in the sky (see Box 1.1, p.19).

How times have changed. Nowadays, few of us even blink an eyelid when we hear that an extreme parachutist, Felix Baumgartner, plans to break the Sound

Barrier – without an aircraft. And the same is likely to be true, eventually, of those who are pressing toward the Sustainability Barrier. Once we have achieved the trick of breaking through at scale, we will wonder why we ever thought it impossible.

Think of the runner Roger Bannister, who ran one mile (1609 meters) in under four minutes in 01954, a feat previously thought physically impossible. But he viewed the challenge pretty much as pilots did the Sound Barrier, as a mental rather than just a physical barrier. Strikingly, a short time later another runner broke through – and by the end of 01957 no less than 16 other athletes had done so.[5]

Again, as in so many areas of science, technology, and business, a growing number of pioneers are rivaling one another to be the first to break through the Sustainability Barrier – though they don't yet call it that – in different markets and sectors, whether they are designing new cars, new aircraft, or even entire new cities such as Dongtan in China or Masdar in the United Arab Emirates.

Some are succeeding. In fact, one of my favorite phrases from the work of science fiction author William Gibson applies nicely: "The future is already here – it's just not evenly distributed." Yet. Our challenge is to get out there and find the early innovators, building a better sense of how their experiments are turning out, of what seems to be working, and what, at least to date, seems not to be. That is what we aim to do in *The Zeronauts*. Before introducing the later sections of the book, however, it may be worth taking a quick look at the history of zero itself.

The zero story

Few of us, aside from mathematicians, understand just how great a breakthrough the invention of zero was. We know of no single Eureka! moment when someone came up with the notion of zero for the first time; indeed, it is thought that it was independently discovered several times.

Historians tell us that zero was invented at least four times: by the Babylonians around 4000 years ago; by the Chinese some 2000 years ago; by the Mayans between the fourth and ninth centuries of the Common Era; and in India from around 650 CE – from where it spread to the Arab world and, eventually, the West.

These days, zero is generally understood to mean either nothing, as in Sun Microsystems chairman Scott McNealy telling us in 01999 that "You have zero privacy. Get over it", or by those of a mathematical bent as a key tool in what is called positional mathematics, enabling us to calculate in ways that would have been a mystery to the ancient Greeks and Romans – who appear never to have grasped the concept of zero.

But there is another meaning of zero which is also relevant here – and it tracks back to exactly the time period when those pilots were trying to break through the Sound Barrier.

In this case, however, scientists such as John von Neumann and Oskar Morgenstern were opening up the whole area of game theory, exploring its applications in such fields as national security, diplomacy, and economics. A key distinction made was between zero-sum games, in which one player could only gain at the expense of others, and non-zero-sum games, where not only does a win by one player not automatically result in a loss for others, but the total result potentially can be greater for all. The question of who tackles greenhouse gases, and how quickly, is a classic zero-sum challenge, says Gideon Rachman in his book *Zero-Sum World*.[6] His question, toward the end of the book, is why we can't mobilize in the same way that America did around the Manhattan Project or, later, the historically unprecedented Marshall Plan for the reconstruction of war-torn Europe.[7]

One of the most interesting books I have read in this area is Robert Wright's *Nonzero*, in which he uses non-zero-sum logic to explore the underlying dynamics of human and cultural evolution – and concludes that new forms of "non-zero-sumness" are tending to displace older forms of "zero-sumness".[8] While the universe may be running down to ultimate heat death, here on Earth evolution is driving us toward greater complexity.

In the same way that wars bonded particular peoples in the past, Wright argues, new forms of environmental stress now have the potential to bond us at the global scale. Anyone who attended the Copenhagen, Cancún, or Durban climate summits may have raised their eyebrows at this optimistic projection; but even Wright admits that none of this means that "combating global warming will lead to a transnational lovefest".

Instead, he believes, working toward the resolution of complex global challenges offers us the opportunity to evolve new social and cultural forms that permit citizens, cities, corporations, and countries to compete, while protecting and increasing our common wealth, in the form of our cultures, natural systems, and wider biosphere.

As I began work on *The Zeronauts*, such thinking seemed wishful. It was not just that the international jockeying over climate change threatened to wreck the UN's carefully laid plans for its Conference of the Parties (COP) process, but that countries were clearly beginning to compete for natural resources in new ways, dramatized by the political collisions in 02010 between China and Canada over potash – and between China and Japan over rare earth minerals.

With the "peak oil", "peak water", and even "peak fish" challenges now looming increasingly large on the horizon, it is hard to be totally optimistic about the future of the global economy.

But while such resource and security issues almost certainly will result in new outbreaks of the sort of zero-sum conflicts that so scarred the twentieth century, it is at least conceivable that the stresses imposed upon our economies, business models, and technologies – and upon our thinking around accounting and economics – could trigger the necessary jump to new mindsets, behaviors, and cultures, and ultimately to a new paradigm.

You are certainly beginning to see early evidence of that in the military world. Energy and climate security issues are perceived as being among the growing constraints that "could place the United States at a strategic turning point", argued Navy Admiral Mike Mullen, as chairman of the US military's Joint Chiefs of Staff.[9]

"Glaciers are melting at a faster rate", he warned in 02011, "causing water supplies to diminish in Asia. Rising sea levels could lead to a mass migration and displacement similar to what we saw in Pakistan's floods last year. And other shifts could reduce the arable land needed to feed a growing population in Africa, for example. Scarcity of water, food and space could create not only a humanitarian crisis, but conditions that could lead to failed states, instability and, potentially, radicalization." He concluded: "Business as usual won't cut it."

The quest is not new

Just in case this quest for zero seems new, the first time I was involved in helping the leaders of a major business think through elements of the zero agenda was over 20 years ago and involved, of all companies, BP – the brand now indelibly associated with America's largest pollution disaster, to date.

The question a small group of us were asked by the oil giant was whether it would make sense to set internal targets specifying zero accidents or zero pollution? Our advice at the time was that, as long as people inside the company did not forget that this was a form of thought experiment to help them think the previously unthinkable, and as long as the concept did not appear in external propaganda, it was a worthwhile experiment.

Nor has my thinking changed; rather, my sense of urgency has intensified. At a time when growing numbers of CEOs and other business leaders around the world are embracing the sustainability agenda, it is hard not to worry that most still have a poor grasp of the agenda – and of its implications for their markets and businesses.

In a survey of 766 CEOs carried out for the UN Global Compact by the consultancy Accenture, for example, no less than 81 percent insisted that they had already "embedded" the concept in their businesses.[10] With the greatest respect, I think not.

We will come back to this; but our experience suggests that, at best, most companies now have at least a basic understanding of the corporate social responsibility (CSR) agenda – a term that has achieved a growing profile during the period of economic globalization. But many still assume that the sustainability agenda is subsumed within the CSR and corporate citizenship agenda. That may be the reality in their own thinking and in their boardrooms; but the truth is that these are quite distinct challenges.

To put it starkly, CSR is often about how a given company can do good, "give back to society", whereas the sustainability agenda is ultimately about the long-term survival and health not only of individual companies or value chains, but of our civilization and planetary biosphere. Business people are trained to believe that everything is negotiable, and certainly a given company can bargain with its various stakeholders; but – as Bill McKibben has put it – we can't bargain with Nature.[11]

Viewed from this angle, the great, hard-fought UN climate change conferences in places such as Copenhagen and Cancún are likely to be about as useful in fending off the worst effects of global environmental change as animal sacrifices were in changing the minds of the Roman gods.

Poke even thoughtful business leaders on the subject of zero, though, and you are likely to get at least flashes of recognition and interest, even if the degree of understanding will vary considerably. Some people may have heard of one or more of the small but growing number of initiatives that have the word "zero" somewhere in their title: the Zero Emissions Research Initiative (ZERI),[12] for example, the "Mission Zero" website,[13] or the "Get Zero" campaign and design competition launched in the US by Metropolis and the General Services Administration.[14]

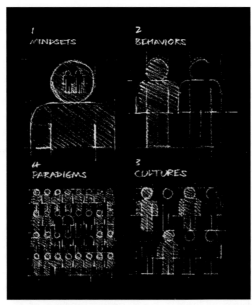

Figure 1.1 Toward a 1-Earth Paradigm

The end game

So what should be our end game in transformative change? Not long ago, the global management consulting firm McKinsey & Company asked me to distil my thinking on possible ways forward.[15] The result was an essay built around a two-by-two matrix, shown in Figure 1.1. This was the first time that I had tried to work out how the various elements of the social innovation agenda fitted together.[16]

Let's quickly work our way around the matrix, cell to cell. In the first, *Mindsets*, the emphasis is on changing our mental operating systems at the individual level. The last century taught us that most forms of brainwashing don't work very well, so how do we rewire our brains?

Well, happily, there is some evidence that leading social entrepreneurs are helping CEOs and other C-suite leaders – and a growing spectrum of intrapreneurs – to spot new market risks and opportunities, prototype innovative business models, and test out novel leadership approaches.

Great, but even the best-intentioned leaders can hit the wall when attempting the transition from cells 1 to 2. They make the announcements to signal the intention to change mindsets, but their own *Behavior* remains unchanged: critically, they fail to introduce the right incentives and, even more damagingly, often fail to model the new behaviors. If you get this bit right, though, the process can go viral.

Those who do make it into cell 2 must then make the even tougher transition to cell 3. Here the focus is on integrating new values within corporate, urban, national, or even global *Cultures*. Cultures lock in behavior.

Culture is the new frontier – and we're going to have to get dramatically better at cultural engineering, or perhaps catalysis would be a better word. And now, as we probe the margins of cell 4, the spotlight is beginning to shift to *Paradigms*.

The notion of paradigms is much discussed – and much misunderstood. There are those who would try to persuade us that a new formulation of toothpaste constitutes a paradigm shift. Not so, if you go back to the original work of Thomas Kuhn, whose book *The Structure of Scientific Revolutions*[17] transformed the way in which I see the world when I first read it during the 01960s.

True paradigm shifts take decades, even generations, to work their way through – partly because those infected by old paradigms have to retire and die, clearing the way for the new order.

Without wanting to sound millennial about this, my sense is that we are over 50 years into a shift toward a 1-Earth – or Gaian – paradigm. One way to track its origins is to look for mentions of the concept of *Spaceship Earth*,[18] a term possibly first used by Adlai Stevenson in 01965. It was then used the following year both in an essay by economist Kenneth Boulding[19] and in the title of the book *Spaceship Earth*,[20] by Barbara Ward, a friend of Stevenson's – but these days who knows which way the debt ran? The phrase was also popularized by Buckminster Fuller in his 01968 book *Operating Manual for Spaceship Earth*, which I bought and devoured at the time.

This series of events helped to catalyze both the Environmental Revolution and the sustainability movement that evolved from it. And now the trend seems to be accelerating toward some sort of systemic transformation in key world regions by the late 02030s or early 02040s. In the process, zero-based strategies will be central to the intensifying attempts to break through the Sustainability Barrier.

100 percent joy, 0 percent emissions

For most business people, the term "zero" most likely triggers associations with the total quality management (TQM) agendas, as in "zero defects". The approach's champions argue that it "is a way of thinking and doing that reinforces the notion that defects are not acceptable, and that everyone should 'do things right the first time'. The idea here is that with a philosophy of zero defects, you can increase profits both by eliminating the cost of failure and increasing revenues through increased customer satisfaction."

They also see the approach as "adaptable to any situation, business, profession or industry". The inevitable question then is "whether or not zero defects is [sic] ever attainable. Essentially, does adopting a zero defect environment only set users up for failure? Zero defects is *not* about being perfect. Zero defects is about changing your perspective."[21]

Yes, it is clear that we need to change our mindsets, behaviors, cultures, and, ultimately, our underlying paradigm. But as we push toward a 1-Earth Paradigm, business leaders must be careful about how they talk in public about all of this. Italy's Enel, for example, claims – under the banner headline "Our energy will always be powered by your dreams" – that "starting with the dream of zero emission energy, we developed power stations … with technology that can capture and store CO_2, which means they don't use chimneys". Sounds nice, doesn't it; but what proportion of their production does this now account for? Is it more than one plant? And still perhaps not the sort of thing, despite the dreamy words, that you would perhaps want in your back garden or in the heart of your community.

One well-known firm that has been producing ads spotlighting its ambitions for zero emissions and zero waste is the BMW Group. Among the taglines: "We're bringing zero emissions within reach" and 'We're the first company to recycle 100 percent of our waste." Well, in relation to that last claim, not quite 100 percent: more like 96 percent; but as they modestly continued: "ahead of us is perfection, and we're not slowing down".

It's hard not to admire the panache; but at least one of those ads got the German automaker into hot water in one of its major markets: the UK. The caption of the ad read: "The BMW Concept ActiveE is the first BMW to be powered purely by electricity", and used the tagline "100 percent joy, 0 percent emissions". Inevitably, someone complained that the claim of "zero CO_2 when driving" could not be substantiated because the car would be charged with electricity from the relevant utility, which would result in emissions. BMW retorted that the inclusion of the phrase "when driving" limited the claim, and did not suggest the ad was referring to the vehicle's entire life cycle.[22]

However, the Advertising Standards Authority referred to a previous judgment when it banned a Renault ad for its "zero emissions" electric car range. Viewers had complained that Renault's "zero-emission vehicles" line did not take the full life cycle of the vehicle into account, and the complaint was upheld.

This was a small skirmish in a series of battles in a wider war to adapt our economic and business models to 1-Earth realities. In the context of the infinitely greater challenge of pushing our entire civilization through the Sustainability Barrier, BMW's problems are small beer, but they hint at the complexities that will characterize this entire area.

While I was drafting this chapter, for example, two CEOs clashed in public on the issue of zero emissions at the imaginatively branded TechCrunch Disrupt event in New York.[23] Don Runkle, CEO of Michigan-based EcoMotors, which makes more efficient combustion engines, said that his firm's engine technology allowed car companies to produce diesel-powered vehicles that have a lower overall carbon footprint than any available electric automobile.

Electric vehicles are not zero-emission vehicles, he charged, something that the other CEO – Craig Bramscher of Oregon-based Brammo – quickly retorted that he didn't claim for his firm's all-electric motorcycles. Bramscher went on to say, tellingly, that he didn't want his children fighting to defend an oil field as petroleum resources became strained. Clearly, this is a landscape crowded with risks and opportunities.

When I covered the potential role of the military in driving the zero revolution in a *Guardian* blog,[24] I heard back within hours from James Swanston, a veteran of the war in Afghanistan.[25] "I run a business called Carbon Voyage and we are doing some work in London with the Ministry of Defence", he began. "I'm also a Territorial Army officer, having been a regular officer in the Australian army, and was very frustrated by the lack of sustainability within the MoD, both here and on operations. With that in mind, I found a part of the MoD in which we can do some work focused on energy and transport. Short term, we are looking to do a pilot on five MoD sites, focused on taking them off the grid as much as possible through a mix of renewable energy and energy reduction strategies, plus a range of measures to reduce their transport impact."

And there was more: "From my time in Afghanistan and elsewhere, there are concepts that I am looking to get into the MoD once the pilot schemes are up and running." By way of example, the lack of electricity in Helmand is a major stumbling block in gaining local consent from the population. From my perspective, efforts to set up big infrastructure (such as hydro schemes) are flawed as they present targets for insurgents and criminals to attack. A better option would be to provide households with "micro-generation" of some sort.

As we see in Chapter 4, the armed forces are increasingly interested in all of this. "As the military gets involved in nation building or rebuilding", Swanston argued, "there is a massive opportunity for green technology. I also see opportunities for renewable energy to cut the need for logistics missions, which would have a significant impact on reducing the threat of IEDs (improvised explosive devices). Clearly, there is a wider issue about climate change as a catalyst for conflict and how the military might proactively – or reactively – respond to this. The US military certainly seems to be way out in front in terms of this!"

The US army, meanwhile, has established a special unit to process proposals for weaning the armed forces off fossil fuels – and switching them on to energy efficiency and renewables. Using its vast holdings of land, it wants to draw at least 25 percent of its electricity from clean sources by 02025.[26] It notes that it has both "the land and the demand". Peace advocates may not want to know, but this doesn't mean the military is softening: US Navy Secretary Ray Mabus insisted that the idea "is to make us better war fighters".[27] He added that he was more concerned about the fact that a Marine is killed or wounded for every 50 convoys of fuel brought into Afghanistan than about cutting greenhouse gas emissions.

This is a subject to which we will return; but first let's take a broader look at the challenges facing us – and introduce the first wave of Zeronauts. As Box 1.2 suggests, these people use zero to cut through complexity, getting to the core of an issue – just as Alexander the Great is said to have done with the fabled Gordian Knot.

Box 1.2

Zero and Gordian Knots

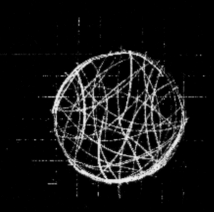

GORDIAN KNOT

With a single bold stroke, Alexander the Great is said to have undone the infernally complex knot that symbolized the power of the ruler of ancient Phrygia. There are different accounts of how the deed was done: some say he used his sword to cut through the knot, others that he changed the rules of the game by pulling the knot off the post or shaft that concealed the ends that needed to be untied. In either case, he reframed the challenge to win. In the same way, zero helps us to reframe wickedly complex sustainability challenges to make them easier to solve. To achieve such feats, as Chapter 8 explains, our thinking must go wider, deeper, higher, and longer.

2

Houston, We Have A(nother) Problem

It may not have been designed that way, but conventional capitalism increasingly looks like a giant Ponzi scheme – where the interests of (at least some) people alive today are wildly favored over those of future generations. The example of soil is used to demonstrate that, without intending to do so, we are in the process of crashing the biosphere.

Anyone who recalls their space exploration history will know that the "Houston, we have a problem" line was a slight misquotation of Apollo Astronaut Jack Swigert's super-cool warning to ground control when the ill-fated *Apollo 13* mission had to be aborted. An oxygen tank had ruptured en route to the Moon, severely damaging the spacecraft's electrical system.

Three men in a tiny space capsule went through an excruciating series of life-threatening events which in many ways symbolizes where our species may be headed in the twenty-first century.

But if you were coming the other way, inbound toward Earth, how would you get any sense that we were pressing up against the limits of our small planet? One thought experiment that has been used with good effect over the years revolves around a related question: how would ET, or some other intelligent alien, know that there was life (intelligent or otherwise) on Earth?

One answer might be that they would look for radio signals as a sign of a reasonably advanced civilization. Many years ago, the desktop Mac on which I wrote a number of books had a screensaver churning away in the background that helped scientists scan for radio signals from outer space. As far as I know, they have drawn a blank, to date.

This quest was organized by SETI, the Search for Extraterrestrial Intelligence. Just two years after the Soviets launched their *Sputnik* satellite, which I can still remember excitedly watching arc through the night sky, two physicists at Cornell

University published an article in the journal *Nature* noting the relative ease with which radio messages could be sent between the stars.

This led to the suggestion that it might be possible to detect the presence of extraterrestrial civilizations using radio telescopes. SETI projects scan for two different types of signal: first, deliberate "Here we are" signals and, second, the sort of background noise that a radio-based civilization inadvertently beams out into space, as Earth has been doing for the past 70 years.

One problem with this second approach is that Earth has become a much quieter radio object over recent decades – as more efficient, less powerful systems replace earlier sources of radio leakage.[1]

The sort of TV transmitters used in the last century, which might have sent a megawatt of radio energy into space, are being replaced by low-power digital, cable and satellite systems. "Very soon", one of the scientists involved predicted, "Earth will become undetectable."

A different approach would be to look at Earth's atmosphere for chemical signs of life. One of my heroes, after whose Gaia Hypothesis my first daughter was named in 01977, is James Lovelock. He qualifies as an early example of a Zeronaut, with his work demonstrating that our species is leaving very distinct chemical fingerprints – and footprints – in both our biosphere and atmosphere.

In 01961, the same year that I was raising money for the World Wildlife Fund (WWF) at school, he was already busily working for the National Aeronautics and Space Administration (NASA) on the evolution of sensitive instruments for the analysis of extraterrestrial atmospheres and planetary surfaces. The Viking mission, visiting Mars in the late 01970s, was partly motivated by an interest in finding out whether the red planet supported life.

The emerging paradigm we are groping our way toward draws on the work of people such as Lovelock, whose thinking around what he calls geophysiology – which treats the Earth as if it is a living organism – feels like a critical building block for the coming decades. Interest in his Gaia Hypothesis (now Theory) spiked from the publication of his book *Gaia: A New Look at Life on Earth*[2] in 01979.

Lovelock became interested in the composition of the Martian atmosphere, concluding that life forms on Mars would be obliged to make use of it and, in the process, alter it. Disappointingly, for those who were keen to find life, the atmosphere was found to be very close to its chemical equilibrium, with very little in the way of evidence of life – in particular, gases such as oxygen, methane, or even hydrogen. By contrast, anyone who chose to look at Earth's atmosphere would quickly find evidence of a pretty volatile mix of gases that only life could keep going.

As if that was not enough, during the late 01960s Lovelock went on to invent one of the most important scientific instruments of the past century: the electron capture detector. This played a crucial role in discovering the presence not only of persistent organochlorine compounds (used as insecticides) in the natural environment, helping to inform Rachel Carson's work on the landmark book *Silent Spring*, but also the spread of chlorofluorocarbons (CFCs) in the atmosphere, which subsequently turned out to be tearing a ragged hole in the Earth's protective ozone layer.

Mercifully, major progress has since been made in reining in the worst effects of such chemicals – although the continuation of the problem can be seen in US beehives. Scientists have found that bees are "entombing" certain cells in their combs that subsequent analysis shows have dramatically higher levels of pesticides and other chemicals.[3] Often it seems that for every problem solved there is a Hydra-headed series of additional threats, constantly morphing and mutating.

Take, for example, the issue of acid rain, which was such a major concern in countries such as Germany a couple of decades ago. Recent tracking of media coverage of the acidification story around the world shows a striking tailing off in the level of attention given to it by editors and journalists. But we have also seen a very different form of acidification surfacing in the world's oceans, with growing concern that the increasing carbon content of our atmosphere is leading surface waters of our seas and oceans to become more acidic – posing a growing threat to life forms, including coral reefs, that evolved to cope with very different conditions.

Such emerging challenges are a key reason that most current definitions of sustainability are too weak, too supportive of business-as-usual complacency.

Have we created a global Ponzi scheme?

It is not hard to see where at least some of that complacency came from. There was jubilation in the capitalist world when growing numbers of communist states failed in the late 01980s. Much was made of their inability to protect the interests of their own citizens and their natural environment.

Nor was the criticism misplaced, though the triumphalism definitely was. Our own capitalist economic system, it turns out, has many characteristics of what economists and regulators would call a Ponzi scheme: a scourge of markets for centuries.

Most of us had probably not heard much of such schemes before the collapse of Bernard Madoff's "investment" operation – the largest fraud caused by a single individual in history. Such schemes, which pay returns to separate investors from their own money or from money paid by subsequent investors who have been lured in, rather than from any actual profits earned, are named after Charles Ponzi, who became notorious for using the technique in the early 01920s.

Like a shark, a Ponzi scheme needs to keep swimming, or it dies. The perpetuation of the scheme's returns demands an ever-increasing flow of money from new investors. Ultimately, however, such frauds are doomed to collapse because, inevitably, the earnings, if any, are less than the payments to investors.

Think about it for a moment and there seem to be an uncomfortable number of parallels with the environmental costs we are imposing on future generations with our current economic models. From the destabilization of our climate to the destruction of major natural resources such as forests and fisheries, evidence of failure has been building for decades – and hasn't gone unremarked.

But, once again, we have been surprisingly blind and deaf to the early warnings. Partly this is because, as with Ponzi schemes, there is a logic that suggests that it makes financial sense to stay in the game until the last moments.

In the case of Western capitalism, our incomes and – in many cases – our pensions depend on the continuation of returns that are only achievable by running down ecological assets that by rights should have been handed over in good working order to future generations.

The difference here is that there is a clear intent to defraud in Ponzi schemes, whereas the fact that most current economic models defraud both a proportion of people already alive and, on an even greater scale, future generations, is generally an unforeseen consequence of the way in which these models value, price, and manage the biosphere and a broad array of natural resources.

At the very heart of our civilizational fraud sits a deceptively simple equation: $I = P \times A \times T$, where I is the total impact upon the biosphere, upon people, and upon future generations, while P stands for population numbers, A for affluence and T for the technologies used to provide for current needs and wants. Critics of current economic models sometimes talk in terms of "affluenza", a contagious, socially transmitted condition of sensory overload, status anxiety, debt, and waste.

True, there has been growing global media coverage of the climate change challenge, but often in terms that leave ordinary people (and even many experts) confused. Where our leaders choose to embrace the sustainability agenda – not surprisingly – they have tended to go for "weak" rather than "strong" definitions of sustainability.

Weak sustainability is often at the heart of the agenda that CEOs have been signing up for, by which they tend to mean corporate citizenship and philanthropy – generally with a fraction of one percent improvements in their environmental performance year on year. Such initiatives are typically poorly linked to the core business, being seen as an inevitable expense incurred to ensure a continuing license to operate – a form of "social lubrication" for the business.

Strong sustainability, by contrast, should be based on a thorough understanding of biosphere dynamics and the environmental impacts and footprints associated with a business, through the entire life cycle, from cradle to cradle. And it should lead to coherent, effective, and transformational action to restructure businesses and economies alike.

If we were truly advocates of strong sustainability, we would be shutting down entire industries, among them coal-fired power production and many – all-too-often state-subsidized – fisheries.

Strong sustainability would involve our species making the scale of transition we made during the early years of the Industrial Revolution, when we switched from potentially renewable sources of energy to fossil fuels – a process in large part triggered by the fact that in the early industrializing nations we had already removed much of the available tree cover. Indeed, one of the most depressing definitions of humankind I ever heard described us simply as "a disease of trees". And you can see the process continuing if you fly over the tropical forests of places such as Brazil, the Congo, and Indonesia – despite the "zero deforestation" pledge used by at least one company targeted by Greenpeace (see p.113).

What I want to do next is to look at a few key aspects of the current intergenerational Ponzi scheme, before turning to the question of how we drive the necessary system change to put the twenty-first century on a more sustainable footing.

Follow the soil

One of the people I sat down with while researching *The Zeronauts* was Lester Brown of the Earth Policy Institute, one of the world's leading environmental analysts. If World War II was about the future of democracy, he told me, what's coming is about the future of civilization. And the problem with the language of sustainability, he mused, is that "it doesn't stir our souls".[4]

Rather than taking the Martin Luther King route of stirring people's souls with his oratory, however, Lester Brown has carefully marshaled the facts over more than four decades – and they paint an ever-bleaker picture.

Box 2.1

At war with our soils

Follow the money, we are advised – but we might be better off if we were to track what is happening to soils. Often overlooked, they are a critical resource that we damage or destroy at a potentially crippling cost to future generations.

As you wing across the coastlines of countries such as Madagascar or Malaysia, you see the results, with rivers clogged with topsoil sluiced from land denuded of trees - giving the impression, where the soils are of a reddish hue, that the land is hemorrhaging into the sea.

"The thin layer of topsoil that covers the planet's land surface is the foundation of civilization", observes Lester Brown of the Earth Policy Institute. "This soil, typically six inches or so deep, was formed over long stretches of geological time as new soil formation exceeded the natural rate of erosion. But sometime within the last century, as human and livestock populations expanded, soil erosion began to exceed new soil formation over large areas."[5]

Not that this is new, as Brown points out. "In 1938", he recalls, "Walter Lowdermilk, a senior official in the Soil Conservation Service of the US Department of Agriculture, travelled abroad to look at lands that had been cultivated for thousands of years, seeking to learn how these older civilizations had coped with soil erosion. He found that some had managed their land well, maintaining its fertility over long stretches of history, and were thriving."

Strikingly, however, "others had failed to do so and left only remnants of their illustrious pasts. In a section of Lowdermilk's report entitled The Hundred Dead Cities, he described a site in northern Syria, near Aleppo, where ancient buildings were still standing in stark isolated relief, but they were on bare rock. During the seventh century, the thriving region had been invaded, initially by a Persian army and later by nomads out of the Arabian Desert. In the process, soil and water conservation practices used for centuries were abandoned."

I visited the very same area some years back - and, while we were struck by the beauty of the ruins, the ecological lessons were stark for those with the eyes to see.

Travel south and east to Ethiopia, a mountainous country with highly erodible soils, and the situation is heading in pretty much the same direction, with the country estimated to be losing around 2 billion tons of topsoil a year. As Brown comments: "This is one reason Ethiopia always seems to be on the verge of famine, never able to accumulate enough grain reserves to provide meaningful food security. Soil erosion from the deterioration of grasslands is widespread. The world's steadily growing herds of cattle and flocks of sheep and goats forage on the two-fifths of the Earth's land surface that is too dry, too steeply sloping, or not fertile enough to sustain crop production."

Nor is this problem confined to what some would see as basket case countries. Perhaps surprisingly, given the awe in which its recent development is held, China faces similar challenges.

"After the economic reforms in 1978 that shifted the responsibility for farming from large state-organized production teams to farm families", Brown continues, "China's cattle, sheep, and goat populations spiraled upward. While the United States, a country with comparable grazing capacity, has 97 million cattle, China has a slightly smaller herd of 82 million. But while the United States has only 9 million sheep and goats, China has 284 million. Concentrated in China's western and northern provinces, sheep and goats are destroying the land's protective vegetation. The wind then does the rest, removing the soil and converting productive rangeland into desert. China's desertification may be the worst in the world."

China "is now at war. It is not invading armies that are claiming its territory, but expanding deserts. Old deserts are advancing and new ones are forming like guerrilla forces striking unexpectedly, forcing Beijing to fight on several fronts." It is worth remembering that, within living memory, two of the world's great countries – the US and the erstwhile Soviet Union – have seen agricultural booms followed by ecological busts, with devastating dust bowls forming.

In the US, this overexpansion of farming onto vulnerable lands culminated during the 01930s in the "Dust Bowl", chronicled by John Steinbeck in his harrowing novel <u>The Grapes of Wrath</u>. "In a crash program to save its soils", Brown recalls, "the United States returned large areas of eroded cropland to grass, adopted strip-cropping, and planted thousands of miles of tree shelterbelts." The Soviet Union followed pretty much the same downward track, beginning in the mid-01950s. The result, as agronomists had predicted, was another dust bowl.

Now, though it is not a popular thing to say in the region, we see a third massive cropland expansion taking place in the Brazilian Amazon Basin and in the <u>cerrado</u>, a savannah-like region bordering the basin on its south side. "Land in the cerrado, like that in the US and Soviet expansion, is vulnerable to soil erosion", Brown warns. "This cropland expansion is pushing cattle ranchers into the Amazon forests, where ecologists are convinced that continuing to clear the area of trees will end in disaster."

The system's crashing – slowly

All of this may seem happily remote for those sitting in the comfort of rich world cities, but impending system crashes periodically reach out and affect our comfortable realities.

One of the most distressing books I have read recently was the account of what happened to Abdul Rahman Zeitoun in New Orleans when Hurricane Katrina struck the region in 02005. In his account of one of the world's costliest natural disasters to date, *Zeitoun*, Dave Eggers describes how what we take for the fundamental building blocks of civilized society can quickly break down under such stresses – particularly where the government itself is somewhat deranged, as the US was in the aftermath of the 9/11 attacks of 02001.[6]

Think, too, of the plight of the communities affected by the earthquakes and tsunami that tore into northern Japan as I was developing the first draft of *The Zeronauts*. Intriguingly, it turned out that Tepco (Tokyo Electric Power Company) had published a number of ambitious zero targets a few years ago, but they applied to waste – not to the challenge of ensuring that there was zero risk of the company's (and country's) nuclear reactors teetering on the edge of melt-down in the event of the sort of earthquake that hit on Friday, 11 March 02011.

Some of us may have been obsessing, albeit not always very effectively, about climate change for some time; but the work of highly respected scientific organizations such as the Stockholm Resilience Centre shows that we are now infringing natural limits in multiple dimensions. In fact, the degree to which we are destabilizing the climate is overshadowed in Figure 2.1 by the extent to which we have already overshot key limits in two other dimensions – biodiversity loss and nitrogen cycles. The science suggests that in the process we are losing significant freedom of maneuver in our attempts to keep ourselves within the remaining boundaries.

How to wake up political and business leaders to such threats? Sometimes Nature itself takes a hand. As Katrina knocked out or crippled scores of Wal-Mart stores across the American south, for example, Lee Scott, the giant retailer's CEO at the time, had a powerful awakening. He was quoted as saying that he suddenly realized that all the challenges that environmentalists had been warning of, among them the destruction of fisheries, forests, and soils, were in effect "Katrina in slow motion".

The long-term environmental goals that the company adopted were these: to be supplied 100 percent by renewable energy; to create zero waste; and to sell products that sustain our resources and environment. For a blow-by-blow account of some of the adventures along the way, read *Force of Nature*, subtitled "The Unlikely Story of Wal-Mart's Green Revolution", by Edward Humes.[7]

It's not just that we are approaching possible peaks in the production of environmental goods such as oil, water, and fish, but that we are undermining the Earth's capacity to keep those resources flowing. This truly is going to be a zero-sum game, with future generations pretty certain to be the big losers.

Perhaps every politician, worldwide, should be sent a free copy of Jared Diamond's book *Collapse*? This describes how environmental factors have so often been complicit in the fall of great powers – and even entire civilizations.[8] He recalls the civilizations – from Easter Island to various empires of Central America and the Middle East's Fertile Crescent – brought to their knees wholly or in part because they overtaxed their environmental resource base.

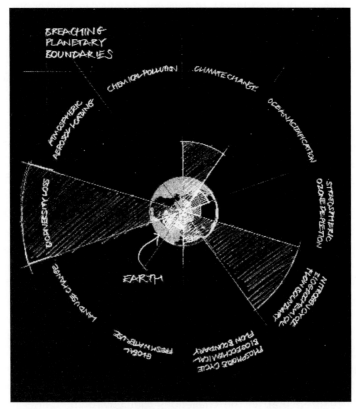

Figure 2.1 Breaching planetary boundaries

A Plimsoll Line for Earth?

It seems increasingly clear that what we need for our planet is something akin to the Plimsoll Line, which shipping lines use to ensure that their vessels are not overloaded to the point where they are likely to founder.[9]

While writing *The Zeronauts*, I sailed over the site of one of the world's most extraordinary wrecks, at Ulburun on the southern coast of Turkey.[10] This tragedy dates back to the fourteenth century BCE. Interestingly, the first known official loading regulations were even older, dating back to legislation originating in the kingdom of Crete in 02500 BCE, when it seems that vessels were required to pass loading and maintenance inspections. Roman sea regulations also contained similar regulations. Later, in the Middle Ages, the Venetian Republic, Genoa, and the Hanseatic League required ships to load to a "load line".

During the 01860s, after increased – and often stupefyingly horrible – loss of ships due to overloading, a British MP, Samuel Plimsoll, took up the load line cause. The resulting Plimsoll Line was designed to be painted amidships, indicating the legal limit to which a ship could be loaded – with some variation for specific water types and temperatures, given that warm or salty water can be more buoyant.

The basic idea is to ensure that a ship has sufficient "freeboard" (the distance from the water line to the main deck) and sufficient buoyancy to cope with the conditions likely to be experienced once at sea. All commercial ships, other than in exceptional circumstances, now have to have a load line symbol painted on both sides of the vessel. The load line, which is calculated by an independent authority, makes it easy for anyone to determine if a ship has been overloaded.

Someone who knows the Plimsoll story inside out is Nicolette Jones, who wrote an extraordinary biography of the innovator, *The Plimsoll Sensation*.[11] The battle to force ship-owners and other interested parties to adopt the new approach was at times exceedingly bitter, raging back and forth for years, at one point almost bringing down the government of the day.

Jones notes that one recalcitrant ship-owner even went so far as to offer to paint the Plimsoll mark on the funnel of his vessel. Almost funny, but once again recent decades have seen the evolution of extremely sophisticated lobbies designed to sow confusion in the minds of those called upon to decide whether or not to act on the sort of challenges spotlighted by the Earth Policy Institute and the Stockholm Resilience Centre.

"Doubt is our product", wrote one tobacco industry lobbyist, and in their remarkable book, *Merchants of Doubt*,[12] Naomi Oreskes and Erik Conway take the lid off the secretive world of influence for money. Among the most conspicuous practitioners of this dark art are the Koch Brothers, who own Koch Industries, and who have aggressively funded deniers of climate change.[13]

Still, the forces of good seem to be making real headway, this time on the issue of fitting our planet with the equivalent of the Plimsoll Line. Take the work of the Global Footprint Network (GFN). Founded in 02003, GFN notes that "Humans are the most successful species on the planet. But we are using more resources than the Earth can provide. We are in global ecological overshoot."[14] GFN was founded to "enable a sustainable future where all people have the opportunity to live satisfying lives within the means of one planet. An essential step in creating a one-planet future is measuring human impact on the Earth so we can make more informed choices."

At the heart of their approach is the use of the "ecological footprint", a resource accounting tool that measures how much nature we have, how much we use, and who uses what. Like bank statements, such footprints show whether we are living within our ecological budget or consuming nature's resources faster than the planet can renew them.

For me, GFN cofounders Mathis Wackernagel and Susan Burns are prototypical Zeronauts. Summarizing the challenge we face, they conclude that "If everyone lived the lifestyle of the average American we would need five planets."

To publicize the planet-scale implications of their work, which also focuses on individual citizens, companies, cities, and countries, GFN is involved in Earth Overshoot Day (see Figure 2.2), an idea first dreamed up by the New Economics Foundation. The day is designed to spotlight the point in time each year when our species will have consumed all the ecological services that Nature can sustainably provide in a year – from producing the raw materials for food through to filtering carbon dioxide from the atmosphere.

From that point until the end of the relevant year, we are effectively meeting our ecological demands by liquidating resource stocks and accumulating problem gases such as carbon dioxide in the atmosphere.

Worryingly, Earth Overshoot Day has been moving earlier in the year as human consumption levels have grown. Human demand for ecological services first began to exceed nature's ability to regenerate in the 01970s. Since then, we have depleted our annual budget earlier and earlier in the year. GFN data show that it now takes about one year and six months to generate the ecological services that humanity requires in one year. Clearly, this is not sustainable.

But how can we help people see all of this? How do we move across the "chasm" (see Figure 2.3) that so often appears when we are pushing forward new areas of innovation, standing between the point where the early enthusiasts and visionaries understand what is needed and the point where the pragmatic mainstream players, the conservatives, and even some of the skeptics switch on?

One way is to show people the evidence in new ways. And one of the most interesting visualization tools I have come across is the GFN Trendalyzer, developed with the help of one of my favorite ventures in the field, Gapminder,[15] recently acquired by Google.[16] This tool allows users to explore how statistics relating to various ecological and quality-of-life factors interact. You can choose

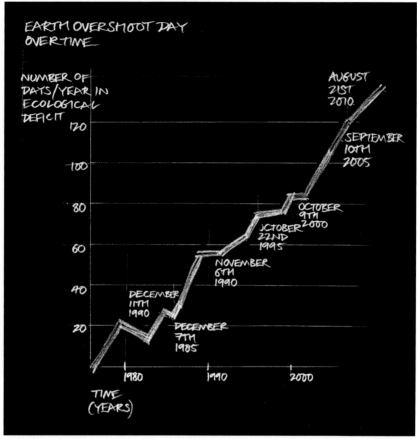

Figure 2.2 Earth Overshoot Day over time

from internationally recognized data sets on development, quality of life, and ecology, and rapidly see how these factors relate to one another over time – and across geography.

The Trendalyzer features the ecological footprint as one of the key ecological indicators, along with carbon emissions, energy use, fossil fuel consumption, and other factors. You can plot these, for example, against others such as literacy, mortality, income, and population to investigate trends and correlations.

A growing number of organizations are now using the ecological footprint approach to underpin their work and campaigns, one of them being WWF, with its One Planet program. Like the software that underpins the World Wide Web and specialist services such as Amazon, eBay, and iTunes, we may hope to see GFN spawning new waves of innovation designed to bring the necessary information and intelligence to citizens, consumers, corporations, cities, and countries – all covered in Chapter 4.

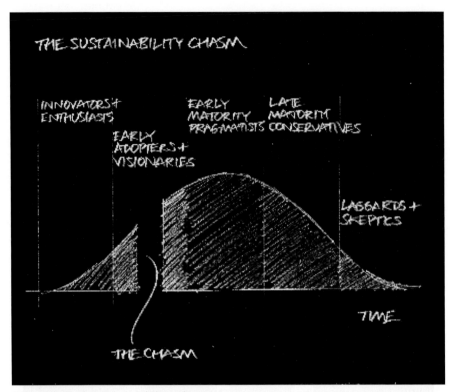

Figure 2.3 The Sustainability Chasm
Source: adapted from Geoffrey Moore, 01998[17]

But first let's take a closer look at some Zeronauts leading the charge in different areas. The first Zeronaut Roll of Honor appears in Box 3.1 (see pp.44–6), linking out to the various parts of the book where their ambitions, adventures, and achievements are described. Whatever language they may use, they are all involved in shaping our accelerating global Race to Zero.

3
Enter the Zeronauts

Transformational systemic change is generally driven by unreasonable people – who refuse to take the world as it is as any guide to how it might be in the future. We introduce the first Zeronaut Roll of Honor, spotlighting 50 pioneers – referring to coverage elsewhere in the book.

High above Ground Zero in New York, new generations of sky-walkers – ironworkers skilled at operating at dizzy heights – have been helping a new skyline rise above the ruins of the World Trade Center.[1] Inspiring, but essentially an exercise in rebuilding the status quo. Now the time has come to build toward what we call the "future quo", evolving very different forms of wealth creation, which could well throw up very different skylines.

It's time to meet some of the main characters of our story, though none of the pioneers spotlighted here – even in our first "Zeronaut 50" Roll of Honor (see Box 3.1, pp.44–6) – would yet self-identify as a Zeronaut. To my knowledge the term hasn't been employed to date in the sense in which I use it, though it did turn out to have been used by a band I stumbled upon through Google: formed in 02003 and called "The Zeronaut", their play-list contained songs with cheery titles such as "Napalm death", "Destruction", "Rage", and "Wormed".

And the origin of the word Zeronaut, as I plan to use it? Well, in the years before the Trojan War, the Argonauts (a name meaning sailors in the ship *Argo* – and reputed to be 50 in number) sailed in pursuit of the Golden Fleece, which may have been linked to lamb fleeces pinned to the bed of rivers to capture flecks of alluvial gold washed downstream.

These days, we might consider the Golden Fleece as a powerful symbol of the processes of wealth creation based on conventional natural resources. The challenge for gold-miners has always been to extract the maximum amount of precious metal for the minimum effort, a process that generally left immense mountains of spoil and huge plumes of toxic materials such as mercury.

I have been down a deep gold mine in the Rockies and it left me with a deep respect for those who work in the bowels of our Earth. But I am in even greater awe of those who have gone outward from our planet. During the second half of the twentieth century, Astronauts (meaning space sailors) and Cosmonauts (their Soviet/Russian equivalent) launched into the heavens, some in pursuit of the new commanding heights in the Cold War, others in search of new worlds to colonize. In the process, they helped to catalyze the evolution of everything from non-stick frying pans and minicomputers to satellite telecommunications. But the biggest, priceless gift was the outside-in view of our home planet.

So, first, to set the scene, I want to go back to the 01930s, to a time when space flight was a distant dream, the stuff of science fiction novels. And I want to return to a moment that, for me, underscores the vital role of innovation in warding off the great challenges that we face – and the crucial role of apparently unreasonable individuals in catalyzing transformational change.

Box 3.1

The First "Zeronaut 50" Roll of Honor

The Argo is reputed to have had a crew of 50. What follows is a first stab at a selection of leading Zeronauts, which will be launched as part of the Zeronauts.com website. Most of the nominees are individuals; but in some cases organizations or teams are listed, with several key individuals spotlighted.

One clear area of weakness is in relation to the financial markets – although a number of the Zeronauts flagged here are in that world to some degree, among them Bill Gates, Generation Investment Management, Richard Sandor, Jeff Skoll, Pavan Sukhdev (with his background at DeutscheBank), and Muhammad Yunus (though he has now been shaken out of the Grameen Bank). Another is that so many of the current honorees are American. This speaks volumes about the role of the US as a source of breakthrough ideas, technologies, and business models in recent decades – but it's perhaps significant that the last honoree in our list, thanks to the tyranny of the alphabet, is Zhengrong Shi, who is Chinese. Watch that space.

- SHAI AGASSI, Better Place (US/Israel; see pp.109–10, 138).
- MORTON ALBAEK, Vestas (Denmark; see p.86).
- RAY ANDERSON, Interface (01934–02011, US; see pp.84–5, 144).

- BAN KI-MOON, <u>UN Secretary-General</u> (South Korea; see pp.199, 218, 231).
- JANINE BENYUS, <u>Biomimicry Guild</u> (US; see pp.231, 232, 249).
- MICHAEL BRAUNGART AND WILLIAM MCDONOUGH, <u>Cradle to Cradle and MBDC</u> (US/Germany; see pp.4, 208–9, 237).
- LARRY BRILLIANT, for his work on smallpox (US; see pp.193, 235).
- LESTER BROWN, <u>Earth Policy Institute</u> (US; see pp.15, 34–7, 118, 185–6, 234).
- SUSAN BURNS AND MATHIS WACKERNAGEL, <u>Global Footprint Network</u> (US/Switzerland; see pp.4, 40, 107, 232).
- GARY COHEN, <u>Health Care Without Harm</u> (US; see pp.171, 228).
- GRETCHEN DAILY, <u>Center for Conservation Biology, Stanford University</u> (US; see p.113).
- RON DEMBO, <u>Zerofootprint</u> (Canada; see pp.134–5).
- POORAN DESAI AND SUE RIDDLESTONE, <u>BioRegional</u> (UK; see p.254n15).
- PETER DIAMANDIS, <u>X Prize Foundation</u> (US; see p.151–2).
- JOHN FRAZIER, SANTIAGO GOWLAND, HANNAH JONES, AND SARAH SEVERN, <u>Nike</u>, for their work on "Race to Zero" (Argentina/UK/US; see pp.202, 205, 227–8).
- BUCKMINSTER FULLER, geodesic engineer and champion of "ephemeralization" (01895–01983, US; see pp.26, 49).
- BILL AND MELINDA GATES, <u>Gates Foundation</u> (US; see pp.75, 187, 190, 194–5, 197, 235).
- AL GORE AND DAVID BLOOD, <u>Generation Investment Management</u> (US; see p.233).
- GREENPEACE INTERNATIONAL, zero toxics and zero deforestation (The Netherlands; see pp.227–8).
- JAMES HANSEN, <u>NASA Goddard Center for Space Studies</u> (US; see p.247).
- GODERT VAN HARDENBROEK AND EELCO RIETVELD, <u>Formula Zero</u> (The Netherlands; see pp.135–41).
- PAUL HAWKEN, environmentalist, author, and entrepreneur (US; see pp.68, 70, 144, 223, 240).
- PETER HEAD, <u>Arup/Ecological Sequestration Trust</u> (UK; see p.210).
- MARTHA JOHNSON, <u>General Services Administration</u> (US; see pp.109, 240).
- JERRY LINENGER, former Astronaut and Cosmonaut, <u>Circle of Blue/Volans</u> (US; see pp.48–51, 229–30, 243).

- EVE ENSLER, author of The Vagina Monologues, translated into over 48 languages and performed in over 140 countries, prime mover in global V-Day campaign to end violence against women (US; see p.123).
- JAMES LOVELOCK, independent scientist (UK; see pp.31-2, 232, 250).
- AMORY LOVINS, Rocky Mountain Institute and author of Reinventing Fire (US; see p.235).
- HUNTER LOVINS, Natural Capitalism Solutions (US; see pp.87, 224-5).
- DONELLA MEADOWS, DENNIS MEADOWS, JØRGEN RANDERS AND WILLIAM W. BEHRENS III, Limits to Growth team (US/Norway; see pp.54, 114-15, 250).
- HERMAN MILLER, INC. (US; see pp.163, 263).
- ELON MUSK, Tesla (US; see p.156).
- RAMEZ NAAM, Microsoft (US; see p.104).
- GUNTER PAULI, ZERI (Belgium; Japan; see pp.5, 145, 147, 232).
- MICHAEL PAWLYN, Exploration (UK; see p.246).
- KARL-HENRIK ROBÈRT, The Natural Step (Sweden; see pp.71-3, 232).
- RICHARD SANDOR, Chicago Climate Exchange (US; see p.211).
- ALLAN SAVORY, Savory Institute (Zimbabwe; see pp.234-5).
- FRIEDRICH SCHMIDT-BLEEK, Factor 10 Institute (Germany; see p.6).
- JEFF SKOLL, Global Zero (Canada/US; see p.218).
- DAVID STUBBS AND FELICITY HARTNETT, London Olympic and Paralympic Games (UK; see pp.172-4).
- PAVAN SUKHDEV, TEEB (India; see pp.113, 232).
- PAUL TEBO, former DuPont "Hero of Zero" (US; see pp.1, 5, 206, 208).
- RALPH THURM, Deloitte Innovation and Zero Hub (The Netherlands; see pp.12-13).
- MECHAI VIRAVAIDYA, PDA (Thailand; see pp.187-8).
- GEOFFREY WEST, Santa Fe Institute (UK/US; see pp.97-9).
- MATTHEW WRIGHT, Beyond Zero Emissions (Australia; see p.245).
- MUHAMMAD YUNUS, Grameen movement (Bangladesh; see pp.200-2).
- JOCHEN ZEITZ, Puma/PPR (Germany; see pp.4, 232, 242).
- ZHENGRONG SHI, Suntech Power (China; see p.88).

For more details, see www.zeronauts.com/rollofhonor.

Lady Houston: We have a problem

It is hard not to admire Lucy, Lady Houston – though she was, by all accounts, a bit of a handful. A London chorus girl, she eloped to Paris aged sixteen with a member of the Bass Brewery family, who was twice her age – and already married. When he died she was, as they used to say, set up for life.

Today she is probably best remembered for her last-minute gift of £100,000 to Supermarine, which allowed the British firm to refine their racing seaplane and go on to win the world-famous Schneider Trophy in 01931.

You can view the trophy, which Supermarine won outright after three successive triumphs, in London's Science Museum. The sculpture shows a young female nymph with dragonfly-style wings kissing a young man (who may be dead, unconscious, or simply ecstatic) floating on a breaking wave. The symbolism, however, probably goes much deeper than suggested by the young girl's naked, winged form – linking to the basic idea of spurring innovators to reach for the skies, even the stars.

And this is where, in retrospect, the world's democracies owe an immense debt to Lady Houston – who helped to fund critical experiments at a time when democracies were largely blind to the risks looming on the horizon. At the time of her Supermarine gift, Britain's Air Ministry had refused a last minute request for funds for the country's air racing team. Worse, it had banned the use of the plane that had won in 01929, forbidden Royal Air Force (RAF) pilots trained to fly these seaplanes to take part, and – the final nail in the coffin – refused to police the course, which was laid out in the midst of busy shipping lanes.

The Lady was not without her flaws, however. I wrote these few paragraphs while in Bellagio, not far from Dongo, where Italian dictator Benito Mussolini and his mistress would be intercepted in 01945 as they tried to escape to Switzerland – and were then shot and hung from a lamppost. And he comes to mind because, strangely, Lady Houston was also a sometime supporter of Mussolini. Still, strongly on the plus side, she saw a great challenge coming that her country was ill-equipped to respond to.

Her gift not only gave Supermarine – and its legendary designer Reginald Mitchell – the opportunity to build the winning plane, but also helped Mitchell learn how to build the Supermarine Spitfire, which would go on to play such a pivotal role in turning back the Nazi onslaught during and after the Battle of Britain.

Stepping back a little, I see this story as one part of the immense decades-long collective effort that would take us from the early flying experiments of people such as Germany's Otto Lilienthal, Brazil's Alberto Santos-Dumont, or America's Wright Brothers out into Earth orbit – and, eventually, way beyond.

Zeronaut in orbit

Jerry Linenger, for me both a striking expression of *Homo volans* and a prototypical Zeronaut, was a founder member of the Volans advisory board in 02008 – and is a rare bird indeed in that he has been both an Astronaut and Cosmonaut. He traveled roughly 50 million miles while aboard the Russian space station *Mir*. The equivalent, he explained, "of going to the Moon and back 110 times". He spacewalked more than three orbits around the planet.

By his own account, he returned a changed man. In his book *Letters from Mir*, he has collected all the emails he sent to his family while on the space station.[2] The original idea was to write to his first son, John, as a way of showing him in later life that his father had been thinking of him out there. But things, as Linenger put it, "did not go as planned".

After a relatively calm first month, a raging fire broke out aboard the space station, with 3 foot flames roaring out of a solid-fueled oxygen generator. "Choking smoke filled every nook and cranny of the station." The first respirator he tried on failed and, with the smoke so dense he had to feel his way by touch, he only just made it to a second, which mercifully worked.

Nor was that the end of the three-man crew's travails. Later, losing computer control, they raced to regain control as *Mir* tumbled through space. For weeks they worked in 90 degree Fahrenheit heat when the cooling systems went down.

When he finally got back to Earth, safe and sound, after five months in space, Linenger was asked a question by a Detroit trauma surgeon – a question that stuck in his mind. "He asked if I had any solution to solving the problem of the senseless violence of man against man that he sees the deadly consequences of almost daily in the Detroit hospitals. He asked me, I think, because he knew that I could see the planet as one, without boundary or division."

Linenger had certainly seen mankind's impact from space. "Black soot, residue from burning coal, covers the white snow and distinctively outlines the towns of Siberia and Western Canada", he wrote to his son. "In Amazonia, the jungles are ablaze. I can see literally hundreds of fires burning daily. The rising smoke forms great palls that are clearly discernible from space. Our planet's oxygen-generating jungles are being converted into short-lived farms."

"The people on the ground probably do not realize the extent of the damage they're causing", he wrote in a later letter. "The view from space makes it all too clear." And as to the question asked by the surgeon, as he read the news reports from places such as Bosnia, from his place in the heavens, he reported that he "could see no boundaries, no artificial divisions, only beautiful mountain ranges. That the people of the planet would be slaughtering one another *for whatever reason* made no sense."

His conclusion was that "the broad perspective is one that would serve us all well. I can attest to the fact that given a broad enough perspective, all conflicts appear senseless. We are all in it together on Planet Earth."

Linenger, too, came back from space with an overriding sense that we were hitting environmental limits – although in his case his conclusion was that water would be the defining issue of the coming decades. I had first met him through our joint involvement in the World Economic Forum in Davos, where he spoke on behalf of Circle of Blue,[3] an international network of journalists, scientists, and communications experts that builds and communicates the intelligence necessary to respond to the global freshwater crisis.

When I later interviewed Linenger for *The Zeronauts*, he compared being in the space station with being on Earth. "On *Mir* you had three people in a tightly closed ecosystem", he noted.[4] "You quickly realize that your actions have immediate effects on the others. An ethylene glycol leak one day, for example, resulted in one of my Cosmonaut crewmates having eyes swollen like golfballs the next."

By contrast, aboard our "Earth spaceship", he continued, "you have a closed ecosystem containing billions of people, but there's no immediate accountability for your impacts. Hey: the other guy's actions are always worse, right?"

Successful failure

As the planet's human population heads toward the projected 9 billion mark by mid-century, the emerging challenge requires us to radically cut our dependence upon natural resources and shrink our impact upon the biosphere. To get a sense of what this could involve, let's turn our eyes to space once again.

For several days through April 01970, as we have already recalled, the world held its collective breath as the three-man crew of *Apollo 13* struggled to deal with a cascade of life-threatening challenges. They were forced to conserve resources such as power, heat, and water to a totally unimagined degree – and then had to jury-rig a complex carbon-dioxide removal system, designed on the fly by engineers back here on Earth.

As a result, NASA would later call *Apollo 13* a "successful failure". But you would be hard pressed to use the same phrase in terms of our attempts to wrestle with the great challenges that our species faces as our numbers, activities and ecological footprints begin to overwhelm the carrying capacity of what in the early years of space flight would become known as "*Spaceship Earth*".

Indeed, someone who had an enormous impact upon my thinking at the time was R. Buckminster Fuller, whose books included 01968's *Operating Manual for Spaceship Earth*. Fuller's language was mind-bendingly complex, but often he surprised you with a visual gem. When we had breakfast together in Reykjavik in the summer of 01977, he told me that if you breathed on the surface of a 6 foot diameter steel sphere, the depth of the condensation on the sphere was equivalent to the average depth of the world ocean. This brought home the fragility of the apparently immense oceans in a very powerful way.

Way more influential, though, was his geodesic dome, for many a defining product of the era because of its ability to enclose living or working space with a minimum of materials – and a maximum of elegance.

Bucky, as he was sometimes known, bucked the underlying trends in so many ways, arguing that "we can make all of humanity successful through science's world-engulfing industrial evolution provided that we are not so foolish as to continue to exhaust in a split second of astronomical history the orderly energy savings of billions of years' energy conservation aboard our *Spaceship Earth*. These energy savings have been put into our Spaceship's life-regeneration-guaranteeing bank account for use only in self-starter functions."

A huge amount has been written on the space effort; but a book that powerfully shaped the way I see that era of our history was Marina Benjamin's *Rocket Dreams*, subtitled "How the Space Age Shaped Our Vision of a World Beyond". Sometimes described as a recovering space addict, Benjamin described how the frustration of our space ambitions, beyond a certain point, was compensated for by a shift into cyberspace. Instead of pushing ever outwards, we started to probe ever inwards.

Over the years, I have met a number of people who were part of that pioneering push into space, among them Dave Scott (the seventh person to walk on the Moon) and Jerry Linenger, already mentioned. A fair few Astronauts came back converted to religion, or with their faith strengthened.

One key reason, as *Apollo 13* Captain James Lovell would explain, was that:

> The lunar flights give you a correct perception of our existence. You look back at Earth from the moon and you can put your thumb up to the window and hide the Earth behind your thumb. Everything you've ever known is behind your thumb, and that blue-and-white ball is orbiting a rather normal star, tucked away on the outer edge of a galaxy. You realize how insignificant we really are. Everything you've ever known – all those arguments and wars – is right behind your thumb.[5]

That said, Linenger – as a scientist and engineer – is concerned that environmentalists too often crusade. That said, having overflown places such as China, he says he has seen "total obliteration, incredible pollution. They are using old-style coal-burning plants that other countries abandoned years ago."

Cosmonauts tended not to talk about religious experiences when they returned, for perhaps obvious reasons; but some of them also came back with a new way of looking at the world – like Salizhan Shapirov, a Cosmonaut from

Kyrgystan, who took part in space missions in 01998 and 02004.[6] Echoing Linenger, he spoke of the "catastrophic environmental damage we are doing. There are great swathes of Russia and China where the snow is blackened by industrial pollution."

Breaking the Sustainability Barrier

Jerry Linenger came back from space convinced that water would be the next big issue – and, as it happens, a global survey of CSR and sustainability experts carried out in 02009 by GlobeScan and SustainAbility would come to pretty much the same conclusion. Water topped the chart in terms of challenges rated as urgent or very urgent, ahead of climate change – despite the fact that the Copenhagen climate summit was about to open its doors.

Even more striking was the sheer number of challenges – many interlinked – that were now seen to be crowding the agenda for politicians and business leaders. They ranged from air pollution and electronic waste through to the acidification of the oceans.

Standing back from the results, one conclusion seemed to jump out. With 12 of the 14 issues tested seen as urgent, among them a number of social issues such as poverty, food security, and diseases such as HIV/AIDS and malaria, we were no longer talking about a set of single issue agendas, but a growing challenge linked to system malfunction – and the need for systemic change.

Spaceship Earth, in short, is having its *Apollo 13* moment. The more I thought about it, however, the images of the F/A18 jet fighter breaking the Sound Barrier and of Apollo 13 dissolved into another image, which seemed to represent a different dimension of the global challenge we increasingly face. Rather than simply smashing through an inconvenient impediment to our collective progress, it seemed to me, the 1-Earth challenge could equally be seen as akin to the infernal complexity of solving the world's favorite puzzle, Rubik's Cube.

The original cube was designed by Ernő Rubik in 01974 – the year I first started working professionally in what would later be called the sustainability field. I remember holding the baffling thing in my hands, but never really tried to solve it. Those who did try, once the original order of the "facelets" had been disturbed, typically found the solution hovering just out of reach, time after time. Even when you got all the "facelets" on one face of the cube sorted, the chances were that you would have cascaded a series of problems through to other faces.

You could scarcely have a more exact symbol for the complexities of dealing with our systemic challenges. People tried all sorts of ruses in their efforts to prevail over the puzzle, just as people have denied the reality and urgency of the 1-Earth challenge we face. According to one enthusiast, some so-called "cubers", after spending hours and days twisting and turning in vain, "resorted

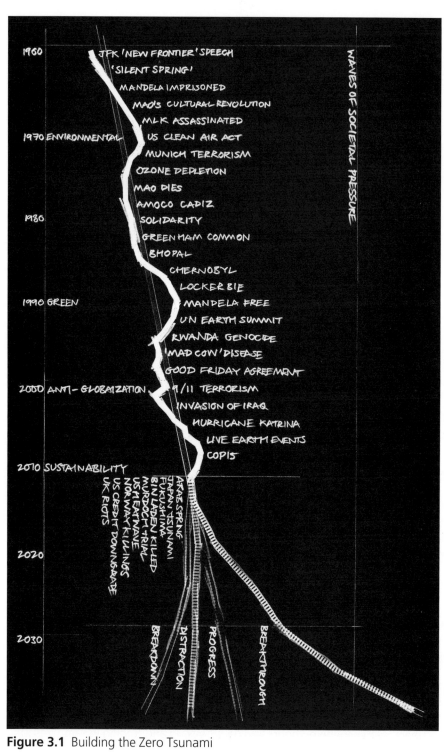

Figure 3.1 Building the Zero Tsunami

to removing and replacing the multi-colored facelets of the cube in a dastardly attempt to cheat the seemingly infallible logic of the cube, while others simply tossed it to the side and dubbed it impossible. The Rubik's cube, it seemed, had defeated all."[7]

Well not quite all. A few determined souls pressed on and, amazingly, found not just a single solution, but many solutions, ranging from beginner level to advanced. Over time, these pioneers also developed a series of algorithms (or move sequences) that made it possible for anyone to crack the cube. That is what the Zeronauts spotlighted in the following pages are also attempting with a whole spectrum of sustainability puzzles, all linking back to the one big overarching challenge of building a 1-Earth economy.

So where are we in all of this? Are we about to crack the Rubik's Earth code? Having surfed (and, in some cases, helped to build) earlier societal pressure waves, I have tried to capture where I think we are – and where we need to head next (see Figure 3.1).

Box 3.2

Preparing for the Fifth Wave

In the sketchiest of fashions, Figure 3.1 maps the course of four great pressure waves since 01960 – which is pretty much when modern environmentalism started.

The first wave moved toward a peak in 01969–01970, which extended through 01972 when The Limits to Growth study[8] was published and the first United Nations environmental summit was held in Stockholm. A key catalyst had been Rachel Carson's book Silent Spring, which spotlighted the deadly impact of persistent insecticides upon wildlife. The focus at this point was on the need for government action, so, for example, we saw the formation of the US Environmental Protection Agency (EPA) in 01970.

The first great downwave began in 01973–01974, paradoxically when the first OPEC (Organization of the Petroleum Exporting Countries) oil shock seemed to bear out the Limits to Growth analysis – but with the resulting recession helping to distract leaders around the world.

I asked Jørgen Randers, one of the Limits to Growth co-authors, why he felt their analysis had failed to gain long-term traction. "The reason," she said, "is that both capitalist society and its potential regulator, the voter, are inherently short term, and are not going to act until after the problem is sufficiently acute to bother both the system and the voter in the short term (which may take into account a period as long as a couple of years, but probably much less)."

In retrospect, however, the downwaves have proved to be the times when the really useful work gets done, so the period 01973–01987 saw an accelerating tempo of environment ministries being founded around the world, and the number of new laws threatened to go off the scale. Business was pretty much on the defensive during this period, fighting against the new rules before they were introduced and, at best, operating in compliance mode thereafter.

There were exceptions, however, one of them 3M, with its Pollution Prevention Pays (3P) program – launched in 01975 and covered in a bit more detail in Chapters 5 and 6. Such companies began to talk about moving "beyond compliance"; but their numbers remained precariously small. One contribution I made during that period, in 01984, was to coin the term environmental excellence, which then went viral (though we didn't use the word in that sense then) in big footprint industries like the chemical and oil sectors.

The second great pressure wave was triggered by a number of factors, key among them the discovery of the Antarctic ozone hole, with ordinary people told that something they were doing every day – using aerosols – was tearing a ragged hole in the skies, letting in damaging ultraviolet radiation that, among other things, could cause skin cancers in children.

With my colleague Julia Hailes, I managed to catch that second wave just before its peak, which ran from 01988 to 01991. In 01986, I had coined the term green consumer, and in 01988 we published The Green Consumer Guide, which went on to sell around 1 million copies in the original edition and some 20 foreign language versions.

We discovered that many ordinary citizens were no longer willing to subcontract their consciences to non-governmental organizations (NGOs), instead wanting to do their bit, sending market signals by choosing "greener" products over their less environment-friendly competitors. This was something of a shock for big business, which had learned how to lobby to slow down new regulations, increasingly using the resulting rules to their own competitive advantage by imposing greater costs on smaller or less skilled competitors.

The shock was amplified by the fact that new specifications could be imposed virtually overnight by market gatekeepers such as the supermarkets. Suddenly major fast-moving consumer good companies were scrambling to keep up. With the pressures building in many countries, CFCs were driven out of aerosols and many other applications, mercury and cadmium out of many batteries, lead out of petrol, and chlorine out of paper-making.

Then the second downwave began, again triggered by recessionary pressures and such distractions as the first Gulf War. This period ran from 01992 (coinciding with the 20-years-on-from-Stockholm UN Rio Earth Summit) to around 01997. The focus this time around was on the travails of companies such as Nike, Shell, and Monsanto as globalization threw up new environmental, social, and governance challenges through increasingly extended supply chains. In retrospect, my most successful contribution during this period was probably to coin the term triple bottom line in 01994 and the linked phrase people, planet, and profit, which both spread rapidly around the world.

The third wave kicked off, symbolically at least, in the streets of Seattle, with the protests against the World Trade Organization (WTO). This pressure wave revolved around the processes of globalization - and the agenda of the anti-globalization movement. I recall being in the boardroom of a major international financial institution in Washington, DC, with protestors massed in the streets outside and with one senior figure peering out of the top-floor window and asking: "What do these people want?" To him it was self-evident that globalization was a good thing: to the protestors it was anything but.

Over the space of a couple of years, the pressures mounted on institutions such as the International Monetary Fund (IMF), the World Bank and the World Economic

Forum (WEF). As a result, changes were made; but then the events of 02001 tore that reality apart. In the aftermath of the 9/11 attacks, the agenda – which had been opening out to include issues such as climate security – was rudely (and shortsightedly) hacked back to a much narrower view of security.

When the recovery came, and the fourth pressure wave began to build, the spotlight was very much on sustainability – often, though, defined as a slightly advanced form of corporate social responsibility. There were many reasons for this. Take Wal-Mart. Hurricane Katrina had hit the giant retail company very hard in 02005, as already mentioned, triggering something of an epiphany in its then CEO, Lee Scott.

When he switched on to "green" and "sustainability", a new set of requirements began to cascade through Wal-Mart's vast global supply chain. A parallel reason was the rapid growth of the cleantech movement, which offered potential solutions to a growing number of the challenges that were starting to pop up in boardrooms and C-suites.

Underlying all of these ups and downs in societal interest and pressure, there is a progressive upward trajectory – which, I believe, is tracking toward an eventual 1-Earth Paradigm. If wave 1 was primarily about environment, wave 2 was about green, wave 3 about globalization, and wave 4 about (somewhat diluted versions of) sustainability, then wave 5 could now be the 1-Earth or Zero Wave, with the Zeronauts perfectly placed to build, shape, and surf it.

The Fifth Wave is not as inevitable as the tsunami was after the earthquake off Japan in March 02011; but the seismic shifts that have been building for over half a century are generating huge energies. There will be many failures, as we see in our case on Formula Zero (see pp.135–41). But failure often provides the mulch from which the future grows.

Box 3.3

Some Zero Memes

- Formula Zero: pp.45, 135–41, 151
- Generation Zero: p.75
- Get Zero: p.24
- Goal Zero: pp.57, 158
- Global Zero: pp.46, 213, 245
- Mission Zero: pp.24, 84–5, 223, 245
- net zero: pp.11, 117, 250
- non-zero sum: pp.22, 250
- Pathways to Zero: Chapter 6, from p.142
- Race to Zero: pp.45, 57, 189, 227–8, 235, 241
- Zero Beat: pp.9–11
- zero carbon: pp.11, 100
- zero deforestation: p.113
- zero desertification: p.234
- Zero Discharge of Hazardous Chemicals: p.227
- zero emissions: pp.5, 135–41, 145, 210
- zero footprint: p.133
- Zero Hub: pp.12–3, 46, 57, 227, 241, 245, 246, 251
- zero impact growth: pp.12–13, 57, 251
- Zero Planet: p.210
- zeropreneur: p.145
- Zero Rush: pp.159–61, 247
- zero sum: p.22–3, 38, 57, 63, 78, 204, 251
- zero-till (and zero-kill) agriculture: p.239
- zero tolerance: p.207
- zero toxics: p.11, 227–8
- zero waste: pp.5, 10, 38, 57, 87, 114, 158–61, 173, 206–7, 240, 248
- Zeronaut/s: Chapter 6, from p.142
- Zeronautics: Chapter 6, p.142
- zeronomics: p.247
- zerowashing: pp.57, 247

For these energies to be put to good work we must get the politics right. That was borne in on me as I read about America's largest net-zero energy office complex, the headquarters of the National Renewable Energy Laboratory (NREL). When I visited the lab in 01981, it was the Solar Energy Research Institute (SERI).[9] I was there to see SERI Director Denis Hayes, to whom right-wing, pro-fossil-fuels President Reagan gave the boot just a few days later.[10]

Denis, who had been one of the founders of the Earth Day movement in 01970, was an early precursor of the Zeronauts. Serving on his international board for the first international Earth Day, in 01990, I got to know him a bit better. And so I was not surprised to hear him so competitive about the prospects of solar America versus solar China recently. "Back in the early days of SERI, we had a huge lead over the rest of the world", Hayes said.[11] Now head of the non-profit Bullitt Foundation in Seattle, his competitive instincts are still strong. "Now we're trailing Europe and China", he said. "The question is whether we'll catch up and pass them. I think we can."

For that to happen, the US government must switch on to sustainability, in general – and to renewable energy, in particular. At the time of writing, this looked supremely unlikely; but they say it often looks darkest just before dawn.

Meanwhile, the NREL HQ is one indication of where America may go tomorrow. Its 800 engineers, managers, and staff occupy a US$64 million building designed as a template for affordable, super energy-efficient construction.[12] "Nothing in this building was built the way it usually is", said Jerry Blocher, a senior project manager at Haselden Construction.

The aim: to find the sweet spot where net zero energy is neither too complicated nor too expensive. Now our challenge is to move citizens, corporations, cities, countries, and, ultimately, our entire civilization into that damnably elusive sweet spot.

II

CRACKING THE
1-EARTH CODE

Alice laughed:
  "There's no use trying", she said;
  "one can't believe impossible things."
  "I daresay you haven't had much
practice",
  said the Queen.

Alice's Adventures in Wonderland,
                              Lewis Carroll,
                                        01865

LING

4
Turbulent Teens
Our Detox Decade

> The decade to 2020 is set to be our Detox Decade, in which we are forced to abandon unsustainable mindsets, behaviors, and valuation models. Three scenarios are presented: breakdown, change as usual, and breakthrough. We dig into five key domains (the 5Cs) where innovation is taking place: citizens, corporations, cities, countries, and, ultimately, our civilization.

Lenin said that "There are decades where nothing happens; and there are weeks where decades happen."[1] Recent times have seen plenty of weeks of that sort – and the evidence suggests that this century's second decade will see change becoming endemic. "The Turbulent Teens", is one name suggested by a leading business organization for the decade through to 2020.[2] And almost everywhere we look, the evidence suggests that our species is in for a period of profound detoxification. Perhaps a better label would be the "Detox Decade"?[3]

But whatever label finally sticks, spotting early clues as to where the future may take us is never easy. It gets slightly less difficult, however, if you have some sense of where to look. So where in the world would you look for evidence that Zeronauts are creating the foundations of a better future? Let's open a window on the worlds of some of the innovators, entrepreneurs, and investors who are trying to turn a number of impossibilities into real-world possibilities.

The metaphor that springs to mind here is that of the humble Petri dish, in which scientists grow colonies of micro-organisms, in search of useful insights and, if all goes well, new sources of well-being, health, and wealth. So let's explore five distinct zero zones, where potentially transformative innovation is under way. And, in the process, let's also remember that many earlier transformations have exploded out from niches and early experiments that looked desperately unpromising at the time – even to those in the driving seat.

But first a few words about Petri dishes. As someone who generally works at a supremely untidy desk, I have taken great comfort in the achievements of Sir Alexander Fleming. Best remembered as the brilliant researcher who discovered penicillin, he partly owed his renown to the fact that he ran a pretty messy laboratory.

Famously, on a September day in 01928, he left a stack of Petri dishes of staphylococci on a bench, in a corner. On returning, he spotted something strange: one culture had been contaminated with a fungus, with the unexpected result that the colonies of staphylococci immediately surrounding it had been destroyed, while other colonies further away seemed to be unaffected. Some unknown active principle seemed to be at work.

Luckily, Fleming's mind was primed for just this sort of serendipity. During World War I, he had discovered that some antiseptics used to treat infected wounds made matters worse by killing off benign organisms that are part of the body's natural defenses, yet leaving harmful bacteria untouched.

Some part of his brain was still looking for something that would tackle those hard-to-kill microbes. Sadly, there is no time to tell the extraordinary story of how he and his colleagues fought to extract enough of the active principle, penicillin, to tackle infections, nor of how eventual mass production was started in time to treat Allied wounded during and after the D-Day landings.

Instead, I recall the Fleming saga here not to justify untidiness, but to make the point that tomorrow's solutions are often to be found in unlikely places.

So where in the world might we now look for the equivalent of Fleming's Petri dishes when it comes to the Race to Zero? And where they exist, what sort of future do they herald? We will look in five places: the minds of citizens, the C-suites of corporations, the booming global network of cities and megacities, an A-to-Z of countries, and – the ultimate bottom line – our civilization itself.

Breakdown, change as usual, or breakthrough?

To sort the evidence into meaningful clusters, it may help to sketch several possible future trajectories, or scenarios.

The first of our three scenarios is the 100 percent negative one, "breakdown", a world in which early experiments and enthusiasm fade in the face of wider incomprehension and resistance to change – and our businesses, cities, and economies overshoot ecological limits, bringing the planetary roof down on our heads.

History shows that the end can come suddenly. Those with long memories may remember that 17 April 01975 was declared "Day Zero" by the Khmer Rouge, who had just taken Cambodia's capital city, Phnom Penh, after a bitter war – and were about to decant its inhabitants into what became known as the "Killing Fields". Cambodia recovered, to a degree, but most previous civilizations didn't.[4]

This was the "breakdown" scenario on an almost unimaginable scale; but extreme situations often create the preconditions for history to take one of its periodic excursions into the hell of wars and, on occasion, genocides. Those who think it impossible that the world can turn around in time forecast zero-sum outcomes driven by climate change and ecological overshoot. Individual regions, countries, and communities may hope to isolate themselves from the worst effects, they say, at least for a while; but the general outlook, they assert, is grim.

If we imagine the breakdown scenario in a Petri dish, it would probably involve a set of cultures that are breaking down, leaving a noisome sludge – possibly even melting the bottom of the dish itself.

The second scenario, in which things muddle along for some time, is "change as usual" – where change does happen, but political leaders, investors, and the global C-suite proceed at a dangerously relaxed, incremental pace. There are plenty of projects designed to boost efficiency and effectiveness, to satisfy and even exceed customer needs and wants; but the need for – and possibility of – system change is not understood by most people, even by so-called leaders.

If you look into the change-as-usual Petri dish, you may see some sort of balance, with potentially aggressive cultures largely held in check by adaptive mainstream cultures – but with the ever-present risk that a shock to the system could send things spinning out of control.

And the third scenario, underpinning the transformative change agenda that sits at the heart of *The Zeronauts*, is "breakthrough". For Zeronauts, however, it has to be based on new forms of 1-Earth thinking – and have the potential to help us work our way through the looming Sustainability Barrier.

The breakthrough scenario assumes that, with the usual ups and downs, ins and outs, the trajectory of our societies and economies is pointed toward a very different set of outcomes – in fields as disparate as population growth, pandemics, poverty, pollution, and the proliferation of weapons of mass destruction, as described in Chapter 7.

There is nothing automatic or guaranteed about this, clearly. The process will have to start with the biggest "detox" in history, a progressive weaning off the cornucopian lifestyles that the world's better-off inhabitants have accustomed themselves to in the post-World War II era.[5] And the detox process must involve all five of the levels we will explore in this chapter: citizens, corporations, cities, countries, and, ultimately, our taken-for-granted civilization. So let's take a peek into each of these in turn:

1 The first Petri dish we inspect is the brain – and mind – of the ordinary **citizen**. Each of us, to some degree, can help to drive (or impede) change, among other things as voters, consumers, innovators, entrepreneurs, or investors – if we decide to do so. So what are we now thinking about the great challenges outlined earlier? And what are the most important brakes and accelerators in terms of the necessary behavioral changes?

2 The second Petri dish we look into is the world of business – and particularly the **corporations** that have emerged as the most powerful engines of global capitalism. We consider how some of the challenges already discussed are perceived, prioritized, and tackled in boardrooms and C-suites. But while corporations remain our best hope for breaking through the Sustainability Barrier, we also need to engage those who shape their thinking most powerfully, including stock markets, financial analysts, and standards agencies, investors, city administrations, and national and intergenerational government agencies.

3 Third, we investigate the way in which **cities**, where over half the world's population now live, are emerging as some of the most interesting zones of experimentation, pulling together concentrations of talent, risks, and opportunities that look set to spur the next great transformation in human values, priorities, and economies.

4 Fourth, we take the lids off a series of even larger dishes, representing entire **countries**. These not only powerfully shape our sense of identity but also – for better or worse – provide the platforms from which at least some of our political leaders are trying to respond to the great global challenges.

5 Fifth, and most taxing of all, we explore an even bigger Petri dish, looking at the prospects for rewiring our entire **civilization**, and guiding it toward more sustainable outcomes.

Our biggest Petri dish: Earth

As we peer into these five zones of ferment and change, we should keep in mind a sixth Petri dish, the biggest of them all: Planet Earth. If, as I believe, we are headed toward a 1-Earth Paradigm, future generations will see the world very differently. Imagine what they might say to us today if they could find some way to get in contact. They would almost certainly observe that we are acting as if whenever we need money we can sell – and have surgically removed – one or more of our organs: a kidney, a lung, a length of artery, even parts of our brain.

That, in effect, is what we do when we clear-fell forests, exhaust oceanic fisheries, run down aquifers that have taken millennia to build up, or expose children to environmental toxins that stunt their development. Normally, because trade links and supply chains separate out producers and suppliers, we can't see what impacts our priorities, choices, and lifestyles create – many of the adverse impacts and outcomes are felt a long way away.

You can't miss the evidence, though, when you are in orbit around Earth. No surprise, then, that several of the earliest Zeronauts had been into space. The *Apollo 13* crew, with their failing life-support systems, provide an unnervingly close parallel to the breakdown scenario, where we sometimes seem to be headed on this small planet of ours.

But what if, like the returning Astronauts and Cosmonauts, we learned to see a world without boundaries? What if we could learn to appreciate this planet's unique fitness for life – and appreciate its vulnerability to the nature and scale of the ecological footprints that we are now imposing?

And what if, as the Zeronaut would ask, we turned the current economic model on its head – deciding instead to invest in a non-zero-sum future? What if, instead of drawing down our biosphere reserves, we began to invest in restoring and extending our ecological assets?

Impossible, many will say. But in each of the Petri dishes we will investigate there seem to be areas where the envelope of impossibility is being stretched and, in some cases, punctured. In each case, we will spotlight a small sample of innovators who seem to be moving in the right (or at least promising) directions. They can be compared to the small colonies of incalculably important organisms discovered by Sir Alexander Fleming on that far-off day in 01928.

But as he probably suspected – and others would soon discover – taking such solutions and producing them at industrial scale would involve overcoming immense new challenges. This is the side of things that is addressed in the emerging discipline of Zeronautics, explored in Chapters 5 and 6. Chapter 7 then digs into some of the complexities of "going for zero" in five key areas: population, pandemics, poverty, pollution, and the proliferation of weapons of mass destruction. For those at the leading edge of change, Lenin's dictum is very likely to apply – in that a normal century's worth of change is about to happen in a decade or two.

Figure 4.1 Petri dish 1 of 5

CITIZENS

> Never doubt that a small group of thoughtful, committed citizens can change the world; indeed, it's the only thing that ever has.
>
> Margaret Mead[6]

Margaret Mead's much-quoted comment on the power of citizens to change the world is much quoted; but mobilizing the citizen to act remains a formidable challenge. And there is simply no way that business or politicians can drive transformative change on their own: ordinary people have to support change – as voters, consumers, employees, parents, or investors – if critical mass for change is to be built.

For this to happen, our communities, cultures, and prevailing paradigm must themselves change, profoundly. It is increasingly clear that we must wean ourselves off big footprint lifestyles. Easy to say, but there are few tougher challenges than behavioral and culture change. So let's peer into the first of our Petri dishes, in which sits a typical human brain – the ultimate source of our minds, thoughts, behaviors, cultures, and, in the final analysis, civilizations.

Breakdown/citizens

Some environmental campaigners picture humans as a version of those mythical lemmings, streaming inexorably toward some sort of chasm. True, for the ordinary human brain navigating its way through early twenty-first-century realities, the fact that we all create daily globally damaging ecological footprints is a matter of little interest and even less concern. I was shocked to learn that 64 percent of Americans have less than US$1000 in savings, for example.[7] If you can't (or won't) take care of your own future, what chance is there that you will do so for the future of others?

Still, whether or not we choose to worry about it, our world is incontrovertibly in ecological overshoot. By the 02030s, according to even moderate forecasts, we will need – on average – the environmental services of at least two planets. Europeans, strikingly, already consume at the rate of three planets a year, and the Americans are burning along at five. Then when I was in Abu Dhabi recently a senior government official told me they are now running at the rate of six planets.

So why aren't we more concerned about our own environmental footprints – and other people's? Among the obvious reasons: the underlying science has been challenged in areas such as climate change; there have been very different views on how real all of this is and, if real, how significant, who is to blame, and what should be done; the time scales involved, at least for most citizens, politicians, and business leaders, often seem remote; and, perhaps most important, we are too wrapped up in our daily lives to consider whether we might be part of the biggest Ponzi scheme in history.

Worse, having seen ordinary people pile on massive amounts of debt in good times – for example, during the build-up to the "Great Recession", it is hard not to conclude that our species will forever choose to surf the booms and endure – or succumb to – the inevitable crashes. Worse still, there are those who see evidence of a "Great Splintering", where the traditional social contract has, in effect, been torn up, creating lost generations. Effective looting of society's wealth by oligarchs, many bankers, and hand-in-the-till CEOs has largely escaped the rule of law – encouraging the dispossessed (or those who feel they are dispossessed) to descend into anarchy, as (some suggest) in the London riots.[8]

This was the context for an invited essay I did for McKinsey, referenced in Chapter 1, in which I tracked the cycle of changes in mindsets, behaviors, and cultures through to deeper shifts in our underlying paradigm. Successful Zeronauts – and other change agents – operate across all of these levels. But increasingly they acknowledge that a critical challenge is to change the prevailing culture.

However big a social movement may eventually become, it generally starts out in the mind of just one person. Often their life to date has in some way primed them to recognize where the future might be headed, as was the case with Alexander Fleming. And for many change agents there has generally been a particular moment when they woke up to a different reality. Whether it was Lee Scott of Wal-Mart waking up to climate change or James Lovelock to Gaia and geophysiology, there was a gradual – or, in some cases, quite abrupt – opening of the eyes and of the mind.

Change as usual/citizens

As individuals, we vary enormously in the extent to which we worry about such issues – and in the degree to which we are prepared to take action. At one extreme, we have the man who vigorously complained that his can of Pepsi had too many bubbles; on the other hand, the millions of people who know that carbon dioxide is building up in the atmosphere and oceans, and yet who prefer to say and do nothing.

This was a situation we tried to tackle in the late 01980s and early 01990s with a series of books building on our 01988 million-selling book *The Green Consumer Guide*. The branding was critical, with the combination of "green" and "consumer" suggesting a more relaxed – even sexy – approach to critiquing consumerism than was typical at the time among more fundamentalist Greens.

Coupled with growing concern around issues such as the Antarctic Ozone Hole, the eventual impact of such consumer-driven initiatives upon product design and formulation turned out to be fairly profound, at least for a time, with chlorofluorocarbons (CFCs) coming out of a broad range of products, lead out of gasoline, chlorine out of paper-making processes, mercury out of batteries, and phosphates out of many detergents.

But there are many areas where there was little or no impact – and many where big issues were ignored or where new evidence on the nature and scale of our environmental footprints is only now emerging. Take marijuana, with recent research suggesting that in the US alone indoor cannabis production results in energy expenditures of US$5 billion a year. This, in turn, involves electricity use equivalent to 2 million average American homes – that's 1 percent of national electricity consumption, or as much as 3 percent in California. In greenhouse gas terms, even the 1 percent figure is equivalent to 2 million cars.[9]

Thankfully, recent decades have seen a boom in NGO activity around the world, with Paul Hawken talking in his book *Blessed Unrest*[10] of civil society organizations as an evolving global immune system. So where are we in terms of public awareness of – and concern about – major environmental issues? I asked colleagues at GlobeScan, a Toronto- and London-based research group that I have worked alongside for nearly two decades.[11]

Doug Miller, GlobeScan's founder and chairman, was bullish. He replied: "Through the global recession, GlobeScan tracking shows both prompted and unprompted (top-of-mind) environmental concern has been growing across a range of developed and developing countries. Environment is second only to the economy as the most important issue facing the world. This increase is a more recent phenomenon outside the developed West – perhaps as the environment has been forced onto the media agenda in developing nations as never before."

Chris Coulter, senior vice-president, dug deeper: "More specifically on climate change", he noted, "after the largely abortive Copenhagen climate summit in 02009, GlobeScan research identified an important shift in global views of climate change. Until then, for most of the decade citizens of the developed economies of the OECD [Organisation for Economic Co-operation and Development] had expressed more concern than those in developing and middle-income economies about the changing climate. But in 02010, we saw climate concern in non-OECD countries surpass levels in industrialized nations."

So how can the ordinary citizen get a better sense of – and a better grip on – his or her environmental footprint? One answer is to try the calculator offered free by the Global Footprint Network. While the original tool was based on data for the US and Australia, two of the biggest footprint societies on Earth, the range of countries is being expanded to make the results more relevant in other countries.

If you want to dig further into your footprint, another fascinating pioneer is Dara O'Rourke of *GoodGuide*.[12] His firm aims to provide authoritative information about the health, environmental, and social performance of companies and on tens of thousands of the products that they make. Even the most everyday products, as *GoodGuide* notes, "often have hidden and sometimes disturbing stories – stylish apparel made in Asian sweatshops, or baby care products containing cancer-causing chemicals."

"Our mission is to help consumers make purchasing decisions that reflect their preferences and values", they say. "We believe that better information can transform the marketplace: as more consumers buy better products, retailers and manufacturers face compelling incentives to make products that are safe, environmentally sustainable and produced using ethical sourcing of raw materials and labor."

I was on the advisory board of San Francisco-based Physic Ventures when it invested in *GoodGuide*, founded in 02007 by O'Rourke, a professor of environmental and labor policy at the University of California at Berkeley. Users scan products, for example, with their iPhones, either in the store or at home, and can then access in-depth information about both them and their manufacturers. When I dropped in on them early in 02011, they showed me one of their latest applications, designed to slot into people's Amazon search windows, enabling them to investigate the sustainability credentials of different products and rival producers.

Finally here, as in any area of business, it can pay to address citizens and consumers where they are, rather than where you would like them to be. There have been many attempts to crack the code of green marketing, with the ultimate goal being to reach and convert consumers who are skeptical or cynical.

One approach I came across recently was the Shelton Sustainability Segmentation, which distinguishes between three kinds of environmental skeptics. Key to success, they argue, at least in America, is to "disarm the skeptics by showing that you understand that they view the green movement as a scam. Then suggest that China is beating the US in sustainability, or conversely, that China doesn't want US consumers to be sustainable. Focus on purity – the lack of toxins and pollution created by your products. And avoid discussing global warming at all costs!"[13]

Such advice is being listened to partly because green products lost out badly during recessionary times. Take Clorox, which introduced its environment-friendly cleaning line in 02008 and achieved sales of US$100 million that year. But not long afterwards sales had plunged closer to US$60 million.[14] Big blue-chip firms offering green lines have been harder hit than smaller green-chip firms, but there is clearly an Everest to climb here.

Breakthrough/citizens

Online technologies are helping to evolve new online networks and communities, joining a considerable number already in existence, some of which may well hold the potential for true breakthrough – given the right circumstances. These include Sustainable Communities Online, which evolved out of a ferment of community activity in the US in the 01990s,[15] and WiserEarth, which is more international in its coverage.

Certainly, civil society movements are now on a scale that would have been unimaginable a few decades back. "There are more than one million organizations and many millions of us around the world who are actively working toward ecological sustainability, economic justice, human rights protection, political accountability and peace – issues that are systemically interconnected and intertwined", says WiserEarth. Yet:

> Our effectiveness to prevent harm and institute positive change is undermined by our lack of collective awareness, duplication of efforts, and poor connectivity. What has been missing is a map and directory of our network that includes the resources for communication and cooperation; in essence, an infrastructure through which to coordinate our efforts. WiserEarth provides this infrastructure. It provides a way for us to become better connected and more effective at working together.

The founding vision of WiserEarth came from Paul Hawken, who recognized the need for such an initiative when researching his book *Blessed Unrest*, subtitled "How the Largest Movement in the World Came into Being, and Why No One Saw It Coming".[16] As he explained: "I knew that if we could understand the connections and visualize the breadth of global efforts on behalf of social and environmental justice, we would recognize the largest movement the world has ever seen. WiserEarth is where this movement can begin to see itself."

The fact that most such ventures have not yet broken through in the way that Amazon or eBay did is no reason to believe that something of the sort mightn't do so when the conditions are right. Among the hopeful signals: the way protestors during the so-called "Arab Spring" used Facebook, Twitter, and other social networks to mobilize and coordinate their campaigns.

Just as Fleming had his epiphany while staring into dirty dishes, so one of the most interesting champions of sustainable lifestyles had his breakthrough moment when inspecting cancer cells under a microscope – cells taken from one of his patients.

Dr. Karl-Henrik Robèrt, a Swedish doctor and cancer scientist, had been treating children suffering from various forms of cancer. Looking at the cells, he was seized by a simple idea. What if we could use our agreement on the basics of cell biology as a platform to understand the requirements for wider human well-being? He noted how families, care providers, and the wider community usually come together quickly and efficiently to support cancer patients – in stark contrast with their response when faced with the confusion and debate over the health of the planet.[17]

Viewing the world through the lens of the cell, the smallest unit of life, linking all life forms in ways that go way beyond politics and belief systems, Robèrt wondered whether it might be possible to build real consensus among governments, business people, and environmentalists?

To test out the idea, he founded The Natural Step in 01989. With colleagues, he drafted a first version of a "consensus document" and sent it out to a cross-section of scientists, including over 50 ecologists, chemists, physicists, and medical doctors in Sweden, asking for their input. Twenty-one drafts later, there was broad agreement about what we need to do to sustain human civilization on Earth.

With the support of Sweden's king, Carl XVI Gustaf, the document was then sent to every household and school in the country. Next came a first version of what were called the "system conditions for sustainability" and what later became known as The Natural Step framework.

Robèrt recalls that this took people "beyond the arguments of what is and is not possible; of what may be left or right wing. Instead, [it built] on a basic understanding of what makes life possible, how our biosphere functions and how we are part of the Earth's natural systems." It's no accident, however, that the movement started in Scandinavia, where Nature is viewed in a rather different light, and The Natural Step has sometimes struggled to gain traction in other cultures – although real progress has been made over the past couple of decades.

I asked Karl-Henrik what was one thing he wished he had known when he started The Natural Step?[18] I found his answer surprising. "The framework we have explored, tested, and refined in peer review since the launch is a dream coming true", he said. "This part of it all – the outcome of the idea – has beaten my expectations, no regrets. The idea was to develop a framework, use it as a shared mental model for inclusive group dynamics in science, strategic planning, decision-making, and community building, and, during this process, test and refine the framework in an action-research mode. That bridge between science and practice has worked beautifully. However, it is fair to say that the reverse is more true; there are things I am glad I *didn't* know upfront."

He explained:

> Most of the learning journey has been pleasant, but there have been some really dreadfully unpleasant experiences of how far a threatened establishment of obsolete paradigms can be prepared to go. There have been two large-scale attempts in Swedish society, orchestrated within alliances of threatened groups, to eradicate The Natural Step from the map by use of rigged campaigns in mass media, applying misquotes, lies, and various kinds of intellectual dishonesty. On both occasions it was possible to prove the allegations false to the public, but at tremendous costs of time, manpower, and peace of mind. Those two moments have been the most challenging of my professional life, and I am glad I didn't need to worry about them prematurely!

Next I asked what problems he wants to drive to – or toward – zero? "The ignorance and incompetence of our current leadership in business and policy", he began. "Good hearted and intelligent leaders still operate in line with old paradigms, looking at unsustainability as something requiring some added elements, rather than a correction of course."

"Our greatest sustainability problem", he stressed, "is not climate change, decline of freshwater, shrinking fertile cropland, declining biodiversity, poverty, or any other global challenge. It is not greed or any other negative aspect of human character, either. Our greatest problem is the lack of understanding of how those things are interconnected, from a systems perspective, and how they can be strategically tackled by use of clear objectives. The greatest challenge is incompetence in our mainstream leadership."

And the key lessons in spreading The Natural Step agenda to other cultures?

Peer-reviewed science is an international and democratic language. On this front, we have not met any resistance in any culture. So far the intellectual contents of the framework itself – a sort of unifying "chess-rules" – have been received well everywhere. However, the way the framework has been applied has been highly different in different cultures just like chess can be played with many different preferences and cultural styles.

   In some cultures, inclusive and transparent processes are not as prominent. You can apply the intellectual contents of the framework also in top-down demand-and-control cultures; but the potential of the framework for community building and really smart solutions is not fully exploited unless there is a bottom-up dynamic as well.

Finally, looking to the future, I asked what the challenge through 02020 looks like? "By then", Karl-Henrik concluded, "my hope is that The Natural Step will be mainstream amongst leaders in business, policy, and science. They should understand the enlightened self-interest involved in applying these boundary conditions when developing their organizations' values, visions, missions, and strategic goals."

Time to share

Inevitably, all of this translates into new business risks and opportunities. One acronym you hear from green marketing people is LOHAS, which stands for "lifestyles of health and sustainability". The estimated value of the US marketplace for goods and services focused on health, the environment, social justice, personal development, and sustainable living now exceeds US$200 billion a year. Some 19 percent of adults in the US, or 41 million people, are considered to be LOHAS consumers.

   But how do we start the detox process? Well, there are a number of other early-stage initiatives that aim to help shrink consumer footprints. Why buy, as *The Economist* asked recently, "when you can rent? This simple question is the foundation stone of a growing number of businesses. Why buy a car (and pay for parking) when you can rent one whenever you need to load up at IKEA? Why buy a bike (and risk having it stolen) when you can pick one up at a bike rack near your home and drop it off at another rack near your office? Why buy a DVD when you can watch it and return it in a convenient envelope?"[19]

There is nothing new about renting, the paper was quick to note. "Hotel chains and car-hire firms have been around for ages", it pointed out, "and the world's oldest profession, one might argue, involves renting. But for most of the past 50 years renters have been conceding ground to owners. Laundromats have been closing down as people buy their own washing machines. Home ownership was, until the financial crisis, rising nearly everywhere. Rental markets grew ossified: hotels and car-hire firms barely changed their business models for decades. All this is now changing dramatically, however, thanks to technology, austerity and greenery."

The trend has resulted in a flurry of books, including *What's Mine Is Yours: The Rise of Collaborative Consumption*, by Rachel Botsman and Roo Rogers; and *The Mesh: Why the Future of Business Is Sharing*, by Lisa Gansky. You can now rent a car, for example, from companies like – or modeled upon – Zipcar.

But at the same time, *The Economist* noted that "people are renting things they never used to rent, such as clothes and toys". Bag Borrow or Steal, for example, applies the Netflix principle to posh handbags. Freecycle helps people to give things away so that they do not end up in landfills: its website has 7.6 million members.

At the heart of all this, we seem to be growing impatient with paying to own things we don't use much. The average American, for example, spends 18 percent of his or her income on a car that sits in the street or garage most of the time. Even more striking, "half of American homes own an electric drill, but most people use it once and then forget it".

One of the most interesting findings is that people who used the Zipcar car-sharing scheme in Baltimore reported that they had changed more than their driving habits.[20] While researchers found that only 12 percent of users had taken more than five trips by car in the previous month, down from 38 percent before joining Zipcar, they were walking more (up 21 percent), biking more (up 14 percent), and using public transit more (up 11 percent). If these sorts of improvements could be sustained – and boosted over time – we might be headed toward real culture change.

Here comes Generation Zero

It's amazing how many things we seem to be allergic to these days, but carbon isn't one of them – at least not yet. Still, if climate-related stresses continue to intensify we may well see political pressure building, with growing numbers of citizens using their political muscle to pressure governments for an annual carbon ration to be imposed.

This will encounter enormous resistance, obviously; but champions see the idea of a personal carbon allowance or account as the fairest way of meeting national carbon targets. As with a bank account, we would receive statements showing the carbon weight for each purchase and how much of our ration remains. If we used up our ration within a year, we would have to buy extra credits from those who had not used their full allowance purchases. Those who lived frugally and did little traveling could make a significant profit from selling their unused credits.

Whatever the longer-term prospect for such rationing schemes, we are beginning to see at least anecdotal evidence of the "zero" language going viral. In recessionary times, growing numbers of young people have been embracing minimalist lifestyles, to the point where some parts of the media have started to talk of "Generation Zero".[21] Not all of them go so far as listing everything they own on a website, as software engineer Kelly Sutton does at the cultofless.com,[22] let alone attempting to sell or give away the majority of the possessions they do own, but growing numbers of young people have clearly decided to live their lives more online than in the material world their parents were raised to focus on. It will be interesting to see whether this trend outlives the downturn.

Icons of the emerging movement have included Facebook founder Mark Zuckerburg, who listed "minimalism" as an interest in his profile on the social network, while – perhaps paradoxically – we have seen a small growth industry in the publication of minimalist books. Among their titles: *The 100 Thing Challenge: How I Got Rid of Almost Everything, Remade My Life and Regained My Soul*; *The Art of Being Minimalist: How to Stop Consuming and Start Living*; and *The Joy of Less: A Minimalist Living Guide*.

Less minimalist was Indian steel tycoon Lakshmi Mittal, who announced plans to build a low-carbon mega-mansion in Surrey's green belt. It was promptly dubbed "Zero Towers" by the media.[23] Such efforts may help to develop new technologies, but it is hard to imagine such greening activities doing anything more than putting an infinitesimally small dent in the overall Lakshmi family footprint.

Another man who won't be too bothered if the price of carbon goes sky-high is one of the world's very richest people – and one of the unlikeliest Zeronauts of recent years: Bill Gates. Following his own awakening to the threat of climate change – and his encapsulation of that challenge in the equation $CO_2 = Population \times Services \times Energy \times Carbon$[24] – he says that he would prefer to be able to drive the climate threat to zero over the next 50 years rather than to be able to do the same with any single disease or to pick the US presidents over the same period.

But most of us are still light years from zero

It's sadly true. Yet, the sense that capitalism has a fundamental design flaw, and that it sits at the system's consumerist heart, is spreading. Even the World Economic Forum, that *über*-convening of the capitalist elites, has decided that sustainable consumption is "imperative".[25] It notes that "while sustainable consumption starts with the citizen – as the central actor in the global economy, as consumer, as investor, as voter and as employee – it does not end there".

Instead, the Forum concludes, sustainable consumption is not only about how much we all consume, but about "what we consume, how we consume and who consumes. It is only achievable with the integration of sustainability into business models, production and design. This is not about incremental improvements in the efficient use of particular inputs – conserving water, reducing carbon emissions or saving energy. It is about redefining value."

One of the enterprises we have been working with in this space is Recyclebank, based in New York. Their aim is to use incentives to spur behavioral change in such areas of waste recycling, energy efficiency, and transport. A tremendously exciting initiative.

One of the overarching dimensions of change that needs much further work is the overlap between three areas of what we see as the Venn diagram of forces, overlapping the challenge of breaking the Sustainability Barrier with, second, the need for disruptive innovation and then, third, the aging trend in so many of our societies. It isn't an iron law; but older people tend to vote more assiduously, they are well connected and have the time to campaign, and they tend to become more conservative with age. Their pensions are often invested in incumbent businesses, which gives them an incentive to keep things as they are.

This is an area Volans has been exploring with Accenture, the Doughty Centre for Corporate Responsibility at Cranfield University, and others – in what we call the Second Half program.[26] This is not an area to play a defensive game in, however: we must positively engage older people in addressing the great economic, social, and environmental challenges we face. This is something that Nigel Topping of the Carbon Disclosure Project is pursuing in his research on how to tap into – and further evolve – what he calls the "Wisdom Economy".

Still, the uncomfortable fact is that most of us, most of the time, remain sublimely ignorant of the overarching challenges we face, and as a result have little interest in possible solutions and little faith that what we might do as individuals could ever help drive real system change. We are most likely to take part – and sustain our efforts – if we feel part of something much bigger, and if there is prompt and usable feedback – for example, via new forms of online footprint monitoring. To truly engage, we need to feel part of something much bigger (for example, citywide or countrywide initiatives).

Before looking in those directions, let's peer into our second Petri dish, the fast-paced world of business.

PETRI DISH
2/5

Figure 4.2 Petri dish 2 of 5

CORPORATIONS

> After all, sustainability means running the global environment – Earth Inc. – like a corporation: with depreciation, amortization and maintenance accounts. In other words, keeping the asset whole, rather than undermining your natural capital.
>
> Maurice Strong[27]

Few people have done more to get the sustainability agenda airborne than Canadian Maurice Strong – that rare combination of a successful business leader who has also been willing and able to provide political leadership. His line of thought has been that if we treat our planet like a perpetual cash cow and fail to invest in its maintenance, ultimately it will fail us too. Seen as the man who globalized the environmental movement, he has argued that our challenge is to adapt the corporate form to future needs.

Yes, it looks impossible, particularly if you work inside one of today's giant incumbent corporations; but the Zeronauts believe that it is possible – given enough will, effort, and time – to rewire and reprogram corporations so that they automatically, reflexively, pursue 1-Earth strategies, build zero targets into all key operations with significant environmental footprints, and increasingly hold in mind both intergenerational time scales and equity.

Corporations are one of our truly great inventions. Having spent well over three decades working with them in different ways, though, I know how hard it can be to get them to embark upon even incremental change – let alone truly transformational change. Part of the problem is that the incentive structures they use tend to spur short-term thinking, a point that Roger Martin has made in books such as *Fixing the Game*.[28] This is what makes the protests by groups like Occupy Wall Street so important in that they force people to wake up and rethink.[29]

A business colleague I talked to in Amsterdam while writing *The Zeronauts* described companies as like ants following market pheromone trails, leaving little room for true leadership. A slight exaggeration, perhaps; but the reality is that we are going to have to get much better at laying the market pheromones in directions that we want business leaders to travel.

Breakdown/corporations

No question, at their worst, corporations can help to push the biosphere toward the breakdown scenario. Zero-sum competition is likely to be the fast-track to Armageddon.[30] Most corporations are highly skilled at spreading consumerist dependencies and even virtual addictions; indeed, their very existence often depends upon their success in doing so. As a result, the imminence of Doomsday was a constant refrain of some early environmentalists, including some I knew quite well – such as the late Teddy Goldsmith, founder of *The Ecologist*.

Over time, the warnings became a bit more tempered; but these days a growing number of entrepreneurs and business leaders have joined the chorus. They note that even if we could hold the world population at the 7 billion point that it hit late in 02011, we could only look forward to a viable collective future if corporations, their supply chains, and entire economies managed to break through the Sustainability Barrier at scale – and in rapidly growing numbers.

True, a growing number of businesses are appointing people with titles such as chief sustainability officer (CSO) to help them think all of this through; but the evidence suggests that the overwhelming majority of business leaders have a precariously weak understanding of what is going to be involved in breaking the Sustainability Barrier. To date, however, most of these people have focused on areas such as legal compliance, reporting, stakeholder engagement, and supplier challenges – all helpful in incremental ways, but scarcely transformative.

Change as usual/corporations

As the sustainability agenda has begun to mainstream, leading businesses have joined a growing array of organizations and initiatives designed to build critical mass for change. Having cofounded SustainAbility in 01987, when the word "sustainability" was hardly used in the current sense, I confess that it was immensely gratifying to see Accenture report in 02010, as already noted, that 93 percent of the CEOs polled in 02010 now saw their success in tackling the sustainability agenda as important to their company's future success.[31]

That would have seemed an extraordinary degree of progress from the perspective of the late 01980s, before the latest era of globalization. But where the results became literally incredible, for me at least, was when no less than 81 percent of those same CEOs – compared to 50 percent in 02007 – insisted that "sustainability issues are now fully embedded into the strategy and operations of their company".

True, a small but growing number of corporations are integrating sustainability-linked incentives within top management compensation packages, as well as within innovation and design functions; however, if you agree that sustainability is not about citizenship and corporate social responsibility (CSR), but about the complete rebooting of our economies, this result looks a trifle over-optimistic, more than a little complacent.

When it came to market drivers, perhaps not surprisingly, consumers still ranked as the top stakeholder group for these CEOs – 58 percent of the respondents named consumers, ahead of employees at 45 percent and governments at 39 percent. But this suggests where part of the problem above may be coming from: if you rely on consumers to signal the future of the sustainability agenda, chances are that you will severely underestimate the nature and scale of the challenge.

When I spoke to George Kell, who runs the Global Compact, in the summer of 02011, he agreed that the previous year's survey had presented an over-optimistic picture. Indeed, he noted that the Global Compact had still managed to attract less than one percent of the world's multinationals as members – and was even having to squeeze down membership numbers to get rid of some of the free-rider businesses that had signed up, but done little or nothing.[32]

Luckily, however, many of the Global Compact's members are among the largest corporations on Earth, with immense supply chains, enabling them to bring considerable pressure to bear on their suppliers – where they are minded to do so.

In addition, there is a growing industry dedicated to ensuring that the pace of progress is not only maintained but accelerated. To take just one example, some 2500 organizations globally now measure and disclose their greenhouse gas emissions and climate change strategies through the Carbon Disclosure Project, a non-profit agency based in London which represents over 500 institutional investors with combined assets under management (a measurement of their market muscle) of more than US$64,000 billion.[33]

And for younger people wanting to work out how to make sense of all of this, there are a growing number of online games designed to get things started. Nissan, for example, has developed its Planet Zero website, where players control an animated traveling electric plug-based character – which can tap into various energy sources to power the transition to a low-carbon future.[34]

Politicians and business leaders like to say that "failure is not an option"; but – as has been pointed out by various management gurus – if failure is not an option, then neither is innovation. And yet breakthrough innovation is precisely what we need, with the risks of failure likely to be even higher than in normal circumstances. Are these CEOs really ready to play this new high-stakes game?

The fact that carbon trading markets stumbled badly in the European Union doesn't make them any less important in future.[35] Take the area of carbon capture and storage (CCS), one of the key ways in which innovators are attempting to tackle climate change – which has been described as the greatest market failure of all time.[36] The risks in this area are immense, as was dramatically underscored when CCS pioneer Powerfuel hit the wall.

Founded by Richard "King Coal" Budge, who bought most of Britain's deep coal mines when the government privatized them in 01994, Powerfuel had attracted UK£36 million in start-up funding from KRU, Russia's second biggest coal-miner.[37] Creating a CCS plant on the scale envisaged by Budge was always going to be a complex challenge. At the time, the only existing CCS plant – built outside Berlin by the Swedish power company Vatenfall – was about 1/30th of the size.

But the UK government made things much more difficult, both by allowing a key competition (designed to award UK£1 billion to one company to allow it to build the country's first CCS plant) to drag on way beyond the original deadline, and also by changing the rules – so that only post-combustion carbon removal plants qualified. The Powerfuel proposal was for a pre-combustion plant, which would remove the carbon before the fuel was fed into the turbines.

The importance of ensuring that government policies and incentives are appropriate, clear, and consistent is amply demonstrated by this case. But we must hope – and I expect – that such mishaps will not deter a growing number of innovators and entrepreneurs from plunging into these new opportunity spaces. Meanwhile, we must also keep a close eye on the darker side of the sunrise industries, including the solar sector. In China, for example, there is evidence that solar equipment manufacturers – lauded in other countries as the leading edge of the renewables revolution – have been causing fairly widespread pollution, with dire consequences for local people.[38]

Breakthrough/corporations

Real breakthrough solutions can only come from business; but with many of the leading corporations still defining sustainability in terms of citizenship, it is clear we need to look farther afield. One key driver of change will be the growing international efforts to put big footprint industries under the spotlight – but the true spirit of sustainability is typically still found outside the business mainstream, in companies such as Yves Chouinard's extraordinary Patagonia.[39] If you haven't come across their *Footprint Chronicles*, the website that tracks the impact of specific Patagonia products from design through delivery, take a peek at what the future might look like.[40]

When Patagonia began, there were no award schemes for "sustainable" companies. Now there are many more. They are part of the market carrot to regulation's stick. I recently found myself helping to judge several award schemes, including the Carbon War Room's first round of their Gigaton Awards, the winners of which were announced at the Cancún climate conference. The intention is to look well beyond the usual suspects, though I have to say that some of the ultimate choices left me worried. Very few of these companies yet integrate sustainability within their DNA as Patagonia has done.

Separately, the Carbon War Room, backed by Sir Richard Branson, kicked off its 25-sector review of the global economy by targeting shipping. One key reason why shipping escapes public attention, unless a disaster happens, is that it's another case of "out of sight, out of mind". In addition, the extraterritorial nature of shipping also partly explains why it has escaped tough greenhouse gas regulations to date. Yet, ships account for over one billion tons of CO_2-equivalent (CO_2e) annually, or around three percent of global emissions from human and industrial sources, in addition to a range of other important pollutants.[41]

Among the things that get in the way of sustainable outcomes – ultimately of a sectoral detoxification – is the fact that ship owners and operators rarely pay for marine or bunker fuel. Instead, the bills are typically paid by the customers (or charterers), meaning that there are few incentives to owners and operators to improve efficiency. Then, too, there is the fact that the majority of shipyards, mainly in Asia, builds to standard types and charge prohibitive premiums for new technologies and vessel designs.

The Carbon War Room concluded that shippers, ports and other stakeholders such as insurers urgently need access to open and transparent environmental performance ratings. Meanwhile, according to the International Maritime Organization (IMO), the UN body that governs shipping, the industry could make money by cutting the first 250 million tons of its CO_2e. The IMO estimates that eco-efficiency technologies could reduce CO_2e emissions from shipping by between 25 percent and 75 percent, with the first 25 percent of reductions likely to be achieved profitably.

It also turns out that of the 100,000 vessels that spend most of their time crisscrossing the world's oceans, making only occasional stops at port cities, a relatively small number – about 15,000 – are responsible for the bulk of emissions and are thus obvious initial targets for efficiency and emission scrubbers.

Future technology developments – including a switch from the heavy sulfurous bunker fuel currently burned by ships to liquid nitrogen gas (LNG) or biofuels – could eventually contribute to even greater emissions reductions and present a market-based solution driven by reduced fuel costs. But for this to happen, the pressure on the industry needs to be sustained over decades, suggesting that the IMO and other government agencies will have to play a key role in persuading the industry to change course.

Resource scarcity is both brake and accelerator

A critical driver of the necessary change is likely to be the market valuation of natural raw materials – with recent years having seen rising prices for everything from oil to potash and rare earth minerals. The latter are critically important for industries churning out a wide range of high-tech products, including the MacBook Air on which these words are being typed.

Higher prices help to focus senior management minds on questions of efficiency and, ultimately, sustainability. But much work remains to be done in developing the underlying footprint methodologies and tools that will help boards and C-suites visualize, understand, and get to grips with these emerging challenges.

The penny, however, is beginning to drop. You see the impact of these trends in companies such as Ford, whose chairman Bill Ford – a long-time environmentalist – recently claimed Ford had experienced a "milestone moment" by embracing the challenge of creating electric cars at affordable prices. Following in the tracks of companies such as Toyota and Honda, Ford said it was planning "the creation of a family of electrified vehicles".[42]

A welcome move, but the company's CEO, Alan Mulally, had earlier underscored the enormous complexities such companies face in making the transition. "We have to have a disciplined technological roadmap", he said, "where all the pieces are in place to make it viable." And, he continued, "the issue with electrification is infrastructure: how the cars are charged, how clean the vehicles are, but also how clean the energy is to produce", which is where governments come in, again.

The longer the time scale for a business activity, the more likely potential future resource scarcity is to be taken into account by intelligent companies. The Swiss bank UBS, for example, recently announced plans for a 12-storey, 750,000 square foot headquarters in the center of London's financial district that (before they announced plans to cut the numbers of staff) were slated to house 750 bankers – but with some big differences over earlier designs.

The solar farm planned for the building's roof, which was also intended to sport a green roof area, is forecast to produce 6 percent of the energy needed each year, for example, and there are fewer windows than usual – to cut solar warming of offices and, in the process, reduce the need for air conditioning. Surplus heat will be recycled, as will waste and water.

More ambitious still are the plans of Deutsche Bahn, which runs Germany's railway system, to raise the percentage of wind, hydro, and solar energy it uses in powering its trains from 20 percent today to 28 percent in 02014 – and to become entirely carbon-free by 02050.[43]

True, most corporations would struggle to be able to afford even this level of greening – let alone a shift to zero impact. Chemical companies, for example, are increasingly exploring green chemistry, where new products are designed according to a dozen principles – among them toxicity reduction, energy efficiency, biodegradability, and renewability. As Dow Chemical's Sustainability Vice-President Neil Hawkins put it: "You have to find customers that want to pay for greener chemistry. Sometimes their value chains will support it – and sometimes they won't."[44] So a strategic challenge for such companies will be to find ways to select and favor customer industries that will help power the greening trend.

Cracking the code of 1-Earth business

Some of the companies most sensitive to such issues – because they are closer to the consumer – are the retailers and fast-moving goods companies. Clearly, there are companies you like – and companies you don't like. Unfortunately, the market performance of those you like doesn't always match that of those you don't.

So, for example, I have always liked much about Unilever and their genetic code in the sense that their founding values and activities made them something of a social enterprise of the day – and one that has cracked the overarching question for social entrepreneurs, which is how to achieve scale. But when I helped the company to launch its new *Sustainable Living Plan* late in 02010, its shares were trading at a significant discount to those of some of their major competitors, something the financial media were not slow to point out.

In the sustainability stakes, however, Unilever is again pushing the envelope, with a set of new targets for the decade to 02020 that potentially jumps them into a clear leadership position. Why is this happening now? There are a number of reasons, but a critical factor is that leading CEOs see the evidence of environmental change with their own eyes. In the process, issues such as climate change, access to clean water, and poverty alleviation are pushing their way onto board and C-suite agendas.

In launching the Unilever *Sustainable Living Plan*, Unilever CEO Paul Polman stressed that "growth at any cost is not viable", insisting that "we want to be a sustainable business in every sense of the word". The company's aim is to increasingly decouple the company's growth plans from related environmental footprints by cutting the amount of water used per ton of product by 65 percent in absolute terms, against a 01995 baseline; doubling internal use of renewable energy to 40 percent; and halving the environmental footprint of all new production plants.

But as Polman concluded, "ultimately we will only succeed if we inspire billions of people around the world to take the small, everyday actions that add up to a big difference – actions that will enable us all to live more sustainably", which is where the links track back to the citizens and consumers covered earlier.

Unilever, meanwhile, is going for a 100 percent solution in one area, pledging itself to buy all of its raw materials from sustainable sources by 02020. Today it buys just 10 percent from sustainable sources, so the stretch will be very considerable indeed – and the political pressures on the company at times intense.

I was told by one senior Unilever official, for example, that the company's top management had been called in by the Indonesian government for a dressing down on the Anglo-Dutch firm's efforts to shunt the palm oil industry to more sustainable production patterns. Such counter-lobbying can only grow as the Zeronauts take on big footprint incumbents. Leaders – and their investors – will often need great stamina to succeed with breakthrough solutions.

Interface still leads in the business of zero

And when it comes to sustained leadership in the business of zero, one company that comes to mind is Interface. "What can be a bigger challenge than zero?", asks Ramon Arratia of Interface. And he notes that in its *Mission Zero Milestones* report, the company is focusing on zero footprint goals in such areas as waste, energy use, and emissions.[45]

"When we set the goal to eliminate all of our negative impacts on the environment, we knew it was aspirational", Arratia has explained. "Our people have embraced this vision, and we've achieved progress beyond our imagined success. However, we do not have all the answers – some solutions are still being imagined, and others are complicated to implement or financially arduous."

To see how things were going with the company's Mission Zero, I talked again to company founder Ray Anderson, as it sadly turned out shortly before his death in August 02011, about how he saw the competitive landscape.[46] "Interface was such an early mover", he recalled, "stealing an early march on our competition in terms of sustainability, that no one has yet caught up." Not that there aren't other companies trying to stake a claim. "Almost every competitor in the Americas and Europe has a green effort", Anderson acknowledged, "with varying degrees of credibility and effectiveness."

Figure 4.3 Interface Mission Zero Challenge icon

But he didn't rate the majority of those claims highly. "Most have taken a knee-jerk, rifle-shot approach", he insisted. "For example, Shaw Industries, our largest competitor, created a carpet tile backing out of polyolefin. It is promoted as a non-PVC backing, but has very poor structural characteristics, and requires a full spread of glue for installation. The material is all virgin and petro-derived, and when we compare it with our recycled PVC backing on a life cycle basis, the Shaw product compared very poorly."

"Another competitor, Mohawk, took a similar approach to carpet tile backing", he continued. "The product failed to the tune of more than $100 million in replacement costs. They are still digging out of that mess. There are numerous smaller players – and each one is doing something, generally of a defensive nature, then shouting: 'Mine is greener than yours!'"

Is it any wonder that many business customers and end consumers are a little confused? So I asked about the internal impact of the sustainability agenda – and specifically of Mission Zero. "'Zero footprint', expressed as reaching the top of 'Mount Sustainability', has been the most powerfully motivating initiative I have ever seen in 55 years of business", Anderson replied, "providing a shared higher purpose for 4000 people. For this to take hold throughout the business world, a change in the business paradigm is needed."

As to the future, he forecast that "a new generation of CEOs will emerge. There could be astounding progress by 2040." And the impact of such pioneers goes wider. "Our biggest successes", Anderson concluded, "at least in terms of exerting influence, have been outside the carpet industry. Wal-Mart sent two teams to visit us in LaGrange (our US carpet tile operation) and went away convinced that their supply chain could do it, too. Those teams were led by Mike Duke and Doug McMillan, Wal-Mart's top two executives today. Heaven only knows how many others we have influenced similarly. Lorraine Bolsinger, GE's first head of Ecomagination, once said to me: 'You showed us how to do it.'"

And what about that push to zero? How confident was Anderson of ultimate success? "The technologies are in hand to get us about 97 percent of the way there", he said. "The main external factor that needs to change is the price of oil. Internally, we need persistence and effective execution, plus a little more invention."

Cleantech is coming – but is no panacea

A little – or a lot – more invention is what is going in the clean technology (or cleantech) world. It's always exciting to be in the Golden State, California, particularly when the venture capital community there is working itself up into a new frenzy of hope and, inevitably, hype about an innovation such as the Segway (the upright scooter which you still occasionally see in the streets of San Francisco), Apple's iPad or the so-called Bloom Box – a low-carbon fuel-cell system recently hailed as the most radical technology to have come out of Silicon Valley since the PC.

Only time will tell whether entrepreneur K. R. Sridhar and his company Bloom Energy will fulfill the dreams of their backers, including the legendary John Doerr of venture capitalists Kleiner Perkins, but the initial signs were promising: among the customers already signed up were Coca-Cola, eBay, FedEx, Google, and Wal-Mart.

At the heart of the Bloom Box system, the launch version of which weighed 10 tons and cost around US$800,000, is the seed of something that could sprout into a key industry of the low-carbon economy. And that is only one of the big cleantech stories.

Traveling around Silicon Valley in 02010, I was struck once again by the extraordinary role this region continues to play in the evolution of the world's high-tech industries. Nowhere was this more apparent than at the 16th Cleantech Forum I attended in San Francisco.

After trekking through the "Valley of Death", as Cleantech Group President Sheeraz Haji put it, many cleantech firms were seeing operating conditions improving, not least because of the US$512 billion (and counting) in direct government stimulus funding. But he warned that China's US$200 billion cleantech stimulus was way ahead, with China and Hong Kong accounting for 69 percent of cleantech investment the previous year.

One of the missing links in this area, however, is the connection to consumers. That's why I was so interested to come across WindMade, described as the first global "trustmark" driven by a corporation – Denmark's windpower pioneer, Vestas.[47] The idea is that consumers will start to spot (and prefer) products on the shelves that sport the WindMade swirls.

Morton Albaek, who fronted the WindMade campaign at Vestas and co-authored the provocatively titled book *Generation Fucked Up?*, said he aimed to get at least 1000 companies to take part. He was fairly candid, though, when asked whether WindMade will save the world? "No", he said, "it's a step. What we are trying to do is to create a new model. Is it CSR? Is it sustainability? Is it business development? Is it marketing? Is it PR? You can just say yes."

"If this works", said his colleague and project manager Bragi Fjalldal, "it won't just be people buying WindMade products. We could have WindMade neighborhoods, a WindMade Olympics, WindMade cities and even WindMade countries. If we succeed, five years from now, someone will be working on, say, SolarMade. If we do this right, other industries will want to do this. It will be a new model."

Whether or not Vestas succeeds, and it has had its troubles, the great tectonic plates of the global economy are once again in energetic motion – with key drivers including climate change, energy security, water scarcity, and the growing green sensibility of developed world consumers. As the Cleantech

Group's then Executive Chairman Nick Parker told the Cleantech Forum's opening session that "creative destruction is accelerating".

Can business get to zero?

Even with the most optimistic assumptions, the sort of examples outlined here are only the beginning of the beginning of the journey to zero. There will be innumerable hiccups and periods of intense economic indigestion along the way. Among the barriers likely to slow the spread of even the best cleantech solutions are technical challenges, systemic complexity, head-on competition with established technologies, and, often, the uncomfortable fact that customers don't want to pay for the new technology, product, or service.[48]

The tempo of company announcements of zero targets being met seemed to be accelerating, albeit from a small base. Nestlé, for example, announced that it had achieved zero waste to landfill at the York factory that makes products such as Aero and KitKat. By 02015, the company intends to have all 14 of its factories in the UK and Ireland on a zero-waste basis.[49]

But despite the pioneers' confidence, chances are that even the best companies will struggle to get to zero adverse impact – and stay in that zone. A crucial area will be the evolution of accounting and management systems to measure, value, and manage various aspects of the wider ecosystem services on which our economies depend. Working on the *Newsweek* ranking of the world's greenest companies, for example, brought me a bit closer to Trucost, who track and map the environmental footprints of companies – and have even put a number on the total annual cost of human footprints and impacts.[50]

That figure, they estimate, is some $6600 billion. "The top 3000 companies alone are responsible for $2000 billion of that damage", said Richard Mattison, the firm's chief operating officer.[51] Increasingly, however, environmental analysts are getting much better at measuring the value of ecosystem services such as photosynthesis and pollination; the provision of water, crops, and livestock; and the regulation of air quality, local climate, soil erosion, floods, drought, and disease.

None of that will change the way in which business acts on a sufficient scale without a new type of leader; but there is hope there, too. When Boyd Cohen and Hunter Lovins published their book *Climate Capitalism* a couple of years back, for example, Cohen blogged on his top 10 climate capitalists, listing them in alphabetical order.[52] They were:

- **Shai Agassi**, Israel, whose Better Place business focuses on electrifying the global transportation system;
- the late **Ray Anderson**, US;
- **Richard Branson**, UK, the man behind the Carbon War Room and whose Virgin airline was among the first to test biofuels in its aircraft;

- **Christiana Figueres**, Costa Rica, executive secretary of the United Nations Framework for Climate Change;
- **Norman Foster**, UK, the architect behind green building projects such as Masdar City in Abu Dhabi;
- **Al Gore**, US, whose firm Generation Investment Management pursues profit in the transition to a low-carbon economy;
- **Van Jones**, US, who founded Green Jobs for All;
- **Vinod Khosla**, born in India but now living in the US, the Silicon Valley-based venture capitalist who specializes in cleantech;
- **Jaime Lerner**, Brazil, who as mayor of Curitiba launched the Bus Rapid Transit System which has now spread to over 80 locations worldwide;
- **Zhengrong Shi**, China, at the time the country's wealthiest energy tycoon and billed as the world's first solar billionaire.

We can quibble with the definitions used, with several of these people hardly qualifying as mainstream capitalists; but the underlying point is clear: climate capitalism is alive and well. Cohen himself noted that the list misses out huge numbers of innovators, entrepreneurs, investors, and policy-makers now active in this space.

But it's interesting that Jaime Lerner was a mayor of a city, given that this is where we turn next, and that Van Jones was for a short time part of the Obama government in the US, given that after cities we will spotlight the role of countries – and national governments – in shaping the markets of the future.

The reason why business represents such a crucial bridge between the level of the citizen, on the one hand, and cities and countries, on the other, is illustrated by something that Vinod Khosla said recently. Not everyone likes the guy, who is known for his aggressive critiques of competitors, but you can't fault him for ambition.

"Environmentalists are fiddling while Rome burns", was the challenging way he kicked off.[53] "They get in the way with silly stuff like asking people to walk more, drive less. That is an increment of 1–2 percent change. We need 1000 percent change if billions of people in China and India are to enjoy a Western energy-rich lifestyle."

Electric cars, wind turbines, solar cells, and smart grids will all be nice to have, he suggests, but none of them will get us to the point where every Indian and Chinese consumer can enjoy them without a subsidy. He, by contrast, is looking for "black swans", or maybe that should be "green swans", which promise huge environmental benefits, easy scalability, and rapid payback. And he expects at least 90 percent of his investments to fail, something that most city mayors and national government leaders would find insupportable. "My willingness to fail gives me the ability to succeed", he explains.

Even with this amount of *chutzpah*, however, Khosla and his like are going to need cities and countries to embrace transformative change on an unparalleled scale. So let's take a quick look at the cities where most of our species now live.

PETRI DISH
3/5

Figure 4.4 Petri dish 3 of 5

CITIES

Cities are the greatest creations of humanity.
Daniel Libeskind[54]

Architect Daniel Libeskind is right when he says that in many ways cities rank as the pinnacle of human innovation. But urban forms and lifestyles are also now becoming one of our biggest global headaches. So, yes, it may look impossible; but the third thing we have to do is to radically shrink the footprints of the world's major cities, both existing and new, toward the point of zero impact, even if we know we will never get there. And this is going to be hugely complicated because the pace of urban development is now both so fast and furious, and largely adopting unsustainable forms.

Clearly, there are different ways of looking at all of this. In his book *Triumph of the City*, subtitled "How Our Greatest Invention Makes Us Richer, Smarter, Greener, Healthier and Happier", Edward Glaeser notes with apparent relish that "the world isn't flat, it's paved".[55] A Harvard economist who grew up in Manhattan, Glaeser sees the ongoing, rapid urbanization of many parts of the world as a "happy prospect".[56]

The central insight, as *The Economist* nicely distilled it, is that "proximity makes people more inventive, as bright minds feed off one another; more productive, as scale gives rise to finer degrees of specialization; and kinder to the planet, as city-dwellers are more likely to go by foot, bus or train than the car-slaves of suburbia and the sticks". That said, cities – which are now home to over half the total global population – consume over two-thirds of the world's energy, and account for some 80 percent of global carbon dioxide emissions. And there is no guarantee that all that ingenuity will be focused on driving the problematic aspects of our environmental footprints toward zero.

My own position on the urban future has shifted over time. Many years ago, in 01972, I began a postgraduate degree at University College London (UCL) in urban planning – and was spotted early on as a potential troublemaker. One of our professors noted that some of the students had probably started the course with the anti-urban view that cities were "cancers", which was certainly true of me both then and now, and that they needed to be brought under control – another bull's-eye.

In the wake of *The Limits to Growth* study,[57] I was fascinated by the urban spectrum that ran from the sprawling American suburbs, to some degree based on the Frank Lloyd Wright ideal of Broadacre City, with every family having a 1 acre lot, and – toward the other end – the super-dense cities (or arcologies) proposed by architect Paulo Soleri. When I visited Soleri's Arcosanti[58] in Arizona in 01973, I wrote an article predicting that it would make interesting ruins, and probably much sooner than expected. But the underlying idea has to be right. Over time, cities must get ever denser, allowing greater investment in infrastructure, including mass transit systems.

True, when Astronauts and Cosmonauts look down on Earth, they often describe urban areas as brown, spreading across and sterilizing immense tracts of fertile land, and, in the process, souring both the air overhead and the water alongside or underfoot. How would you even begin the detox process for such places? But over time I began to see the immense power and value of the right sort of cities. Sprawling cities, scaled to cars rather than people, are increasingly going to be seen as classic example of the Ponzi schemes discussed in Chapter 2 – with ever-increasing rates of growth needed by local governments to sustain long-term liabilities, alongside reliably cheap fuels.[59]

So the key questions for me became: how do the life cycles of cities evolve and vary? Why do some parts of cities age and die while others flourish? Why do some cities age and die while others flourish? How do different cities compare in terms of their natural resource take and environmental impact? And what can we do to make them more – though we didn't use that word then – *sustainable*?

Breakdown/cities

The environmental footprint of cities is suggested by the already mentioned fact that they now account for 80 percent of the world's greenhouse gas emissions – not just carbon dioxide. They also produce many of the toxins that stress the biosphere. Nor is this picture going to get dramatically better any time soon. Indeed, the converse is probably true. By 02050, an estimated 6.2 billion people will be living in cities, compared to 3.5 billion today.

To cope with the immense influxes of people from rural areas, Asian cities alone must build – every single day – 20,000 new homes, 250 kilometers of road and the additional infrastructure needed, for example, to transport another 6 million liters of drinking water.[60] As a result, worldwide, cities teeter between descending into chaos and evolving into the innovation platforms needed to create a livable, more sustainable future.

"The global effort for sustainability", as the Global Footprint Network (GFN) notes, "will be won, or lost, in the world's cities, where urban design may influence over 70 percent of people's Ecological Footprint. High-Footprint cities can reduce this demand on nature greatly with existing technology. Many of these savings also cut costs and make cities more livable."

A new perspective is now needed – and urgently. "Since urban infrastructure is long-lasting and influences resource needs for decades to come, infrastructure decisions make or break a city's future", as GFN puts it. "Which cities are building future resource traps? Which ones are building opportunities for resource efficient and more competitive lifestyles?"

Like citizens and corporations, they may seem eternal, but cities have their life cycles, too. No need to visit the dead cities of Syria referenced in Chapter 2: there are few more dramatic illustrations of what can happen to a city when its economics start to fail than today's Detroit. Once the red-blooded heart of the American auto industry, I was in and out of the city (and nearby Dearborn) fairly often at the beginning of the last decade.

Even though I was working for Bill Ford at the time, I found myself put in a holding pen at Detroit airport a couple of times, grilled by immigration officials on why Americans couldn't do the work I was doing. No point at all in asking whether they had heard of globalization: the regional economy was already showing signs of meltdown and these people, at some level, sensed it. Almost unbelievably, the city lost 58 percent of its population between 01950 and 02008.[61] Dramatic images of the extraordinary decay of a once-great, albeit economically monocultural, city have circulated widely.[62]

One key factor in the decline was the stubborn failure of the Big Three auto-makers – Chrysler, Ford and GM – to recognize the seismic shifts beginning to affect their markets. These increasingly included concerns around fuel efficiency, peak oil, and climate change, with the profitable (but often hideously gas-hungry) sport utility vehicles (SUVs) that had helped to keep the Big Three afloat being very poorly placed for where the future now seems likely to take us.

Change as usual/cities

Often hundreds of years in the making, cities can be way more difficult to turn around than the proverbial supertanker. But history shows that they can be changed top down or bottom up – or through external factors that simply shunt aside the old expectations.

One interesting example of the bottom-up trend in recent years has been the spread of the "Transition Town" movement. This involves citizens taking the future of their communities into their own hands, on the basis that if we leave the transition to governments we will almost certainly end up with too little, too late, whereas if we leave it to individuals acting alone the outcome generally won't be much better.[63]

So here's how the approach works. It kicks off when a small group of motivated individuals within a community come together with a shared interest in such questions as "How can our community respond to the challenges, and opportunities, of peak oil and climate change?"

The idea of such initiatives is to help communities look the big environmental challenges "squarely in the eye". And a logical question then arises: what does this community need to do in order to sustain itself and thrive, significantly increasing its resilience (to counter the peak oil challenge) and drastically cut its carbon emissions (to reduce its climate footprint)?

Apart from building local understanding of the key issues, transition initiatives aim to connect with existing groups in the community, build bridges to local government, connect with other initiatives, break up the work among different task teams, and – ultimately – launch a community-developed, community-implemented *Energy Descent Action Plan*, mapping necessary actions over a 15- to 20-year time scale.

The central idea is that "We used immense amounts of creativity, ingenuity and adaptability on the way up the energy 'upslope', and that there's no reason for us not to do the same on the 'downslope' – and that if we collectively plan and act early enough there's every likelihood that we can create a way of living that's significantly more connected, more vibrant and more in touch with our environment than the oil-addicted treadmill that we find ourselves on today."

To get an idea of what this sort of community detox process can be like in practice, take a look at *The Converging World*, the book in which John Pontin tracks progress in the Go Zero project adopted by Chew Magna in south-west England.[64] The village decided to go carbon neutral, working toward this goal by helping to create a wind energy project in rural India.

Such initiatives are helpful and timely, of course; but if we are looking to crack the code of sustainable urbanism in ways that help with a broad range of cities and megacities, we must also look elsewhere. One lens on the future of sustainable urbanism is the work of the Global Footprint Network, already mentioned, which is collaborating with a number of far-sighted mayors and city administrations.

One city that has been trying to tackle these challenges head-on is the city of Calgary in Alberta, Canada. It was the first city government to develop concrete footprint reduction targets – and then built relevant targets into its 100-year sustainability vision. The city participated in an ecological footprint study with GFN, which found that its footprint exceeded the Canadian average by over 30 percent, at almost 10 global hectares per person.

With its EcoFootprint program, Calgary plans to cut its footprint to the national average of 7.25 global hectares per capita by 02036. The city became the first in North America to power its public light rail transit system with 100 percent emissions-free wind-generated energy, aiming eventually to purchase all of its electricity from renewable sources. Not a zero outcome, or even a particularly sustainable one, but evidence that even some of the least sustainable cities are waking up to the need to change.

All of which seems highly commendable, but then you recall that this city is steeped in the oil culture – and also at the epicenter of the booming tar sands industry, which many critics see as likely to crash the climate. So it is clear that we are going to have to demand that such cities not only tell us about the carbon footprint of their infrastructures, but also of their economies.

Cities detox together

The closer you look at the carbon footprint of cities, the more surprising the conclusions – particularly if you think that cities are inherently unsustainable. A study published by the International Institute for Environment and Development (IIED) found that the average Londoner produces around half of the carbon emissions of the average Briton, while each New Yorker produces just 30 percent of the average American emissions per head – and citizens in São Paolo are responsible for just 18 percent of the average carbon emissions for Brazilians.[65] Meanwhile, some city administrations are now embracing carbon neutrality – among them Copenhagen, which, as explained in Chapter 6, is committed to becoming the world's first carbon-neutral city.

Even better, it turns out that urbanization may help to defuse the population time bomb discussed in Chapter 7. Yes, there are downsides in such areas as air quality and crime, but urban women tend to have fewer children, partly because they have better access to family planning, and partly because they generally have better employment prospects, too. "Women in cities stay in school longer, have better access to contraceptives, get married later and have their first child later", explained Jocelyn Finlay, based at the Harvard Center of Population and Development Studies.[66]

Now, like individual citizens and corporations, cities are linking up to build critical mass and to share both resources and best practice. This is what the

Clinton Climate Initiative (CCI) has been encouraging with its C40 group of cities.[67] CCI projects aim to lower emissions, save money, and create jobs. New York's Mayor Bloomberg, who chairs the C40 Climate Leadership Group, noted that "No one has a monopoly on good ideas, and the C40 cities, by working with one another on innovative carbon reduction strategies, have an opportunity to show the world what is possible."

The C40 cities and their metropolitan areas are home to over 390 million people and US$8 trillion in economic activity at purchasing power parity, according to the World Bank, and are responsible for over two billion tons of greenhouse gas emissions annually. While C40 mayors generally govern only a portion of their metropolitan area, their leadership can often shape a region's overall approach to climate change. C40 member cities have launched a growing number of innovative approaches to cut carbon emissions, among them deep water cooling in Toronto, bus rapid transit in Jakarta and Bogotá, car-free days in Seoul, and innovative solid waste policies in Dhaka.

PlaNYC, New York City's long-term plan for a "greener, greater" New York, was launched on Earth Day 02007 and quickly resulted in a nine percent reduction in local emissions over 02005 levels, while simultaneously improving New Yorkers' quality of life and infrastructure. By planting trees, improving transit service, and conserving energy, the city is on track to meet its goal of a 30 percent reduction in citywide greenhouse gas emissions below 02005 levels by 02030.

To meet this fairly ambitious goal, the city has launched programs that address the problem on multiple fronts. For example, the *Greener, Greater Buildings Plan*, based on four landmark pieces of legislation enacted in 02009, requires ongoing energy efficiency in large buildings and is expected to result in a 4.75 percent reduction in greenhouse gas emissions, while supporting 17,800 jobs. This program has created a market for many of the businesses housed in the New York City Accelerator for a Clean and Renewable Economy – which promotes alternative energy and clean technology development while creating new local jobs in the green economy.

Sustainability replaces bribery as competitive edge

All of this creates both risks and opportunities for business. One of the companies positioning itself for growth in the world's exploding megacities – and their slums, *favelas*, *barrios*, and shantytowns – is Germany's Siemens. As *Forbes* magazine told the story, mass migrations from rural to urban areas are "creating unparalleled opportunities. Staggering numbers tell the tale. Already 51 percent of the world's 6.9 billion people – 3.5 billion souls – live in cities; by 02050 demographers think it will be 70 percent, or 6.2 billion people. Nearly all that growth will be in emerging markets like Asia, Africa and Latin America."[68]

Siemens economists estimate that the world infrastructure market is closing in on US$3 trillion a year, with 50 percent of world gross domestic product (GDP) generated in the 645 cities with populations over 750,000 – and the largest 40 cities now representing 20 percent of global GDP. The shifting balance is underscored by the fact that while Germany has three cities with populations over 1 million people, India has 46 and China has 160. Perhaps unsurprisingly, Siemens now has no less than 34,000 employees in China, with annual sales of over US$8 billion. And sustainability themes feature regularly, with projects including smart-grid technology, energy-efficient lighting, and the distribution of electricity from wind farms.

One major problem that Siemens collided with, however, was corruption. As *Forbes* reported: "Germany outlawed bribes in 01999, but Siemens clung to its old habits. In 02008 the company pleaded guilty to US charges that it had made $1.4 billion in questionable payments between 02001 and 02007; it paid a $449 million fine."

The resulting pursuit of zero corruption entailed Siemens sacking half of its top 100 executives – and in 02010, adopting an online, real-time compliance system, with whose help it investigated a further 500 "substantial" internal tip-offs. But it wasn't all bad news. "Despite this case", says Siemens CEO Peter Löscher, "our sales went up. We had the highest order book in the history of the company."

Interestingly, Löscher has personally championed a London "sustainability center" designed to champion energy-saving, low-carbon technologies – and he is also backing the Climate Leadership Group, led by New York's Mayor Bloomberg. As *Forbes* summed up the picture: "Instead of bribing its foreign customers, Siemens is trying to proselytize them."

It will be fascinating to see which approach turns out to be the best long-term bet. But if Shanghai is anything to go by, the prospects are brightening for the new strategy. After years of growth at almost any cost in China, the central government has been signaling plans to embrace sustainability as the core of its next stage of development.[69]

Following the 02010 World Expo in the city, with its "Better city, better life" headline, Shanghai is planning to convert the site – which used to be home to some 270 highly polluting factories – into an "eco-friendly zone of parks, conference and convention centers and pedestrian-friendly retail and commercial space (which will help curb automobile pollution). Renewable energy – mainly wind and solar – will be the primary source of power." Mayor Han Zheng positioned the development as a keystone of city plans to cut energy intensity, in terms of energy use per unit of GDP, by 16 percent by 02015.

There is a huge difference, of course, between redeveloping one high-profile site and turning an entire city into a showcase of sustainable urbanism; but there is a growing sense that China has to change – and fast. "We have to invent our own model [of urbanism]", *Time* magazine was told by Yu Kongjan, head of the Beijing-based urban design firm Turenscape. "As China's urbanization continues, the rate at which it consumes energy and water has to change." The alternative, he says, "is that the environment fails, and the economy fails".

As the pendulum begins to shift toward sustainability, there is growing competition between cities to put their greenest foot forward. In the US there is Greentowns.com, for example, a website which partners with *Reader's Digest* and aims to help towns and cities to spotlight their sustainability efforts,[70] while in the UK there has been the Sustainable Cities Index. The latter ranks the 20 largest cities across three areas of performance: environmental performance, quality of life, and "future-proofing", the last a measurement of how well they are addressing issues such as climate change, recycling, and the availability of local food.[71]

In the process of this intensifying competition, however, some fairly sharp practice has been exposed. When Madrid's mayor, Alberto Ruiz-Gallardón, boasted of major reductions in air pollution since he took office in 02003, he claimed: "Today we have better air quality in Madrid than ever before."[72]

Unfortunately for Ruiz-Gallardón, and for the 3.3 million inhabitants of Spain's capital city, an investigation quickly discovered that the improvements were illusory – in 02009 the municipality had quietly moved half of its pollution sensors from the city's traffic-clogged streets into parks and gardens. In reality, Madrid has consistently failed European Union (EU) air quality standards, and nothing had really changed.

Still, anyone who has walked the streets of emerging market and developing world cities will know that having to breathe even Madrid's air would seem like a major improvement for most people living in these intensely polluted places.

The way in which cities cope with the new demands will vary enormously. "In Europe we are used to submerging infrastructure beneath cities", says David Adjaye, a Tanzanian-born architect who works widely in Africa. "But in Africa that won't be done. Instead it will be laid over existing cities – cabling, elevated railways." He sees this as a benefit, allowing fast prototyping of retrofit technologies, before some of them are applied in the West.[73]

God only knows what all this will look like; but the spirit seems akin to that which inspired architects Piano and Rogers to put all the service systems on the outside of their iconic London Stock Exchange building. In the developing world, one suspects, aesthetics will come much lower down the pecking order.

Breakthrough/cities

Recent years have seen fascinating new thinking on the future of cities, with Richard Florida arguing that our decisions about where to live are among the most important we make in life – with the creative economy largely now found in cities.[74] Among other things, urban breakthroughs can be physical, involving new forms of infrastructure, psychological in terms of new understanding of the need for change, or political – with new commitments to change.

One of the most interesting new forms of thinking about cities comes from work done by the Santa Fe Institute – and designed to develop a unified theory of sustainability. The aim is to come up with a predictive framework that can be applied to all cities, worldwide.[75]

To be honest, every time a CEO or politician tells me that the sustainability agenda is too vague, too slippery, I fantasize about pulling out a unified field theory, like Luke Skywalker wielding his light saber. No such luck to date. But then listening to an interview with Santa Fe Institute President Emeritus Geoffrey West, I had one of those Eureka! moments – as had he. I glimpsed the broad outlines of a theory embracing everything from the smallest cell to the world's largest megacity.[76]

Box 4.1

The Eureka! Moment

Geoffrey West, Santa Fe Institute President Emeritus, began: "I spent most of my career doing high-energy physics, quarks, dark matter, string theory and so on. Between 10 and 15 years ago I started to get interested in the question of whether you can take some of the powerful techniques, ideas, and paradigms developed in physics over into the biological and social sciences."

So far so good, but I recall the bitter hostility that greeted Edward O. Wilson's efforts to apply biological and ecological concepts to the social sciences with his giant 01975 book *Sociobiology*, which I bought and devoured at the time. Still, I suspect that West's thinking won't trigger anything like the same negative reaction – much of the world has moved on. "It is very clear from the beginning that we will never have a theory of biological and social systems that is like physics", West admitted. "Nothing approaching that can possibly be in these other sciences; because they are complex systems."

But he continued: "The remarkable thing in biology that got me excited and has led to all of my present work (which has now gone beyond biology and into social organizations, cities, and companies) is that there was data, quite old and fundamental to all biological processes, about metabolism: here is maybe the most complex physical chemical process possibly in the universe, and when you ask how it is scaled with size across mammals (as an example to keep it simple), you find that there is an extraordinary regularity."

His team discovered "a very simple curve, and that curve has a very simple mathematical formula. It comes out to be a very simple power law [where the frequency of an event or characteristic varies predictably in relation to, for example, its size]. In fact, the power law not only is simple in itself mathematically, but here it has an exponent that is extraordinarily simple. The exponent was very close to the number three-quarters. So this scaling law is truly remarkable. It goes from intracellular up to ecosystems almost 30 orders of magnitude. They're the same phenomenon."

Later on he asked: "Is New York just actually, in some ways, a great big whale? And is Microsoft a great big elephant? Metaphorically, we use biological terms - for example, the DNA of the company or the ecology of the marketplace. But are those just metaphors or is there some serious substance that we can quantify with those?"

I found the twin focus on cities and corporations fascinating. "The point to recognize", West suggests, "is that all of the tsunami of problems we're facing, from global warming, the environment, to the questions of financial markets and risk, crime, pollution, disease, and so forth, all of them are urban. They all have their origin in cities. They have become dominant since the Industrial Revolution. Most importantly, they've been with us for the last 200 or 300 years, and somehow, we've only noticed them in the last 10 or 15 years as if they'd never been here. Why? Because they've been increasing exponentially."

One early result of the research related to the number of gas stations as a function of city size in European cities. "What was discovered was that they behaved sort of like biology. You found that they are scaled beautifully, and it scaled as a power law, and the power law was less than one, indicating an economy of scale. Not surprisingly, the bigger the city, the less gas stations you need per capita. You tell me the size of a city and I'll tell you how many gas stations it has."

But then they also discovered that "every infrastructural quantity you looked at from total length of roadways to the length of electrical lines to the length of gas lines, all the kinds of infrastructural things that are networked throughout a city, scaled in the same way as the number of gas stations – namely, systematically, as you increase city size. I can tell you, roughly speaking, how many gas stations there are; what is the total length of roads, electrical lines; etcetera, etcetera. And it's the same scaling in Europe, the US, Japan, and so on."

(An interesting aside: as a rule of thumb, the bigger and denser cities become, the more creative they are. But when the team turned the same lens on corporations, they found almost precisely the opposite. The bigger corporations become, the less innovative they are.)

When investigating cities, the scientists found what they dub the "15 percent" rule. In terms of well-being, it turns out that as city size increases, things such as per capita wages grow 15 percent more than would be expected from normal linear growth. There was a second interesting link. Doubling a city's population only requires an 85 percent increase in infrastructure. On the downside, however, similar growth trends are seen in areas such as traffic congestion, crime, and disease.

This approach is fairly passive, in the sense that the 15 percent rule is simply an observed phenomenon. So how do we ensure a more active detox process? One way, suggested by recent developments in Seattle, is to focus on how to drive carbon, for example, out of the system. In 02010, the city council adopted the goal of making one of my favorite cities carbon neutral. Using such relatively low-cost and feasible measures as energy retrofits of buildings, shifts to electric cars and biking, and increased recycling, they reckon they can cut Seattle's greenhouse gas emissions by 30 percent by 02020, 60 percent by 02030, and fully 90 percent by 02050.[77]

Alternatively, one of the best chances of shifting urbanism toward radically lower environmental footprints comes in building new towns and new cities. One new city that has attracted both praise and criticism is Masdar, in Abu

Dhabi, which has been billed as "the world's first zero-carbon city". Perhaps unsurprisingly, some people dismissed this as one more mega-gimmick, following such earlier projects as Dubai's 828 meter high tower in the desert and an archipelago of man-made islands in the shape of palm trees and of planet Earth itself.[78]

But there is more to the story than initially meets the eye. And a quick glance is all I have had to date, having been whisked past Masdar without an opportunity to venture into its version of a high-tech green utopia. Designed by Foster & Partners, Masdar is partly based on technology evolved in the region many centuries ago. Among the places that architect Norman Foster and his team studied for clues on how to proceed were the ancient citadel of Aleppo in Syria, and the mud-brick apartment towers of Shibam in the Yemen.

The point was to go back and understand the fundamentals, Foster explained, of how such communities had achieved livable surroundings in a region where the air can get as hot as an oven. What they found was that settlements were often located on high ground, partly to catch the winds, and that tall, hollow "wind towers" were used to channel the cooler air down to street level.

Through a combination of traditional and modern techniques, Foster & Partners set out to make the Masdar streets up to 50 percent cooler. In the process, it looks as if they could end up halving the amount of electricity needed to power the city. Better still, of the power used, 90 percent is expected to be solar, with the rest coming from waste incineration.

Air pollution is minimized by keeping out combustion-engine vehicles, instead allowing a network of electric cars to scoot beneath the complex. Critics, though, wonder whether Masdar will ever gain the "richness and texture of a real city", arguing that this is just one more case of the wealthy walling themselves off in a high-tech ghetto. I look at it differently. Like a car-maker producing concept cars to test out new technologies, the city-building professions and industries are using Masdar and similar concept cities to test out some of the urban models and technologies of tomorrow.

Prototyping the future

So perhaps we should be looking out for the urban equivalent of Henry Ford, the man who taught the last century how to mass-produce cars? Somebody who has been promoting exactly this idea, virtually the mass production of cites, is Stan Gale, chairman of Gale International. His first stab was New Songdo, in South Korea. Billed as a green city, it is designed to emit one third of the greenhouse gases of a typical city of its size – and is expected to serve 300,000 people during the day.[79]

Once again, not everyone approves of New Sondgo or of Gale. But then not everyone approved of Henry Ford, either. "With his shock of dark hair and rapid-fire New York accent, Stan Gale looks and sounds like a cartoon villain", reported

The Sunday Times.[80] "The people in Boston certainly see the developer as a Dick Dastardly type: he knocked down the city's landmark Filene's building, hoping to rebuild it, but ran out of money, leaving a vast hole in the ground. Travel halfway round the world, however, and things are different."

Gale, we are told, "is building the world's most high-tech and greenest city. Songdo, he believes, is the blueprint for dozens of new green cities that will be built across Latin America, Africa, India and China. 'We want to crack the code of urbanism, package it *in a box* and replicate it.'" With emerging economies urbanizing at unprecedented speed, he estimates that the market for his assembly line "insta-cities" could be worth US$5 trillion.

"We gotta make green cities a reality", he has insisted, "because the alternative is: 'We're screwed.' The carbon footprint of existing cities, let alone all the new ones that are springing up, is terrifying."

In the end, whoever emerges as the Bill Gates of the sustainable cities sector, the chances are that they will still take a very small slice of the overall urban pie. Many of the solutions will come from entrepreneurs whom most of us have never heard of – and in some cases may never hear of. When we produced our *Phoenix Economy* survey in 02010,[81] for example, one of the 50 social innovators we flagged was Himanshu Parikh – who had pioneered in the field of what he calls "slum networking". This aims to bring water, sewerage, and electricity to poor communities living in cities.

Such people may not make billions, but they may do even more than the self-declared green architects and urbanists to provide many hundreds of millions of people with livelihoods and lifestyles fit for the future. And if emerging economies and less developed countries are to make the transition to better lifestyles without screwing up the global environment in the process, then the urban Petri dish merits a great deal more attention from us all.

And just to give one final indication of how far all this might take us over time, consider the possibility that our cities – and their buildings – might develop lungs in the coming decade. What if they were able to draw in carbon dioxide and make something useful out of it?[82] What if our building began to come "alive"? Rachel Armstrong, a co-director of Avatar, works at the cutting edge of synthetic biology and thinks that it's only a matter of time before our cities can be biologically programmed to behave in ways that seem like science fiction today.

Just as heavier-than-air flight once seemed impossible, let alone breaking the Sound Barrier, so over time our cities might become one of our greatest allies in tackling this century's defining challenges, including climate change. Now to move up a notch, we switch to countries.

PETRI DISH
4/5

Figure 4.5 Petri dish 4 of 5

COUNTRIES

> We can't drive our SUVs and eat as much as we want and keep our homes on 72 degrees at all times ... and then just expect that other countries are going to say OK. That's not leadership. That's not going to happen.
>
> President Barack Obama[83]

Barack Obama is known for his facility with words; but even he struggled to get American citizens, corporations, and cities to change their profligate ways. Indeed, the problems he faced as president underscored the challenges in getting even the most powerful country in the world headed in the right direction in terms of a sustainable energy mix. Today, as the *Financial Times* put it: "US energy policy looks less like a blueprint for the future than a patchwork of bite-sized programs designed to lower dependence on foreign oil and expand the use of alternative sources of energy. Even those are riddled with problems."[84]

A combination of the economic downturn, the Republicans' victory in the polls in 02010 and (admittedly important) distractions such as healthcare and employment conspired to create a form of paralysis in American politics. No wonder people saw the interventions in oil-rich Iraq and Libya as evidence that the world's most powerful nation suffered from a fossil fuel addiction that was driving a muscular attempt to ensure that it could continue to mainline hard, climate-destabilizing forms of energy.

There are profound geopolitical implications. "There's a delusional America which believes oil is as inexhaustible as American power", *The New York Times* noted.[85] "The global power shift underway will be accelerated if American oil dependency is not curbed." It concluded: "A part of America is stuck back in 01990, jabbering about American 'exceptionalism' when the reality is simple: on a planet with more than seven billion people, no nation can be exempt from the need for energy husbandry and invention."

Let's work through the breakdown, change-as-usual and breakthrough scenarios for countries, the second-largest scale at which the detox process has to operate and succeed.

Breakdown/countries

The nation state is another of our great inventions – and now also a major barrier to the transformative change needed to tackle our increasingly global challenges. The evidence underscores an immense (and often distressing) range in the willingness of individual countries to respond to sustainability challenges.

One way to see this is to look for satellite images of the border between Haiti and the Dominican Republic, where the eye can easily detect that the Dominican Republic side is green and tree covered, while the Haitian side is pretty much denuded – due to a combination of overpopulation, environmental mismanagement, and government incompetence.

While it is tempting to blame nation states for the failure of major international climate summits such as that in Copenhagen in 02009, the truth is that climate change is a class of challenge that they weren't designed to tackle. Like addicts who know they have a problem but don't want to deal with it, at least yet, we shy away from the problem.

So, somehow, we must massively strengthen the capacity of individual countries to manage sustainability challenges – and, at the same time, further evolve the international and global policy-making, enforcement, and incentive structures and processes that catalyze action at the levels, for example, of ordinary citizens and communities, of corporations and markets, and of cities and regions.

Despite the frequent assertion that half of the biggest economies in the world are multinational corporations, when it comes to the really big negotiations about our common future, the most important actors have been national governments. The most powerful have tended to be the US, various members of the European Union and of the BRICS countries (which comprise Brazil, Russia, India, China, and South Africa) – plus other groupings of states, among them the Group of Twenty (G20), the EU, NAFTA, and the Association of Southeast Asian Nations (ASEAN).

Anyone who has been involved in negotiations between such actors will know – to their cost and often intense frustration – that the unfortunate reality is that the power of these states often seems to cancel out, rather than build, practical solutions that genuinely promote our global interests as a species.

Viewed from the perspective of 02050, let alone 02100, these countries seem to be obsessed with their own short-term interests to the exclusion of truly long-term considerations. Despite rare examples of leadership by various Scandinavian countries, parts of the EU and sometimes – but not recently on climate change – the US, the state of global governance on issues bearing on the interests of future generations is generally abominable.

Change as usual/countries

So what do we do? The first thing to say is that we cannot give up on politics and governments, at any level – local, national, or global. Indeed, the opposite is true. Indeed, we have to reinvent politics.[86] This is where much of the action is going to be – and where the market and policy frameworks within which corporations and cities operate will be determined. This is as true of population, pandemics, and poverty as it is of pollution and the proliferation of weapons of mass destruction – all of which are covered in Chapter 7. But things have become tougher for national governments as the focus has increasingly gone international and global.

So, let's focus for the moment on an issue that cuts across all of these areas: energy. To date, a great deal of attention has been focused on trying to suppress demand for fossil fuels such as oil and coal to address the climate challenge; but much more important in the long term will be the challenge of driving down the cost of renewables to the point where they increasingly undercut their fossil competitors.

Governments have critical roles to play in such areas as investment in research and development, boosting the willingness of banks and other funders to back the further evolution of the relevant markets, and the use of government bulk purchasing mechanisms to help drive down prices. At the moment when renewable energy technologies are cheaper than the climate-damaging alternatives, the transformation will become irresistible and we will wonder why we ever did things differently.[87]

What governments often overlook is the way in which emerging solutions can reach a take-off point while they are looking in different directions. One of the most exciting aspects of solar energy technology, for example, is the way in which the progressive fall in the cost of photovoltaic arrays is following an exponential curve – very much along the lines predicted for the power of semiconductors by Moore's Law.

"The exponential trend in solar watts per dollar has been going on for at least 31 years now", as Ramez Naam has noted.[88] "If it continues for another 8–10 years, which looks extremely likely, we'll have a power source which is as cheap as coal for electricity, with virtually no carbon emissions. If it continues for 20 years, which is also well within the realm of scientific and technical possibility, then we'll have a green power source that is half the price of coal for electricity."

But it can be hard for governments to develop and sustain the confidence in such trends – and to communicate the urgency of shrinking the environmental footprints of our economies – both of which are necessary to ensure adequate, consistent funding and other forms of support.

Take the UK, which has been fairly aggressive in setting long-term carbon reduction targets. In 02007, the then Prime Minister Tony Blair unveiled the country's climate change legislation that would make it among the first to mandate binding targets for emission reduction. By 02050, it was agreed, the UK would slash carbon dioxide emissions by 60 percent over 01990 levels. And then, just a year and a half later, the target was raised to 80 percent.[89]

The announced price-tag for this part of the carbon "detox" process was put at £200 billion, involving investment in wind farms, solar power, electric cars, and smart appliances. The benefits would include the creation of 400,000 new jobs as new sunrise industries emerged to overshadow and then replace sunset industries such as coal and steel-making.

That remains the ambition; but a great deal has changed in the few years since – not least the Fukushima nuclear disaster, which placed the nuclear energy component of national low-carbon strategies under a dark pall. Within a short time of the earthquake, tsunami, and meltdown, Germany ordered the immediate closure of seven older nuclear plants and then announced that it would pull out of nuclear altogether, while China froze the rollout of what at the time was the world's largest civil nuclear program.

Clearly, moving countries in the right direction is very tough – and unlikely to get easier any time soon. So who is doing well in this field today? One place to look for answers is the Environmental Performance Index (EPI), which ranks 163 countries on 25 performance indicators tracked across 10 policy categories covering both environmental public health and ecosystem vitality.[90]

What was striking in the 02010 version of the survey was that the top countries were relatively small, with Iceland in the number 1 spot, a key reason being its ability to tap into renewable geothermal power. It was followed by Switzerland, Costa Rica, Sweden, and Norway. The first large country in the listings was France, partly because of its nuclear infrastructure, which has helped to cut its carbon footprint.

Cracking the 1-Earth country code

When it comes to working out the ecological footprints of nations, and the necessary detox trajectories, it is clear that there will be a growing number of competing initiatives. One already mentioned is the Global Footprint Network. In 02005, it launched its Ten-in-Ten campaign, with the goal of institutionalizing the ecological footprint methodology in at least ten key national governments by 02015.

By the beginning of 02012, more than 57 nations had engaged with the GFN team directly. More than 20 nations had completed reviews of the footprint approach and Japan, Switzerland, the United Arab Emirates, Ecuador, Finland, Scotland, and Wales had all formally adopted it.[91]

In what looked like a significant move at the time, French President Nicolas Sarkozy created the Commission on the Measurement of Economic Performance and Social Progress to look into the issue of how we might move beyond GDP approaches to broader indicators of progress that would assess whether countries create human well-being in a meaningful and sustainable way. Chaired by Nobel Prize-winning economist professors Joseph E. Stiglitz and Amartya Sen, the commission issued a report including extensive discussion of ecological footprinting as a possible way forward.

Meanwhile, Switzerland was the first country in the world to complete a review of its national footprint accounts. After a comprehensive two-year study of footprinting, the European Commission also found the footprint approach to be a useful indicator for assessing progress made toward the EU's sustainability goals.

The central idea of this approach, once the facts are in, is to "bend the curve", shifting ecological trends in the direction of sustainability. A potentially powerful way of looking at all this is to consider which nations are ecological creditors, and which are debtors.

When what Max Nicholson dubbed the "Environmental Revolution" kicked off in the early 01960s, the vast majority of countries around the world had ecological surpluses — that is, the natural systems within their borders produced more resources than the given country used. Today that picture has changed profoundly: more than 80 percent of the world's population, according to GFN, now lives in countries that are running ecological deficits.

Some critics may see this as an attempt to turn back globalization, but GFN is adamant that this isn't its intention. "In a globalized economy, trade is a fact of life", it accepts. "Though we've introduced the concept of ecological creditors and debtors, we do not mean to imply, by comparing a population's consumption with its own biocapacity, that countries 'should' consume within their borders and not engage in global trade. But", it concludes, "just as a trade deficit can be a liability, so can a biocapacity deficit."

What is particularly useful about this methodology is that it permits realistic comparisons of country footprints. When GFN launched its assessment of Japan's footprint in 02010, for example, it found that it was about 1.5 times the global average, placing it within the 25 percent of countries with the biggest footprints. Compared with the four countries closest to it geographically, only Russia's footprint was (slightly) bigger. Japan's per capita footprint was 10 percent higher than South Korea's and more than double that of China.

But China is catching up. Its ecological footprint has quadrupled in the last four decades, with the country now demanding more from the planet than any other nation, except for the US. "If China were to follow the consumption patterns of the United States", the GFN concludes, "it would demand the available biocapacity of the entire planet."

And we should pay attention not simply because of the implications for climate security, but also because much of that economic activity involves producing goods for export to countries that are fretting most about greenhouse gas emissions. Too often, it's a case of out of sight, out of mind. Between 01990 and 02008, for example, EU countries cut their total carbon emissions in their own territories by six percent.[92] But this progress was almost exactly canceled out by the extra emission-associated goods created in China for export to the EU. Add in other imports of so-called "embedded" or "embodied" carbon, and Europe's overall carbon emissions turn out to have increased by 6 percent over the period.

Breakthrough/countries

Clearly, something must give. Either we trash the biosphere or we find a way to shrink our footprints at every level – whether by cutting back on the levels of consumption or by developing breakthrough technologies that enable different forms of consumption, with radically smaller footprints. The key, concludes Mathis Wackernagel, president of the Global Footprint Network, "is to get countries to recognize that aligning their economies with the wider biosphere should be a corner stone of their competitiveness strategy".[93]

Very few countries have yet set themselves zero targets, though Denmark is one of them – where the country's Commission of Climate Change Policy is talking of zero oil or coal dependency by 02050. It reckons that it can do this without needing either nuclear energy or carbon capture and storage.[94] A small state, surely, but one that hopes to blaze the way for the rest of the world. Now the WWF says that the UK could also go 100 percent renewable by 02050.[95] By mid-century, on these estimates, the world could be saving four trillion Euros a year through energy efficiency and reduced fuel costs.

Back in Scandinavia, Sweden, too, has set an ambitious goal to achieve a completely oil-free economy, this time by 02020 – without building more nuclear power plants.[96] Motivated by global warming and rising oil prices, the Swedish government says it plans to replace all fossil fuels with renewable alternatives before climate change undermines national economies and shrinking oil supplies force huge price increases. Not everyone believes the goal is achievable; but even critics applaud what they see as a compelling and motivating goal. As Kenneth Werling, chief executive of Agroetanol, which runs Sweden's largest ethanol factory, told the *Associated Press*: "I don't think this is realistic, but it is a good ambition. Maybe we can build a society that is less dependent on oil, and that is good in itself."

Interestingly, the competition between nations in this area is now both driving the evolution of new technologies and raising concerns about who is going to end up as top dog in the cleantech space. The year 02010, for example, saw a rash of media stories with headlines such as "Light dims for Silicon Valley as China shines" and "Chinese eclipse America's solar future".

In what President Obama dubbed another "Sputnik moment", Americans began to realize that the terms of trade between them and Asia – particularly China – mean that even if much of the innovation is done in the US, most of the jobs and a growing slice of the profits are being offshored to Asia. To take just one example, Evergreen Solar announced early in 02011 that it would shut a plant in Massachusetts after less than three years and move production to China, with the loss of 800 jobs.[97]

Many firms are trying to drive down their costs in an effort to compete with the Chinese, but others are opting for an approach that will see even more manufacturing sent off to Asia. At Innovalight, a company which has developed what it calls "silicon ink" that can increase a solar cell's efficiency when printed on a standard silicon wafer, the plan is to license the patented technology to the Chinese – and avoid having to raise the hundreds of millions of dollars needed to build their own factories.[98]

"How do you fight against enormous subsidies, low-interest loans, cheap labor and scale – and a government strategy to make you No. 1 in solar?" asked Innovalight CEO Conrad Burke.

Some point to the way in which China has been struggling to boost its capacity to do fundamental innovation, noting that the funds and tax breaks showered on industry by the Chinese government have shown little sign of turning the country into a powerhouse of invention.[99] Among the barriers slowing progress are "poor enforcement of intellectual property rules, an educational system that emphasizes rote learning and a shortage of independent organizations that can evaluate scientific projects". And there's a more fundamental problem still. "There's a political constraint, too", noted Arthur Kroeber, managing director of GaveKal-Dragonomics in Beijing. "In the long run, innovation arises in societies that are really open, where you can discuss anything. And China doesn't have that kind of political culture yet."

In times of national emergency, history shows that at least some countries can innovate fast – as long as there is the necessary political will and funding. Classic examples include the Manhattan Project and NASA's race to the Moon. But when US Secretary of Energy Steven Chu was asked what the prospects were for something similar in green energy, during an event organized by Stanford University's Green Alliance for Innovative Action, he said that the money wasn't there.[100] But politicians said the same sort of thing about defense budgets before World War II.

Chu, a onetime Stanford professor, began his talk with a briefing on the latest climate data and on global temperature records. "This is recent data", he said. "It's more than a smoking gun. The carbon in the atmosphere is due to humans." The question now, he said, "is not will the earth warm up; it's how much will it warm up".

Referencing a quote from hockey player Wayne Gretzky about skating "to where the puck is", Chu warned that "We have to get people in the United States to skate to where the world will be … not wishing oil prices will get back to $30 a barrel." The rest of the world has entered a race "to lead in this technology", said Chu, citing green automotive technologies such as hybrid vehicle batteries, in particular, as an area where the US is lagging behind.

As for China, he said the country is now "spending over $9 billion a month to diversify and clean up their energy industry".

Among other hopeful signs, in 02010, US General Services Administration (GSA) administrator Martha Johnson launched her Zero Environmental Footprint (ZEF) initiative.[101] This could be one of the world's most significant detox programs if it gains real traction. As one of the Obama administration's top sustainability spokespersons, she had a very direct stake in the federal government's green portfolio. Through the Public Building Service, GSA is the steward of all federal buildings. As a result, the ZEF initiative has placed the agency at the "tip of the federal spear" in leading the sustainability charge. As Johnson has told many audiences, "zero environmental footprint is this generation's moon shot. And so it must be ours at GSA."

The competition between countries is heating up. Even in Australia, the world's worst greenhouse gas (GHG) emitter per head of population, Beyond Zero Emissions (BZE) has launched Zero Carbon Australia by 02020 – looking forward to the day when the country's economy could become a net absorber of carbon.[102]

It remains to be seen how the developing struggle between larger economies such as China, Germany, Japan, and the US plays out in clean technology and in other related areas; but a great deal more hangs on the outcome than the stock prices of any listed companies involved or the health of the national economies concerned. Rather, as we will now conclude, this is increasingly a planetary challenge, with potentially civilizational consequences.

Let's give the final word here to one of our 50 Zeronauts, Shai Agassi of electric vehicle start-up Better Place. Working with Renault, they are developing a huge network of recharging points throughout Israel, offering "guaranteed mobility, zero oil use and zero exhaust emissions".[103] Even better, he noted, "the total cost of implementing such a nationwide network in Israel is equal to less than seven days of fuel use by current petrol-engine cars in the country".

And now here comes China. Agassi sees the world's most populous country embarking on a "triple play. First, it wants to avoid the vulnerabilities of an economy built on imported oil. Second, it desperately needs to clean its urban centers of pollutants largely produced by exhaust pipes. And, third, it sees the opportunity to take a page out of America's twentieth-century playbook, making a large domestic automobile industry the cornerstone of global economic leadership."

Strange as it may seem, countries such as Israel and China may now be evolving the new zero-oriented business playbook that will spur competitors who failed to spot the wider market trend – and, in the process, help our entire civilization shift onto a more sustainable path.

None of that means that the old forms of competition will suddenly end, however, as illustrated by China's threat to launch a trade war against Airbus over the EU's plans to make international airlines pay for their carbon emissions.[104] Like it or not, in civilizations since time immemorial, trade has often been another form of competition for the future. Worryingly, the historical records show that the very competitive forces that help to build civilizations can also end up bringing them down.

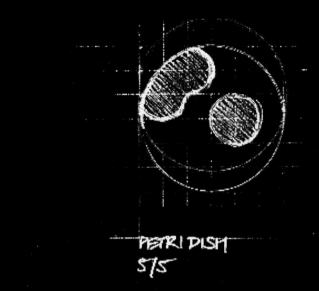

PETRI DISH
5/5

Figure 4.6 Petri dish 5 of 5

CIVILIZATIONS

Civilizations die from suicide, not by murder.
Arnold Toynbee[105]

Just as we breathe oxygen without thinking about it, we tend to take our civilization for granted – as long as it is working. This is a theme that is back in the spotlight with Jeffrey Sachs's book *The Price of Civilization*, though the focus there is very much on America.[106] Few books have had a greater impact upon me than *A Study of History*[107] by Arnold Toynbee, from which the previous quote is extracted. Since the work came in 12 volumes and I was a teenager when I opened the first, I can't say I read them all. Yet those I did read left a deep impression in terms of the vulnerability of our economies, cultures, and civilizations to factors such as environmental degradation.

When we work in a long-established company, or live in a city or a country with long histories, we tend to assume that they are going to be around forever. And unless we are in the midst of world war, depression, or an outbreak of bubonic plague, we tend to think of our own civilization as impregnable, timeless as the mountains. The facts, however, suggest otherwise.

On the upside, the historical record also shows that when the pressure is on, we can sometimes change fairly rapidly. Indeed, if there is one modern book which for me equates with Toynbee's magisterial series, it is the 750-page *Why the West Rules – for Now* by Ian Morris. I read it on a series of flights around Asia early in 02011 and found its 15,000-year account of the rise of humanity to be an extraordinarily powerful analysis of why civilizations rise and fall.[108]

The great question, we are told, is not really whether the West will continue to rule. Instead, "It is whether humanity as a whole will break through to an entirely new kind of existence before disaster strikes us down permanently." Morris proposes what he modestly calls the "Morris Theorem", that "Change is caused by lazy, greedy, frightened people looking for easier, more profitable, and safer ways to do things. And they rarely know what they're doing."

The argument is that each wave of social development, generally driven by demographic changes, creates new generations of problems. Stalking our societies are what Morris calls the "Five Horsemen of the Apocalypse": famine, disease, migration, state collapse, and climate change. Time and again, our civilizations have pressed up against hard ceilings created by the exhaustion of natural resources such as the current forms of energy. In my mind, the ceiling we are now pressing up against, hard, is the Sustainability Barrier.

Breakdown/civilizations

It isn't particularly fashionable to quote Toynbee these days; but in retrospect I liked his brave focus on civilizations – rather than countries or even cultures – as the unit of historical analysis. For him, civilizations tended to evolve in response to a set of challenges, emerging from periods when "creative minorities" came up with novel solutions that, in turn, served to reorient entire societies.

Distilled to its essence, his line of argument ran something like this: the defining challenges could be physical (as when the Sumerians exploited the swamps of southern Iraq, creating a so-called "hydraulic" civilization based on large-scale irrigation projects) or social (as when the Catholic Church resolved the chaos of post-Roman Europe by enrolling the emerging Germanic kingdoms in a single religious community).[109]

When a civilization fails to respond creatively to such challenges, it starts to fail and, eventually, falls. Beyond a certain point, civilizations sink into nationalism, militarism, and the tyranny of despotic minorities. That was the root of Toynbee's much-quoted conclusion that "Civilizations die from suicide, not by murder."

Change as usual/civilizations

If our civilization is not unintentionally to commit suicide, we will need to pay it much greater attention, understanding its internal dynamics – and its interactions with the biosphere – much better.

When I think of civilization these days, my mind turns to Kevin Kelly, whom I visited south of San Francisco in 02005.[110] A former editor of *Wired* magazine and author of some of my favorite books, including *Out of Control*[111] and *New Rules for the New Economy*,[112] he was probably already working on what would become his astounding blog *The Technium*[113] and linked book, *What Technology*

Wants.[114] One of his most extraordinary ideas is this: civilizations are creatures. And, to extend his metaphor, our civilization is a creature in urgent need of a radical detox.

Civilizations "are organisms", he said, "that live very long and that spread very wide over the surface of the earth. Civilizations are beings that consume energy and produce ideas. These ideas materialize as cities, institutions, laws, art, books, and memories. A civilization may persist for thousands of years, evolving constantly. Compared to fleshy animals, or even the wet tissue of the human mind, civilizations are the fastest changing organisms on the planet."

So that's where we increasingly need to focus much of our attention. Among the civilizational risks that we should be obsessing about is the state of the planetary biosphere. People whose work in this space I admire include Pavan Sukhdev, a former Deutsche Bank managing director with his UN-sponsored program The Economics of Ecosystems and Biodiversity.[115] The aim has been "to draw attention to the global economic benefits of biodiversity, to highlight the growing costs of biodiversity loss and ecosystem degradation, and to draw together expertise from the fields of science, economics and policy to enable practical actions moving forward".

The TEEB study concluded that, each year, companies were causing damage to the biosphere – which they do not pay to clean up – costed at US$2.2 trillion. That equates to about one third of their annual profits. On the positive side, it now seems as if the Organisation for Economic Co-operation and Development (OECD) will be building environmental factors, including biodiversity, into its general economic assessments.[116] That would be progress indeed.

Pavan's work links to that of another Zeronaut, Gretchen Daily, a Stanford University professor who has long worked to tackle our ignorance about the value of natural capital. Inspired by Costa Rica's Payment for Environmental Services initiative during the 01990s, Daily cofounded the Natural Capital Project in 02006 – which aims to work out how to include the value of ecosystem services in business, community, and government decisions.[117] These benefits – among them flood protection, crop pollination, and carbon storage – are ignored in traditional economic equations.

Partly as a result, the zero language is beginning to take root in some areas of this debate – for example, Indonesia's Golden Agri-Resources, the world's second-largest producer of palm oil, has been under intense pressure from Greenpeace and other NGOs.[118] Major customers have dropped it as a supplier, among them Nestlé, Burger King, Carrefour, and Unilever. The reason: the worst deforestation outside the Amazon is now found in Indonesia. As a result, it is now the largest producer of carbon dioxide emissions after China and America. And the government wants to double production of palm oil by 2020. Golden Agri-Resources, however, now claims to have undergone a conversion, rather like that which greened Wal-Mart after Hurricane Katrina. In the process, it has committed itself to what it calls "zero deforestation".

One development that promises to jump "NatCap" (as the Stanford initiative is known) from change as usual to breakthrough is the migration of its free-to-download InVEST (Integrated Valuation of Ecosystem Services and Trade-Offs) software onto the new Google Earth Engine platform. The platform already includes a treasure trove of satellite imagery of the Earth's surface. Just maybe we begin to see the emergence of a higher-level global consciousness, of exactly the sort that the Astronauts and Cosmonauts saw as critical to our civilization's survival?

Breakthrough/civilizations

Civilizations also need their wake-up moments, when the urgency of change becomes blindingly clear. Many fail to see the challenge, or fail to develop effective solutions in time; but the optimists among us think that there is also evidence in our history that, in the right circumstances, we can get our act together – and in time.

Ian Morris ends his book with two possible scenarios. The worst-case version sees the Five Horsemen back with a vengeance. In this future, climate change proves to be dramatically non-linear, with agricultural productivity boosted in northern climes such as Canada and Russia, but severely reduced in an "arc of instability" stretching from Africa through Asia. This theme is explored in much greater detail in Laurence Smith's thought-provoking book *The New North: The World in 2050.*[119]

Meanwhile, the US National Intelligence Council has estimated that between 02008 and 02025 the number of people facing food or water shortages will jump from 600 million to 1.4 billion, most of them in that arc. As a result, hundreds of millions people will be on the move. The Stern Report concluded that by 02050 we would see 200 million "climate migrants", most of them poor – five times as many as the world's entire refugee population in 02008.[120] Ultimately, this scenario leads to "Nightfall", truly an apocalyptic vision.

Alternatively, Morris lays out a different path, where our species – or parts of it – break through this new "hard ceiling", what I call the Sustainability Barrier. New forms of renewable energy technology, low-carbon and toward-zero waste economies emerge, together with hybrid forms of man-machine. Cities accelerate to scales unimaginable today. And new forms of global governance emerge to keep the whole process on the rails.

New forms of global governance, to date, have tended to evolve in the wake of major wars. And it now seems as if we either mobilize as if for war, or we face the prospect that World War III will happen well within the lives of many of us today. So when Jørgen Randers – one of the authors of the *Limits to Growth* study[121] in 01972 – asked me to write an essay for a book he was putting together to mark the study's 40th anniversary in 02012, I chose to look at the limits to military growth out to 02050.

I began by saying that only a wild optimist – or a fatalist – would argue that nation states should disarm, following the example of Costa Rica. Indeed, that small Central American state can be seen as the exception that proves the rule. In addition to the ubiquity of death and taxes, we are guaranteed to need armed forces for the foreseeable future – but increasingly with a new purpose, to prevent (and where that is not possible, to deal with the consequences of) large-scale environmental change.

If the armed services – and the defense industries – are to legitimately play this new role, in this Detox Decade and beyond, they will need to go through the same sort of transparency and sustainability revolutions that have hit a broad range of other sectors in recent decades. Think, for example, about the endemic corruption in so much of the defense world – and of the extent to which the military control the economies in countries such as Iran and China.

In this context I was reminded of President Eisenhower's extraordinary farewell speech, in which he warned of the immense power and influence of the military–industrial complex. It is impossible now to read Eisenhower's hard-won words of wisdom from 01961 without being reminded of the insights and foresight that drove the authors of such studies as *The Limits to Growth*[122] and *Our Common Future*.[123] The only general to be elected US president in the twentieth century, Eisenhower had this to say about what we would now call the sustainability challenge:

> We ... must avoid the impulse to live only for today, plundering for our own ease and convenience the precious resources of tomorrow. We cannot mortgage the material assets of our grandchildren without risking the loss also of their political and spiritual heritage. We want democracy to survive for all generations to come, not to become the insolvent phantom of tomorrow.

He went on to warn about the perils of underestimating the often-malign influence of the military–industrial complex:

> In the councils of government, we must guard against the acquisition of unwarranted influence, whether sought or unsought, by the military–industrial complex. The potential for the disastrous rise of misplaced power exists and will persist. We must never let the weight of this combination endanger our liberties or democratic processes.

Among the initiatives designed to view the future of security, defense and the armed forces through lenses other than those typically used by right-wingers, I like the work of the US Truman National Security Project.[124] In particular, I buy into their thesis that:

> Today's world is a dangerous place. Our security is at risk from terrorists, belligerent states, and the proliferation of weapons that can cause unimaginable, massive destruction. We are also threatened by less obvious foes such as pandemic disease, weak and corrupt governments, and the spread of anti-Americanism.
>
> The conservative strategy to meet today's threats is bankrupt. They have missed crucial opportunities. Their rhetoric has squandered world sympathy and support. Allies we need to conquer terror have been alienated. Poor strategic planning has weakened military morale and capabilities. Ideologically based Pentagon-focused policy-making is breeding instability abroad, exacerbating the conditions that make us vulnerable. The conservative strategy is making the world less safe.

And what is true of Americans is true of the rest of us. If we must continue paying for the military, we must also ensure that it does what we really need to get done. Some might argue that this is what the US Army Corps of Engineers did with its massive wetland reclamation and river straightening projects; but true sustainability has often been ignored in the design of such civil engineering works to the point where the impact of natural disasters such as Hurricane Katrina are amplified.

In short, we must learn in the coming decades how to reboot and repurpose military operating systems. By 02052, 80 years on from the first publication of *Limits to Growth*, the armed forces of many countries – if we succeed – will have specialized in helping their economies and societies to adapt to natural disasters, particularly those caused by advancing climate change. This will still mean fighting wars, managing border disputes, and coping with refugees; but I think we will also look back on Mikhail Gorbachev's "Green Cross" as both an idea before its time and an inspiration for the future.[125]

Environmental regeneration, augmentation (including various forms of geo-engineering), and conservation are likely to become a crucial part of military training – and be opened up for a growing proportion of young people, partly as a means of educating, training, and disciplining populations. Ground forces will be tasked with protecting key elements of the biosphere from human depredations. Naval forces will be redeployed to protect the remaining wild fisheries – and the growing number of fish-farming and ocean-ranching operations. Air forces will be used for a range of related surveillance tasks, including future generations of smart sensor networks and drones, the latter often evolved – whether or not its champions approve – on the principles of biomimicry.

Intelligence services – including the satellite remote-sensing branches – will police eco-crime and intervene where there is evidence of the new crime of ecocide.[126] For the moment, however, NGOs and similar are making most of the running here – among them groups such as Greenpeace and Polly Higgins of Eradicating Ecocide, with her mock trial in the UK Supreme Court in September 02011.[127]

Meanwhile, the evidence shows – as intuition has long suggested – that climate change will fuel conflict and warfare.[128] A big question: will we have been forced by 02050 to replace the UN, as we once replaced the League of Nations? Yes, I think so. The United Nations is the best (because only) UN we have, but conspicuously not up to the challenges that we face with seven billion people, let alone 9 to 10 billion later this century.

In the meantime, the potential for "Big Brother" misuse and abuse of such systems is considerable – which is why the transparency, accountability, and sustainability agendas will become central concerns for growing number of countries. There will be new forms of "arms race" between emerging forms of top-down surveillance and novel forms of bottom-up *sousveillance*.[129]

And you can already see evidence of another trajectory in the military, with growing numbers of zero-impact goals being announced in relation to carbon, waste, toxics, and even fossil fuels. Consider the US army's Net Zero Initiative.[130] Those driving this trend in the US are dubbed "Green Hawks".[131]

By the 02020s, in the breakthrough scenario, sustainability versions of Lockheed Martin's "Skunk Works"[132] – which gave disruptive innovators the space and resources to create transformative defense solutions – will hopefully be commonplace in the relevant sectors, with growing interest in spin-off technologies. This won't be confined to idiotic things like lead-free bullets or biodegradable landmines, but to suites of technologies designed to support populations in low-energy, low-footprint ways. Along the way, some exotic swords will be beaten into plowshares, like the North Atlantic Treaty Organization (NATO) bunker transformed into a zero-energy data farm.[133] But relying on happenstance will not be enough.

Leading intelligence services have been adapting for some time, including the Central Intelligence Agency (CIA).[134] By mid-century, however, we will also almost certainly have seen a deeply unwelcome explosion of interest in "environmental weapons". These first really caught public attention with cloud-seeding attempts and with Saddam Hussein's attempts to damage his enemies by draining the Iraqi marshes; but we may well see them expanding to attempts to make incisions in the ozone layer.[135] As a result of bitter experience, new treaties will be drawn up to regulate the development and use of such weapons. Sadly, the current UN is not up to the task of policing them, at least not yet.

The history of conflict shows that virtually every form of technology can be press-ganged (another term, interestingly, was *shanghaied*) into uniform. Our challenge is to draw the military into the sustainability business. I don't know what weapons World War III, let alone World War IV, will be fought with. But it seems a sure-fire certainty that future wars will ensure that we have a World Court of the Generations, where governments, companies, and other actors are arraigned and prosecuted for ecocide and gross damage to the interests of future generations.[136]

As the Earth Policy Institute's Lester Brown has optimistically put it: "We can change course and move onto a path of sustainable progress, but it will take a massive mobilization – at wartime speed. Whenever I begin to feel overwhelmed by the scale and urgency of the changes we need to make, I reread the economic history of US involvement in World War II because it is such an inspiring study in rapid mobilization."[137]

It took Pearl Harbor to throw the switch on the economy, but once thrown there was no stopping the process. "After an all-out commitment, the US engagement helped turn the tide of war, leading the Allied Forces to victory within three-and-a-half years", Brown recalls. "In his State of the Union address on January 6, 1942, one month after the bombing of Pearl Harbor, President Franklin D. Roosevelt announced the country's arms production goals. The United States, he said, was planning to produce 45,000 tanks, 60,000 planes, and several thousand ships. He added, 'Let no man say it cannot be done.'"

Public skepticism abounded, but Roosevelt and his team "realized that the world's largest concentration of industrial power was in the US automobile industry. Even during the Depression, the United States was producing three million or more cars a year. After his State of the Union address, Roosevelt met with auto industry leaders, indicating that the country would rely heavily on them to reach these arms production goals. Initially they expected to continue making cars and simply add on the production of armaments. What they did not yet know was that the sale of new cars would soon be banned. From early February 1942 through the end of 1944, nearly three years, essentially no cars were produced in the United States."

Nor did the changes end there. "In addition to a ban on the sale of new cars, residential and highway construction was halted, and driving for pleasure was banned. Strategic goods – including tires, gasoline, fuel oil, and sugar – were rationed beginning in 1942. Yet that same year saw the greatest expansion of industrial output in the nation's history – all for military use. Wartime aircraft needs were enormous… From the beginning of 1942 through 1944, the United States far exceeded the initial goal of 60,000 planes, turning out a staggering 229,600 aircraft, a fleet so vast it is hard even today to visualize it."

Brown quotes *No Ordinary Time*, the book by Doris Kearns Goodwin,[138] which explains how various firms converted. "A sparkplug factory switched to the production of machine guns. A manufacturer of stoves produced lifeboats. A merry-go-round factory made gun mounts; a toy company turned out compasses; a corset manufacturer produced grenade belts; and a pinball machine plant made armor-piercing shells."

In retrospect, Brown says, the speed of this conversion from a peacetime to a wartime economy was stunning. But, he stresses, "The point is that it did not take decades to restructure the US industrial economy. It did not take years. It was done in a matter of months. If we could restructure the US industrial economy in months, then we can restructure the world energy economy during this decade." Well, the politics would be interesting, but many of the building blocks are potentially already in place. His take: "The world now has the technologies and financial resources to stabilize climate, eradicate poverty, stabilize population, restore the economy's natural support systems, and, above all, restore hope."

And Brown's final critical question: "What contributions can we each make today, in time, money, or reduced consumption, to help save civilization? The choice is ours – yours and mine. We can stay with business as usual and preside over an economy that continues to destroy its natural support systems until it destroys itself, or we can be the generation that changes direction, moving the world onto a path of sustained progress." The choice, he concludes, will be made by generations currently alive, but will affect life on Earth "for all generations to come".

Very few financial analysts or investors yet see the world this way; but there are points of light in the darkness. One remarkably insightful analyst is Jeremy Grantham of GMO, based in Boston, Massachusetts, who is sometimes seen as the financial markets' current version of Thomas Malthus (see pp.119, 245). He notes that we are moving into an era defined not just by "Peak Oil" but "Peak Everything".[139]

To lift the mood, we now take a look at some of the practical ways in which Zeronauts – who are spearheading this great civilizational change movement – can help us to push toward sustainability. We will focus in on the evolving discipline of "Zeronautics" (Chapter 5) and the "Pathways to Zero" model (Chapter 6), before exploring in Chapter 7 five key areas where relevant zero-based solutions are being tested.

Box 4.2

Getting Beyond Eureka!

Having cracked elements of the 1-Earth Code, Zeronauts aim to break through to a fairer, more sustainable future. The second part of the book spotlights, celebrates, and probes the evolving arts and sciences of zeroing. Three panels show the process at work in the areas of water (pp.229–30), hunger and obesity (pp.232–3), and female genital cutting (pp.236–7).

The United States, interestingly, with its profligate "5-planet" economy and lifestyles, shows signs of a strong auto-immune response – producing more Zeronauts, to date, than any other country. Over half of the innovators celebrated in the first round of our Zeronaut Roll of Honor (pp.44–6) are American. Only one is Chinese, but perhaps by 02020 China will have begun to turn the tables?

One of the longest serving Zeronauts in the Roll is Amory Lovins of the Rocky Mountain Institute, who is dedicated to zeroing fossil fuels[140]. As he charmingly puts it, "nearly 90 percent of the world's economy is fueled every year by digging up and burning about four cubic miles of the rotted remains of primeval swamp goo." Just as we now view slavery with horror, so future generations will look back at some aspects of today's economy with disbelief.

The innovators and leaders profiled in the following pages may seem unreasonable, even quixotic at times, but their thinking and work, their failures and triumphs, represent our last, best hope of driving our consumption patterns, communities and cities, corporations, countries, and ultimately civilization through the Sustainability Barrier.

III

BREAKING
THROUGH

STAGE 1

EUREKA!

We can't solve problems by using the same sort of thinking we used when we created them.

Albert Einstein, 01879–01955

LING

5

The Race to Zero

The power of zero has been trumpeted in various areas of business, notably in relation to zero defects. Here we look at lessons learned in the field of total quality management – and introduce a five-stage "Pathways to Zero" model, running through from the Eureka! discovery moment to the point where a new way of doing things becomes endemic in the economy.

The Zeronaut's message is uncomfortable. Instead of devoting most of our efforts to maintaining the current economic system, the time has come to tear down the old order and begin to create the new. In the process, if we are to achieve anything like sustainability in the twenty-first century, we must get much better at fueling and guiding new ventures from the Eureka! moment, where an innovator suddenly wakes up to a new area of opportunity or risk, which we call stage 1, through to stage 5, where the relevant innovation becomes part of the operating systems of entire economies. In what follows, I will draw on a project I carried out several years back with Alejandro Litovsky.

Let's think through what it would take to create a new discipline of Zeronautics. Experience suggests that between the Eureka! moment and the point where it becomes ubiquitous, an innovation (as Figure 5.1 suggests) typically passes through stages 2 (experiment), 3 (enterprise) and 4 (ecosystem), the point at which clusters and wider constellations of actors come together to create the critical mass needed to drive systemic change. Each of these stages has its own dynamics, with transitions becoming almost exponentially more difficult. The boundary between stages 4 and 5 is where I typically draw in the Sustainability Barrier.

While it is often easier to think of zero targets in areas like carbon, waste, or toxics; Zeronauts also work on social problems, as with the work of the Orchid Project on female genital cutting (pp.236–7) or the work of Eve Ensler, author of *The Vagina Monologues*[1] and the driving force behind V-Day, designed to end violence against women and girls[2]. I saw Eve speak at the 2012 Skoll World Forum – and she made me want to help drive the V-Day agenda through all five stages of the Pathways to Zero model.

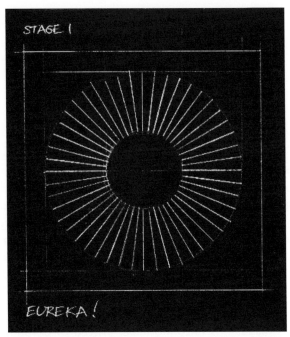

Figure 5.1 Pathways to Zero: Stage 1

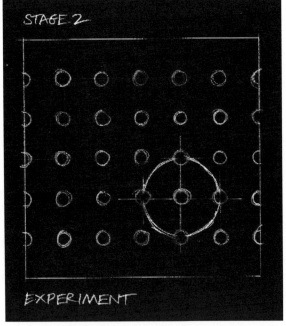

Figure 5.2 Pathways to Zero: Stage 2

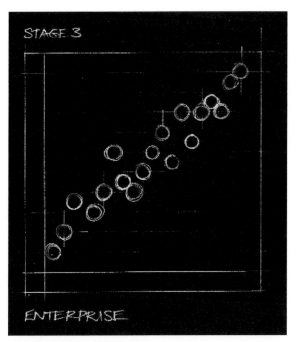

Figure 5.3 Pathways to Zero: Stage 3

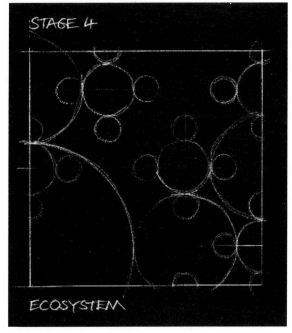

Figure 5.4 Pathways to Zero: Stage 4

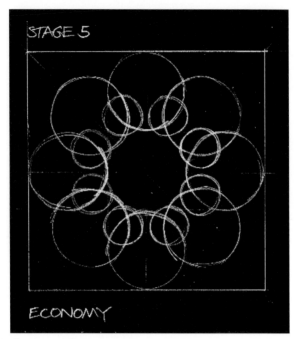

Figure 5.5 Pathways to Zero: Stage 5

As an innovation moves through the stages, the friction and resistance grows. It's very much like the compression waves that build up as a plane tries to crash through the Sound Barrier. But at the same time, the collective capacity of actors operating in higher stages is also typically greater than those at lower stages. That said, timing is key. So before we explore the five stages in detail in Chapter 6, let's take a look at the intertwined history of innovation and – one of the great business innovations of the late twentieth century – the field of total quality management.

10,000 failures

It is clear that the experimenter in stage 2 can fiddle around for ages without achieving a breakthrough: Thomas Edison is well known for having said after working doggedly through 10,000 failed experiments on his way to success in designing the first incandescent light bulb: "I haven't failed, I've found 10,000 ways that don't work."

The bigger the Zeronaut's appetite for change, the more she or he must be able to cope with failure. I have been involved in several significant business failures, among them – tangentially – that of the Norwegian electric car-maker TH!NK. The firm was bought by Ford when we were working for the US company as part of a wider acquisition spree. After investing US$100 million,

Ford span TH!NK out to a group of Norwegian venture capitalists, including a long-time friend of mine, Jan-Olaf Willums. At a TH!NK team session in Provence during the summer of 02006, I predicted that the firm would go bankrupt unless it could create something like an "iPod on wheels", which seemed unlikely at the time.[3] When Jan-Olaf drove me around Oslo in an early version some years ago, the plastic-bodied car felt like a rather nippy wheelie-bin. Sadly, the third and final bankruptcy was announced while I was racing to finish *The Zeronauts*.[4] There were many reasons for this failure, but timing was key among them.

One discipline that aims to reduce the risk of some types of failure is what was originally called quality control and later became known as total quality management (TQM). An interesting tracking of the evolution of the field can be found online.[5] For me, however, there has always been a distinction between work designed to create something totally new and work that aims to make existing systems more effective and efficient. And I was forced to think long and hard about this when, early in 02011, I heard that I had been awarded the Spencer Hutchens, Jr. Medal[6] by the American Society for Quality (ASQ) – and that part of the deal was that I was invited to keynote a major ASQ conference in San Francisco.

To my growing concern, I discovered that the medal – this was only the second time it had been awarded – recognizes "the achievements of an individual who demonstrates outstanding leadership as an individual, business leader, and cause advocate for social responsibility, primarily focusing on the marketplace, environment, workplace, and community. The medal seeks to showcase how the individual's impactful results have led to societal change."

And yet I have often said that in much of the work I do I find myself envying James Bond. Every time he finds himself in the command center of a global villain like Goldfinger or Dr. No, he seems to know exactly which buttons to press. Too often, I have found myself in corporate boardrooms and C-suites, pressing everything that comes to hand to see what connected to what, what worked, and what didn't.

So I started a high-speed journey to see what the ASQ toolkit – particularly TQM – has to offer in the push for a zero footprint economy. A key question, linking back to the discussion of scenarios in Chapter 4, is whether TQM can help to avoid "breakdown" by helping drive us toward "breakthrough" scenarios, or whether it largely focuses minds and effort on what we might call "change as usual".

More modestly, can it help us to drive the necessary cultural change in organizations and in society? And even if we find that quality is more about incremental improvement and refinement than revolutionary reimagining, perhaps there are lessons would-be zeronauts can learn from the history of quality as a movement.

Is sustainability the new TQM?

I confess that I began the quest with something of a prejudice. It had long seemed to me that the quality movement can aggravate the siloing that my concept of the triple bottom line (variously rendered as 3BL or TBL) has sometimes promoted, at least when poorly understood.

That said, few people today would challenge the value of TQM. Consider the International Organization for Standardization (ISO). It launched its first ISO 9000 quality standard in 01987, focusing on the management of quality in business. Later, in 01996, it came up with its family of environmental quality standards, starting with ISO 14001. And more recently we have ISO 26000, released in 02010 and designed to bring social responsibility into the fold.

But there is as yet no overarching framework that pulls all of this together and searches for what my colleague and friend Jed Emerson has called "blended value" in the context of the push for a sustainable – or 1-Earth – economy.

As a consequence, I have long suspected that the TQM approach can potentially stifle innovation at a time when we need disruptive solutions to drive the necessary system change. So I was somewhat surprised, as I Googled my way around the quality landscape, to stumble upon a Korn/Ferry International white paper suggesting that "Sustainability is the next TQM".[7] Maybe sustainability can take over quality, rather than vice versa?

One challenge in terms of combining the sustainability and quality agendas, Shelly Fust and Lisa Walker noted, is that too often discussions about sustainability "foster confusion thanks to terms like global warming, carbon footprint, green products and greenhouse gas emissions".

That theme had been picked up by others, among them Mike Fraser of San Diego-based Source 44. He has argued that TQM can become "even more compelling and exciting" where it works out how to embrace sustainability.[8] "It's not about cap and trade", he says. "It's not a Democratic or Republican or Tea Party thing. It's about good business." And he referenced the 02009 article by Ram Nidumolu, the late C. K. Prahalad, and M. R. Rangaswami in the *Harvard Business Review* that declared sustainability to be the "key driver of innovation".[9] Their research of 30 large corporations was summarized in one key statement:

> Our research shows that sustainability is a mother lode of organizational and technological innovations that yield both bottom-line and top-line returns. Becoming environment-friendly lowers costs because companies end up reducing the inputs they use. In addition, the process generates additional revenues from better products or enables companies to create new businesses. In fact, because

those are the goals of corporate innovation, we find that smart companies now treat sustainability as innovation's new frontier.

On the sustainability side, meanwhile, we often forget the intense evolutionary curve that the quality movement raced up in the 01980s as new standards and expectations triggered immense changes in how corporations operated. So the fact that TQM does not fully embrace sustainability and 1-Earth thinking today does not rule out a powerful convergence within the coming decade.

Indeed, looking back at the early years of the quality revolution, there are strong parallels with where we find ourselves today. A few businesses decided to view "quality as an opportunity rather than a cost, and their investment in TQM paid off handsomely". To make this happen, leaders had to think completely out of the box.

"Rather than simply posting an inspector at the end of an assembly line", Fust and Walker recalled, "Toyota, Motorola, General Electric and others integrated quality considerations earlier in their assembly lines and into processes that preceded manufacturing, such as product design and R&D. Next, those companies pushed quality considerations even further upstream by working with suppliers to develop quality standards for the materials flowing into their organizations." This sounds very much like the arc that many sustainability efforts have followed – moving from initially being add-ons to being an integral part of operations, then on into product design and outward into the supply chain.

The quest for zero defects

A key reason for looking back at the history of TQM is that it also embraced zero, to a degree. The term "zero defects" was coined by the late Philip Crosby, who came up with a 14-step quality improvement process. This enjoyed considerable popularity through the 01960s and 01970s. A central concept was the need to "vaccinate" business leaders against what he saw as the poor-quality virus, to prevent a willingness to accept "close enough" outcomes.

Interestingly, given our focus earlier on the space race, the roots of the zero defects movement can be traced back to the Martin Marietta Corporation, later Lockheed Martin, when it was working on the Titan missile program. Titan rockets carried the first Astronauts into space in the 01960s – and were then used as antiballistic weapons, deployed in Europe as part of the mobile Pershing Missile System.

Years later, Crosby recalled that when Martin Marietta embraced zero defects, employees welcomed the program "with open arms. Everywhere it was presented the defect rates dropped, morale improved, and there was a feeling of accomplishment. Ideas for preventing problems emerged by the batch."[10]

The basic ideas that the zero defects (ZD) champions promoted were simple. First, and fundamentally, quality means meeting customer requirements. Second, defect prevention is much better than quality inspection and correction. Third, the ZD mindset must be core to any quality standard. And, fourth, the outcomes can generally be measured in terms of money – both costs avoided and, in some cases, premium prices chargeable.

Unfortunately, the approach soon hit a wall, both at Martin Marietta and elsewhere. As Crosby himself recalled a couple of decades later, "much of the enthusiasm and activity dropped off after a year or so when it became clear in most companies that the management had feet of clay. They still wanted to deliver materials that didn't meet the requirements if that was what it took to comply with the schedule and cost obligations."

The result, he noted, was that "many thought leaders came to think of the ZD approach as an infantile, motivation oriented, impractical program". The Japanese, however, thought different – and engaged differently – embracing much of the thinking and evolving their *kaizen* philosophy, focusing on "continuous improvement" and "change for the better".

Among the critics of the ZD agenda, surprisingly, was a man sometimes described as the "godfather of total quality", W. Edwards Deming – often credited with sparking the Japanese *kaizen* revolution. He pushed back against the concept of zero, promoting the concept of *acceptable defects*, arguing that the pursuit of zero could lead to an immense waste of time, effort, and money. Interesting.

Among Deming's principles was the following: "Eliminate slogans, exhortations, and targets for the work force asking for zero defects and new levels of productivity. Such exhortations", he argued, "only create adversarial relationships, as the bulk of the causes of low quality and low productivity belong to the system and thus lie beyond the power of the work force."

Once again, however, looking beyond the cut and thrust of competitive stances, most Zeronauts would conclude that this cannot simply be a question of "either/or", but instead the challenge is to achieve "both/and" outcomes. And it's the dysfunctional system that we now have to address.

Enter Six Sigma and total quality environmental management (TQEM)

Then came the rapid proliferation of a linked approach, Six Sigma. This is based on the intensive use of statistical methods – a Six Sigma process is one in which, astonishingly, 99.99966 percent of products are expected to be free of defects. Or, to put it another way, that's 3.4 defective products per million produced.

Motorola pioneered this path to zero defects – and it subsequently spread around the world. By the late 01980s, perhaps two-thirds of Fortune 500 companies were using Six Sigma methods. Drawing on the martial arts, those trained in the new science were designated "Champions", "Master Black Belts", "Black Belts", "Green Belts", and so on.

When you work with such people, you know that they often use histograms, Pareto charts, and similar tools to hammer their points home. Over time, as we have seen, their mandate has progressively expanded, first embracing environmental quality with standards such as ISO 14001 and then, more recently, social quality with ISO 26000.

Looking back through the late 01980s and into the 01990s, it strikes me that I was often called upon to speak at business conferences organized by the likes of the Global Environmental Management Initiative (GEMI), the Conference Board, and the World Environment Center (WEC) as new quality approaches evolved, notably total quality environmental management (TQEM).

Among the techniques used in this area were the "4Rs" (focusing, in order of priority, on waste reduction, reuse, recycling, and recovery), energy efficiency, pollution prevention, industrial ecology, cleaner production, design for environment, green procurement, and zero-emission processes, with one of the pioneers in the last area being the Zero Emissions Research Initiative (ZERI), covered later.

One of the vanguard companies was 3M, which as far back as 01975 had introduced its near-legendary 3P program, standing for Pollution Prevention Pays. I visited them several times and wrote about their considerable success in several early books.

In 02010, the 3P program celebrated its 35th anniversary. Over the first period, 3M reported the program had prevented more than 3.2 billion pounds of pollutants and saved more than US$1.4 billion based on aggregated data just from the first year of each 3P project.[11] 3P projects, of which over 8600 have been submitted, have typically focused on product reformulation, process modification, equipment redesign, or recycling and reuse of waste materials.

3M has also been a pioneer in the use of so-called "Lean Six Sigma", a process-improvement methodology and collection of statistical tools designed to reduce process variation and improve product quality.[12] The company's Lean Six Sigma vision, "Achieving Breakthrough Performance for our Customers, Employees and Shareholders", is firmly rooted in 3M's culture of innovation.

The company noted that while Lean Six Sigma projects focused on improving operational efficiency and product yield, direct reductions in energy use, air emissions, waste reduction, greenhouse gas emissions, and other environmental impacts also coincided.

So here is an obvious question: could the history of quality also point to how a new way of operating can be embedded within how companies work, as sustainability now needs to be? As Daniel Aronson of Deloitte put it: "What can sustainability learn from the way quality changed the game for companies? The quality revolution was about innovation in the core set of tools and methods that companies used to manage much of what they do. Quality became a central element of strategy, rather than a tactical tool, smashing previous cost versus fitness-for-use barriers and raising the 'table stakes' for all companies. Sustainability needs to do the same."

Does TQM help – or hinder – disruptive innovation?

Even so, at the back of my mind there has been this nagging sense that something about TQM was inimical to the task of driving system change. And it was reinforced by a *BusinessWeek* article I read in 02007.[13] Written by Brian Hindo, it was entitled "At 3M, a struggle between efficiency and creativity". And it cited two Wharton Business School professors to the effect that the introduction of Six Sigma approaches at 3M had suppressed creativity.

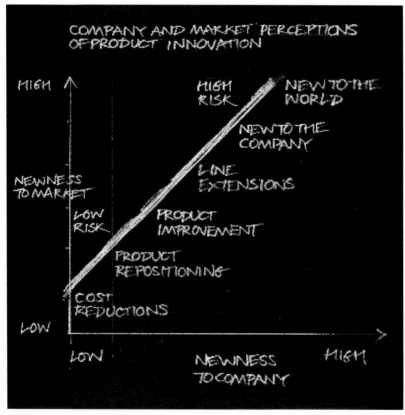

Figure 5.6 Company and market perceptions

More worrying still, a *Fortune* article the previous year had concluded that "of 58 large companies that have announced Six Sigma programs, 91 percent have trailed the S&P 500 since".[14] In retrospect, part of the problem may have been that some of these companies were being encouraged by TQM mindsets to look inwards rather than outwards – at a time when the market was shifting rapidly around them.

No one doubts the power and utility of TQM processes, properly applied; but I have found myself concluding that they are likely to be most helpful when used in the context of the sort of risk avoidance targets embodied in our Pathways to Zero model.

Indeed, as Deloitte's Daniel Aronson put it to me: "Is there a role for quality in the event-avoidance part of the movement toward zero? For example, would a reduction in the chances of a major environmental incident be a significant contributor to the journey to zero? The answer is clearly yes. This is a role quality can play in the context of the new zero and zero-related goals."

But surely there is more to TQM than this? A well-established perspective on how this looks from the TQM angle is shown in Figure 5.2 – running from basic cost reduction as a goal through to the point where the outcome is something completely new to the world. Sustaining the effort can be difficult, however, as the travails of Toyota have shown – between 02009 and 02011, after it fumbled the TQM ball, it was forced to recall no less than 20 million cars.[15] Our aim in what follows will be to push upwards along both axes, measuring newness to the company and newness to the market, both of which almost inevitably involve higher risk.

Inevitably, different Zeronauts have taken different paths from their Eureka! moment. Ron Dembo of Toronto-based Zerofootprint Software recalls that his stage 1 moment "came about six years ago when I attended a TED conference. It struck me that we desperately needed to find a way to live our lives without messing up the planet. The idea I started with is 'Is it possible to live a life with no impact on the environment?' Once you use a resource, can it be replaced?"[16]

There is a fair amount of simultaneous – or parallel – discovery going on. Asked if Ray Anderson was an inspiration, Dembo replied that "I knew nothing about him until after Zerofootprint had already started. I found out about him when I was researching companies that were doing work for the environment. At the time he wasn't using the term 'zero footprint' at all. I started using it for my company because I thought it was a cute name. I got a lot of grief over it because people said it wasn't possible to have zero footprint. I would reply that it was a goal, not necessarily the current reality."

The basis of his business is measuring footprints, en route toward zero. "The original idea revolved around how we don't measure the environment", Dembo recalls. "How can we make any inroads into changing if we don't measure? Big changes are the result of little changes. For example, you are sitting in a room and you have no idea if the air quality is good or bad. How does it compare with the air quality of the room that I am sitting in? How much energy is being used in your room compared with mine?"

Over time, the approach has become "much more focused on data and on what we call 'universal benchmarking'. We are very focused on buildings and what we can do to change, measure and manage them. For instance, our software can now measure an entire city within months." And as the opportunity space becomes more obvious, what does the competitive landscape look like? "The good news is that the market is growing and that helps us. In the early days, when we were ahead of the market, we spent a lot of time educating the public on why this is important, which is expensive. Now we just have to convince people that we have the better mousetrap."

As we discussed earlier when considering a number of CEOs who told Accenture that they have already embedded sustainability within their organizations, it seems that when it comes to zero, there is much more educating of the public to be done. One possibility, raised by Daniel Aronson of Deloitte, is that the lessons the quality movement has learned about this education process could be harnessed to good effect. "Perhaps revolutionary change is quickly assimilated only by a portion of society, businesses and governments – the 'Early Adopters'", he suggests. Those who wait until later – the "Early Majority", "Late Majority", and "Laggards" in Gordon Moore's classic typology – want more refined, complete solutions. Given the strength of quality tools and processes in creating these refinements, perhaps there is a powerful complementarity here.

Dembo, meanwhile, has begun to engage the banks. The aim: to get them to provide "financial incentives for true, measurable green behavior. This is a key part of the Holy Grail." Given the fondness of banks for hard numbers, perhaps some of the experiences that the quality movement has had can help Dembo and his like to gain traction more quickly. And maybe the tools and processes that the quality field has developed can help us all to refine and improve our messages and offerings so that we move past the early adopters sooner and reach our goals in less time.

Growing numbers of innovators will follow the lead of pioneers such as Dembo and experiment with the "Power of Zero". Recently, for example, I bumped into people from Ricoh when I was speaking in Madrid – and three of them later came through our London office to brief us on what they are doing on the zero front.[17]

Founded in 1936, Ricoh has around 110,000 employees and operates in 180 countries. It specializes in industrial products such as semiconductors, imaging technology such as copiers and laser printers, and optical equipment such as cameras and network software. The zero-focused initiative they are leading with is in the field of "zero carbon footprint" printing, achieved partly through energy efficiency and partly through carbon offsetting using carbon credits they have generated themselves. This offer is made to business customers and there are plans to extend it to consumers through retail green print shops – a relatively small start, given the size of Ricoh, but innovation that could well spread to other parts of the group, which has 235 companies.

We will need to keep an eye on such experiments over time to see how they evolve. As our next case study (see Box 5.1) suggests, the power of zero does not guarantee successful outcomes. For that, something more than quality and efficiency is required: innovators have to breed, train, and back the right horse. And they have to work out how to move from the Eureka! discovery moment through to the point where their innovation becomes endemic across the economy. That's where we are headed in Chapter 6. But before that, given that so many inventors and innovators celebrate failure, let's take a closer look at a recent failure in the world of zero.

Box 5.1

Formula Zero

An early experiment in zero-emission mobility, Formula Zero foundered – but not before the founders, including Godert van Hardenbroek, learned lessons with wider applications.[18] I asked him about the experience.

JOHN ELKINGTON (JE): What sparked Formula Zero?

GODERT VAN HARDENBROEK (GvH): The origins date back to an international workshop organized in 01998 by O2, a network of sustainability-focused designers.[19] The theme was Sustainable Business Concepts. So far so good. During the event, however, one of the participants got a phone call alerting him that he could buy a classic car, a Citroën SM. He decided to buy the car, a very special old-timer with a Maserati engine. This stirred up quite a bit of unrest during the workshop. How could you spend several days in a workshop focusing on a sustainable future – and at the same time buy such a gas-guzzling piece of nostalgic machinery?

I was really struck by the question raised, and I think the hard-nosed environmentalists in the group got it wrong. If you extend the trajectory they were promoting, you get to a grim, uncomfortable place. Your lifestyle shrinks to doing the bare minimum with the maximum efficiency, and then only if you have a good justification for it. This is the opposite of what most human behavior looks like, especially the stuff most Western people are passionate about. They obsess about leisure time, sports, partying, fashion, traveling, exotic meals, extravagant cars, and so on.

This led me - and my business partner Eelco Rietveld - to the idea that we should open up a new route, uniting these contradictory ideas. We created Formula Zero, a race class without any emissions. Irrational, emotional, fun, but compatible with a new ecological reality. Doing stuff you like, such as racing, because that is part of what it means to be a human being, but adapting it to fit into the vision of a sustainable future.

In 02002, we decided to "go for it", researching the automotive and racing market, writing a business plan, raising our first €100,000. Formula Zero B. V. was founded in 02003. Our mission statement read: "Formula Zero promotes well to wheel zero emission technologies through racing with fuel cell-powered cars." We created the perfect job for ourselves: we were building a business while doing something we felt deeply passionate about. Salaries were small but we really loved what we were doing.

JE: And the high point?

GvH: This was the promotional tour we made after building a functional prototype of a Formula Zero hydrogen fuel cell go-kart. The road to get that prototype realized was really challenging because to build it we had to raise about €430,000 and build a vehicle that had no predecessor. This was tough, but once the prototype Mark II was there, people lined up to see it. It was special because it was a fully functional race machine, producing nothing but water as exhaust.

With this prototype we went on an international tour giving presentations and demonstrations at over 60 venues. We raced through the streets of Brussels in front of the European Commission; we had business leaders, politicians, celebrities, and racecar drivers behind the wheel. And we always made them drink water from the exhaust in specially branded FZ shot glasses that they could keep to remember the experience.

Discovery Channel caught on to the story and made a piece about it that is still being aired from time to time. This reached millions of people and was the perfect foundation for the next phase, the establishment of the championship.

JE: Were there early signals that the agenda might be shifting?

GvH: Looking back, yes, there were both internal and external signals that electric vehicles (EVs) might become the dominant zero emission solution. Internally, we discovered that the fuel cell, the technology of choice for the car industry, which we had chosen to promote, was really complicated.

In the development stage of our prototype, we built two battery-powered versions to test the drive train and chassis. We found that these were much, much cheaper and much, much simpler to put together and much simpler to control. By contrast, the fuel cell technology was very complicated, many things could go wrong and they did, expensively.

This raised questions internally whether all of this complexity, plus building an entire new fueling infrastructure, would be justified – just to have more range and quick refueling. Because that is what the whole debate between batteries and hydrogen boils down to. They both produce zero emission mobility, though the battery has a better well to wheel efficiency. But we decided to stick with the vision pushed by the car-makers, the oil companies, and government. Everybody knew it would be hard, but this was not a reason not to go for it, right?

Externally, too, there were a few warning signs. One of them came as early as 2004 through research done by a friend of mine. He studied the response of the car industry to the fuel cell and the need for zero emission mobility. His argument in his PhD thesis was that the automotive sector was using the fuel cell to keep public opinion and politicians at bay. They were basically saying: "Listen, we are working on a solution, we are designing the silver bullet, it's complicated, give us seven more years, give us some cash to do the research, because, well ... it's very complicated!"

And all this time they were selling diesel engines and protecting their investment in existing technologies. While I was dealing with the people running these programs at the big car and big oil companies, I was trying to sell them our races, and didn't believe his theory. But in retrospect I think this is exactly what happened. These industries bought themselves a lot of time, and it was relatively cheap.

But then the game-changer came along that rewrote the rules. Tesla single-handedly broke through the barriers created by Big Auto and Big Oil. They had no ties to the car industry, but were linked to Silicon Valley. Their timing was good because when they built their first vehicle, battery technology had improved tremendously through the push and cash coming from laptop computers and cell phones. They literally soldered together 4000 laptop batteries and put them in a sports car. The Tesla Roadster is really fast, looks great and runs for 300 kilometers. It can be charged at a regular socket, which makes it backwards compatible with the entire electric system we already have in place. With hydrogen, this is not an option so that technology could only take off if there was a "big bang" provision of infrastructure.

We have also seen the appearance of fast charging for batteries. This means you can recharge your EV up to 80 percent in 30 minutes. This is really the nail in the coffin for hydrogen as I see it. The only real argument for hydrogen over batteries, being able to refuel quickly, is now gone. The car industry still insists fuel cells will become cheaper than batteries; but I don't see how that is going to happen because this will only occur with economies of scale, and that is only going to be achieved with a "big bang" implementation; and that, in my view, is not going to happen at all.

So, yes, during 02007, I started noticing the hype around the Tesla: people were buying them, making down payments just to be on the waiting list! This was also the time when Project Better Place was launched by Shai Agassi, and its partnership with Renault Nissan was announced. When, early in 02008, the first production Teslas were delivered to customers, we were having urgent internal discussions about what the EV trends meant for our company. By this time, we were heavily invested in fuel cell racing. We had just bought six Hydrogenics fuel cells for €184,000 to help university teams build their own race go-kart.

You asked about the high point of Formula Zero, but of course there was also a low point. For me this was a very counter-intuitive moment because this was the launch of the Formula Zero Championship in August, 02008. It was the first time we had fully realized our plan: there was a race, it was in the city center of Rotterdam, there were six teams from five countries, their machines were marvels of engineering, it was exciting, it was futuristic, there were sponsors, we were on the 8 o'clock news ... but I was really upset.

We'd worked like mad to put together this race; but in parallel I had worked with an MBA student to produce a new investment proposal. This was a plan to take us to the next level - and I figured that the race would be the perfect venue to invite investors. Quite a few of them came to see the action, and some read the proposal, but all said they didn't see hydrogen happening. So there we were, we had accomplished something extraordinary - but things didn't look good at all.

A few months later the global economic crisis erupted - and we found ourselves without sponsors or investors. The teams were disappointed we couldn't deliver all the races we had promised, but one after the other venues and sponsors we were talking to backed out - and that was that.

JE: Were there things you might have done to adapt?

GvH: This is a question I've been struggling with quite a bit. With every option I find myself bringing forth all the old arguments that we had for not following that plan. There are two obvious things we could have done: either switch to racing with EVs or bring EVs under the Formula Zero umbrella.

I suppose that if we had taken the signs in 02007 seriously and learned from our own experience of the difficulties with fuel cells, we should have switched to a battery series, when we still had the chance. We could have built the prototype of a full size battery-powered single-seater in 02008 and built a series around that. But this is a difficult thing to do. I remember a discussion we had in early 02008, when I was raising the EV threat to our business once again, and one of our employees said something like: "But it's all perfectly lined up right now, with the record, the teams, the championship, the involvement of the FIA [Federation Internationale Automobile], the vision for scaling up. It's like domino blocks that just have to be tipped over."

Our vision for scaling up was synched to the timeline of the automotive sector. The PR departments of most of the big auto companies were still saying hydrogen; but the contours of the change were becoming apparent and our competitors were developing their prototypes. So the domino blocks were perhaps not going to be tipped in the way we expected, and they weren't.

Broadening the series to include more technologies, so making Formula Zero an umbrella brand, is something we did try to pursue, but too late. The window had closed. By the time we were working on this, it was already 02009 and EV competitors had an edge on us, and we were super low in cash and energy. We had to "let go" all of our staff and I was personally struggling with my motivation. Looking back, if we could have adapted the broadening strategy in 02007 we might have made it.

JE: If you were starting again, what would you do differently?

GvH: I'd be less inclined to listen to the PR story of multinationals. The classic innovation theory seems to apply, once again: incumbents cannot produce change. This is something that has to come from another source, the new kids on the block, bringing another paradigm. So rather than listening to the PR stories, I would look more at the actual investments being made in new programs.

I'd try to respond faster and more radically to signals of a changing environment. The strong response of early adopters to the Tesla should have told us enough, especially with our own learning from building our own fuel cell vehicle. This implies being more courageous in challenging the assumptions you are working with and acting quickly when the time is there.

JE: Was the concept of zero attractive to people, or not?

GvH: We got tremendous positive response. And it was the young people that loved Formula Zero the most. Especially in the beginning, a lot of people that heard about us were almost relieved. They were very concerned about climate change and the world running out of oil, but didn't like fuel efficiency races like the Ecomarathon. We redefined that challenge from "Extracting as much power out of a kilojoule of fuel" to "going as fast as possible using zero emission technologies". This is something people really understood intuitively. With us they found something they could be enthusiastic about and at the same time feel good about. This is also what resonates with the Tesla owners today.

The reservations mostly came with considerations about making money. This was a very difficult point: nobody was making any money out of hydrogen. This is still a difficult point because hardly anybody is making money on zero emission mobility ... yet. But battery companies and car companies are well positioned to get a good return on their investment. The EV is coming, so the possible returns are clearer than with the hydrogen proposition. So now the proposition of zero emission mobility begins to have it all: the feel-good factor, cool, and the prospect of profits.

We hope to sell the Formula Zero brand to another organization. The idea is that they would turn it into a brand for organizing zero emission events such as EV rallies, Segway races, scooter races, and so on. These potential new owners see the power of zero.

As The Zeronauts went to press, I contacted Godert to see whether the potential new owners had put their money on the table. Not yet, he said.

6
Zeronautics 101

Five stepping-stones take transformative change agents from their breakthrough insight to the point where their impact is so evident that it is increasingly taken for granted. Introducing the emerging discipline of Zeronautics, we move through the five stages (the 5Es): Eureka!, experimentation, enterprise, ecosystems, and economy.

Innovation is tough. From the moment when an innovator wakes up to the potential for driving a particular problem toward – or beyond – zero, there is typically a long, arduous journey of experimentation, of failure, of competition and collaboration, and of all the sundry adventures that are inevitable as efforts are made to replicate and scale the new solutions.

One way to look at the dynamics of all this is to think of negative change exponentials (problems with the potential to dramatically worsen over a relatively short time period) and positive change exponentials (solutions with the potential to replicate and scale).

In nature, the equivalents would be whirlpools which threaten to drag sailors down into the depths, and whirlwinds which create such destruction in the form of tornadoes, typhoons, and hurricanes – but which, at least in the form of thermals, can potentially be harnessed and ridden by those with sufficient skills and courage.

Our species is singularly poor at thinking in terms of exponential effects, but it is something that most Zeronauts are determined to master. Whereas environmentalists have tended to see exponential trajectories as an unmitigated bad thing, many Zeronauts are trying to work out how they can unleash exponential growth trajectories to power solutions – and help break the Sustainability Barrier.

Before we look at some of the ways in which leading Zeronauts are addressing challenges in such areas as population, pandemics, poverty, pollution, and proliferation in Chapter 7, let's move quickly through each of the stages of the Pathways to Zero model, recognizing that the move from stage to stage is far from guaranteed – indeed, as when pushing quality programs to the ultimate

EUREKA!

Figure 6.1 Pathways to Zero: Stage 1

STAGE 1: EUREKA!

degree, the costs in time, effort, risk, and money can sometimes grow almost exponentially as we close in on a stretch target.

Zeronautics will live or die based on its ability to catalyze breakthrough insights and action. Not that this is new. It is impossible today to know what it felt like as the recognition dawned in the minds of quality pioneers such as Philip Crosby and W. Edwards Deming that the old way of doing things was dysfunctional – and likely to become increasingly so. But there has been a long history of people going through such awakenings, or "epiphanies".

Shocks can spur such awakenings. Think of America's *Sputnik* moment. There are those, for example, and they include President Obama, who have seen the rise of China as what he called "a *Sputnik* moment". He was not even born in 01957 when the Soviet Union sent its first satellite into orbit around Earth, but – once again – the achievement proved to be a devastating wake-up call to an America grown complacent.[1] Steven Chu, President Obama's energy secretary, has also harked back to *Sputnik* in arguing that China's growing investment in cleaner sources of energy risks leaving the US bobbing in its wake – unless it ramps up its own spending in the field.

More typically, however, the Eureka! moment is illustrated not by a tiny twinkling object in the night sky, but by images of Archimedes in his bath, understanding that he could measure the volume of irregular objects by measuring the amount of water they displaced on immersion.

STAGE 1

EUREKA!

STAGE 2

EXPERIMENT

STAGE 3

ENTERPRISE

STAGE 4

ECOSYSTEM

STAGE 5

ECONOMY

For the late, great Ray Anderson of Interface, the wake-up moment came when he was being asked to provide his company with an environmental vision – and the best that he could come up with was that they should "comply with all the many rules and regulations that government agencies seemed to love to send our way".[2]

Then, "as if by pure serendipity", Paul Hawken's book *The Ecology of Commerce*[3] landed on Anderson's desk – and triggered an intense personal crisis. Suddenly realizing that mankind is headed into ecological overshoot, Anderson often described the moment he got the message as "an epiphany, a rude awakening, an eye-opening experience, and the point of the story felt just like the point of a spear driven straight into my heart".

What is interesting about Anderson is that he wasn't solely driven by the business case – he saw sustainability as a matter of morality, too. He referred to himself as a "recovering plunderer" because he believed that any company that takes more from the planet than it gives back is involved in plunder. As he told a Technology Entertainment and Design (TED) conference in 02009, "Theft is a crime. And the theft of our children's future [will] someday be considered a crime."[4]

For Lee Scott, at the time CEO of retail giant Wal-Mart, the epiphany involved waking up to the reality of the array of environmental challenges when many of his stores in the southern states of America were crippled by Hurricane Katrina.

Experience suggests that the human brain often needs to be stressed – sometimes over extended periods – before it breaks through to novel solutions. But the record of early Zeronauts suggests that instead of being pessimistic about the prospect of developing solutions, successful innovators often display what Kevin Kelly dubs "radical optimism".[5] Part of his own radical optimism flows from his sense that we are now seeing deep shifts in the nature and scale of change itself.[6]

So, what can business do to open themselves up to the new order? One answer is to find, recruit, and develop high-potential internal change agents – what we some years back dubbed *social intrapreneurs*.[7] One of our most successful reports, published in 2008, was *The Social Intrapreneur*, which spotlighted examples of the breed in a broad range of companies, including Accenture, Banco Real, The Dow Chemical Company, Hindustan Lever, Morgan Stanley, Nike, and Vodafone. Here, in the special case of what we might dub "Zeropreneurs", we should distinguish between those working as free-range entrepreneurs and those working inside larger organizations, as intrapreneurs. Table 6.1 identifies some of the characteristics of zero-focused intrapreneurs, comparing them with those more typically found in zero-focused entrepreneurs.

Homo ZERI

When I think of Zeronauts driving potentially disruptive change, someone who comes to mind as one of the earliest pioneers of the Zero Footprint Economy is Gunter Pauli – who founded the Zero Emissions Research Initiative (ZERI) in 01994. In the terms used in Table 6.1, he has been a Zero-entrepreneur.

I asked him to explain how he sees the link between zero emissions, zero waste, and the wider world of total quality management (TQM). "From an environmental perspective", he replied, "the elimination of waste represents the ultimate solution to pollution problems that threaten ecosystems at both local and global levels. In addition, full use of raw materials, accompanied by a shift toward renewable sources, means that utilization of the Earth's resources can be brought back to sustainable levels."

And what does all this mean for the world of business and industry? "For industry", he explained, "zero emissions means greater competitiveness and represents a continuation of its inevitable drive toward efficiency. First came productivity of labor and capital, and now comes the complete use of raw materials – producing more from less. Zero emissions can therefore be viewed as a standard of efficiency, much like TQM (zero defects) and just-in-time (zero inventory)." Nor, he noted, is this simply a game for business. "For governments, the full use of raw materials creates new industries and generates jobs even as it raises productivity."

When the concept of zero emissions was first introduced, Pauli concluded, "it only referred to the fact that waste of one activity becomes food for another. Over the years, however, this simple principle was further enhanced thanks to observations of natural systems and to projects implemented throughout the ZERI networks." He pointed to the decades of research on biomimetics that was initiated during the 01950s at the University of Reading – and to the work of biomimicry champion Janine Benyus, who argues that the human species is a recent arrival and observes that "Since it lacks the millions of years of co-evolutionary experience, it is bound to make mistakes and [will have to] learn to 'behave' in a symbiotic manner."

Table 6.1 The Zeropreneur, outside and in

	Characteristics of Zeropreneur	Ent	Int
1	Shrug off constraints of ideology or discipline	✓	✓
2	Identify and apply practical solutions to key problems	✓	✓
3	Innovate by finding a new product, service, or approach to problem	✓	✓
4	Focus – first and foremost – on value creation through Zeronautics	✓	✓
5	Successfully navigate corporate culture, strategy, and process		✓
6	Communicate zeroing ambitions and targets in compelling business terms		✓
7	Build and inspire teams across a multiplicity of corporate divisions		✓
8	Jump in before they are fully resourced	✓	✓
9	Have a dogged determination that pushes them to take risks	✓	✓
10	Combine their passion for change with measurement and monitoring of impacts	✓	✓
11	Have a healthy impatience – they don't like bureaucracy	✓	✓
12	Run their organizations	✓	

Ent = Zero-entrepreneur
Int = Zero-intrapreneur

Interestingly, prototypical Zeronaut Ray Anderson had this to say on what it is like to be trapped in the old, unsustainable way of doing things. Quoting Daniel Quinn's book *Ishmael*,[8] he noted that operating by the old rules was like using "those badly designed wings of the early aircraft at the dawn of human flight. Our civilization is like that would-be 'aeronaut' who jumps off a high cliff in his misbegotten craft. He's pedaling away, wings flapping like mad; the wind is in his face, and the poor fool thinks he's flying when he's really in free fall. Though the ground seems far away at first, his flight is doomed because the design of his wings has ignored the laws of aerodynamics."

Similarly, in our world, we cannot ignore the laws of nature or turn a blind eye to the data that tells us whether we are flying or falling. Perhaps this a less obvious way in which the field of quality can be of assistance. As Daniel Aronson of Deloitte asked: "Is it possible to take advantage of the way quality teaches people to think – data-driven, quantitative, using rigorous analysis – to overcome some of the challenges we face in terms of our mindsets? For example, a very large number of people (in the US, UK, and other countries) simply don't believe the data about climate change or environmental issues. Quality inculcates a respect for data – could that make people more receptive to data about environmental issues?"[9]

This is shaping up as a challenging new era of trial and error in which investors, entrepreneurs, and managers evolve new business models to create more value while shrinking the ecological footprints of their enterprises and operations. Some will fly, most won't. As we work our way through the four remaining stages of our Pathways to Zero model, we will focus on how pioneering Zeronauts are moving beyond their epiphanies to develop a growing array of experiments – and what their early successes and failures are telling us about the future.

Box 6.1

How Zeronauts succeed in stage 1

A key point to note about the five stages is not just that you leave one to move into another, but that – like acrobats forming a human pyramid – the skills and strengths achieved in earlier stages are crucial both in moving to and succeeding in later stages. Ask Zeronauts what their golden rules are for getting to the Eureka! moment and they are likely to mention the following:

1 Acknowledge that getting to Eureka! is not something given to everyone – it's a gift, often hard won. Celebrate and develop the skill where it exists, and help others to embrace and support stage 1 breakthroughs.
2 Many critical insights and breakthroughs come from the edges of incumbent systems and organizations.
3 It's critically important to position yourself at what Frans Johansson – a founder member of the Volans advisory board – has dubbed the "intersection", the place where the chances of serendipity operating are enhanced.[10]
4 Multidisciplinary teams and partnerships are crucial.
5 Understand that setting apparently impossible targets can be a key part of the exercise.
6 Don't expect massive breakthroughs every time – often real progress comes through a succession of small steps, through what Peter Sims calls Little Bets.[11]
7 Move quickly from insight to experiment.
8 Recognize that it is critical to get your timing right – and that, at times, it is possible to create your timing.

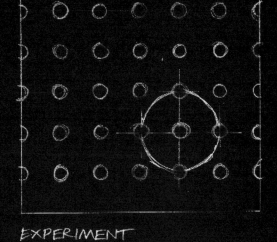

EXPERIMENT

Figure 6.2 Pathways to Zero: Stage 2

STAGE 2: EXPERIMENTATION

Zeronautics, by its very nature, is an emergent, experimental discipline. The quest for zero is not a quest for an absence either of activity or of growth, but a challenge to the current big footprint way of doing things. It is an invitation to explore, discover, and break through into new opportunity spaces.

That's one reason why I was intrigued to discover that the Mayans, who were among the first to discover the concept of zero more or less as we understand it, symbolized zero with a spiral. For many years while I was at the helm, SustainAbility's masthead combined a spiral (representing evolution and breakout innovation) with a trigram (order, balance, and the triple bottom line) that operated in creative tension.

If you want to track the spiraling tips of creativity in our modern societies, one obvious place to kick off is in the laboratory. If you have visited scores of labs and R&D centers around the world, as I have, you will have seen how TQM methods have come to underpin the way in which many research scientists do their work – from designing their experiments through to reporting their findings. And there is huge merit in that. Having visited facilities where some of the world's deadliest organisms are worked on and stored, it's reassuring to know that high-end versions of TQM are in place (we will come back to bio-warfare in Chapter 7).

But TQM, by its very nature, tends to focus on continuous – rather than disruptive, transformative – change. Its quest to avoid failure also typically serves to limit experimentation to incrementalism, not transformative change – let alone true paradigm shifts. For this sort of change, we typically need to look elsewhere.

A key need today is to tap into the innate creativity of our species – mobilizing ideas not just for continuous improvement but also for creative destruction and reconstruction. As Richard Florida put it in *The Great Reset*, "We tend to view prolonged economic downturns, like the Great Depression of the 1930s and the Long Depression of the late nineteenth century, in terms of the crisis and pain they cause, rather than as the opportunities they invariably represent. But history teaches us that these great crises are opportunities to remake our economy and society and generate whole new epochs of economic growth and prosperity."[12] These periods have been some of the most fertile, in terms of innovation, invention, and energetic risk-taking in history, setting the stage for recovery.

I have spent much of the past three decades exploring the leading edge of biotechnology, renewable energy, and clean technology in pursuit of such disruptive solutions – but even when you track them down, time shows that they don't always take off; indeed, most fail. And even those that ultimately break through at scale can take an unconscionable time to do so.

In addition to my day jobs, since the early 01980s I have been involved in a considerable number of award schemes designed to accelerate the evolution of cleaner technologies. And a fair few of the mementos I have collected remind me of ventures that looked exciting at the time, but that ultimately failed. Looking around my study, I see various things that link back to some of those visits, from a small vial of dried white worms (once billed as a waste-to-wealth product) to a bar of glass made from melted waste asbestos.

The worms and glass bar date back to the mid-01980s, when I was a judge for the Pollution Abatement Technology Awards, hosted by the Royal Society of Arts – which subsequently helped to spawn such initiatives as the Better Environment Awards for Industry (BEAFI), which then evolved into a European counterpart and, in the UK, the Queen's Award for Environmental Technology.

More recently, I have been a judge for awards offered by, among others, *Newsweek*, the Carbon War Room, and Katerva. The first of the three focuses on the greening of the US 500 and Global 100 biggest companies. The Carbon War Room frames the climate challenge as a global war, with theaters and battles focusing the spotlight on particular sectors and issues. And Katerva, which aims to become the "Nobel Prize of Sustainability", seeks to find, evaluate, celebrate, and support concepts which can help us to move to 1-Earth lifestyles by mid-century. Specifically, it looks for "true game-changers, the kind of ideas that can create change on the order of 1000 percent rather than 1–2 percent." A pure play in Zeronautics.

Googling the Moon

I love the way in which initiatives like these can mobilize talent – as do both Innocentive, which span out of Eli Lilly, and Open Planet Ideas, developed by Sony and WWF. Innocentive, in particular, has long struck me as a particularly powerful way of using crowdsourcing to tap into the innovative energies of the world's online talent.

But if there are two initiatives I have found even more interesting because you could see the results in the real world, they were Formula Zero and the X Prize.

Formula Zero, which sadly bit the dust as I was writing *The Zeronauts*, is covered in Box 5.1 (see pp.135–41). The X Prize, on the other hand, is still going from strength to strength – and is very much in the spirit of Supermarine's angel investor, Lady Houston, introduced in Chapter 3.

There are two types of X Prize competitions: X Prizes and X Challenges. An X Prize is an award of US$10 million or more given to the first team to achieve a specific goal, set by the X Prize Foundation, which has the potential to positively affect individuals around the world. Rather than awarding money to honor past achievements or directly funding research, an X Prize aims to spur innovation by tapping into our competitive and entrepreneurial spirits.

An X Challenge, by contrast, is a prize of up to US$2.5 million, awarded for solving a well-defined technical problem that has no clear path to a solution, or is perceived as particularly difficult. Unlike an X Prize, which seeks to stimulate or catalyze an entire market, an X Challenge seeks to produce a breakthrough technological or behavioral solution to a specific market need. Both the X Prize and the X Challenge can be developed in one of four different prize groups:

exploration (space and deep ocean); energy and environment; education and global development; and life sciences.

So, for example, the Energy and Environment Prize Group includes the development of prizes that "will end our addiction to oil and stem the harmful effects of climate change. We are looking for breakthroughs in clean fuels, renewable energy, energy efficiency, energy storage, carbon reduction, and sustainable housing."

Among the X Prize initiatives that I have tracked with great interest has been their sustainable mobility competition, with the main winner being the striking Edison2, though I have to admit to an intense fascination with a much less energy-efficient competition, funded by Google. The search engine giant is offering a total of $30 million in prizes to the first privately funded teams to "safely land a robot on the surface of the Moon and have that robot travel 500 meters over the lunar surface and send images and data back to the Earth."

Most such schemes take off in the US for cultural and other reasons; but every so often your heart jumps when you see major private funding coming into big science projects elsewhere in the world. I took time off from writing *The Zeronauts*, and other projects, to attend the launch of a new initiative at the University of Cambridge, England.

An appetite for blue sky thinking

The question in my mind as I traveled east from London on the train was why would you want to give away UK£20 million – over US$30 million at the time – even if you had it? The question was spurred by the case of hedge fund superstar David Harding, who had just made the biggest gift ever to the Cavendish Laboratory at Cambridge University. This was, he explained, a form of compensation for all the physicists his firm had "poached" from the world of science.

He was only partly joking: at the time his firm, Winton Capital Management, employed over 90 researchers with PhDs or other higher degrees, in subjects ranging from extragalactic astrophysics through to artificial intelligence.

But the two main reasons why he decided to fund the Winton Programme for the Physics of Sustainability was that, first, he wanted to provide the "freedom to discover", the ability to invest in what scientists call "blue sky thinking", and, second, in terms of focus, he saw fundamental science as the key to creating the low-carbon, low-impact technologies of the future. Harding noted that Winton Capital succeeds by outsourcing all the things in which it does not excel – and in this case, he quipped, the task they were subcontracting was "the betterment of mankind".

Fine, but why the unusual focus on physics? "While it is not quite as simple as using physics to save the world", Harding explained, "this is an opportunity to use, for example, quantum physics to develop materials with seeming miraculous properties that could combat the growing effect humans are having on the planet."

"In 02100, the sources of energy on this planet will be either solar or fusion", argued Professor Peter Littlewood, who heads the Cavendish Laboratory, "and the preferred means to transport and use energy will be electrical. The 'magic' technologies needed to deliver this new age and make them available to societies worldwide are: photovoltaics, electrical storage, refrigeration, and lighting."

Given the laboratory's long-term focus on nuclear fission and fusion, some people may be surprised to hear that the Winton Programme will largely turn its back on these fields. Instead, at a time when scientists are able to engineer materials at the level of individual atoms, creating new chemical structures with novel properties, it is possible to fine-tune materials by using extreme conditions of temperature, pressure, and magnetic or electrical fields to hunt for emergent properties, such as superconductivity.

One key aim is to find superconductors that can carry electricity while operating at or near room temperature – currently impossible. Other goals include batteries with energy storage properties that rival gasoline and new thermoelectric mechanisms that can scavenge heat from the environment.

Among other things, I saw a project using nanofabrication to create identical copies of the scales that give the spectacular colors to butterfly wings, with the product covering areas of several square centimeters. Longer term, the challenge will involve producing materials that can be manufactured at low cost and used on a massive scale, employing nanoscale products "that can be delivered by the tonne and by the hectare".

The frugal innovators

Massive investment in fundamental research will certainly be needed in the Race to Zero, but a very different – and equally important – trend has been dubbed "frugal innovation". And the first rule in this space, as *The Economist*[13] put it in a Schumpeter column, is "break all the rules".

Rather than trying to adapt Western products to developing world conditions, frugal innovators are "taking the needs of poor consumers as the starting point and working backwards. Instead of adding ever more bells and whistles, they strip the products down to their bare essentials." To date, the idea of zero impact growth is fairly remote from much of this effort, but a sustainable future is going to require cross-fertilization.

Some call this approach frugal innovation, while others – among them General Electric CEO Jeff Immelt – prefer either "reverse innovation" (with innovations developed for poor country consumers catapulting back into rich world markets) or "constraint-based innovation".

Among recent frugal products has been Tata's revolutionary Nano car, which sells for around $2200 and in which I took a ride during a recent trip to India. The effect was quite extraordinary: the car felt modern, spacious, and comfortable, and one could easily imagine driving it in Europe. Despite the problems Tata has encountered in promoting the Nano, and the questions raised about the implications of a private mobility solution to India's humongous transport challenges, this is a trajectory with huge potential.

The point about frugal innovation, however, is that it is not just about redesigning products. As *The Economist* put it: "it involves rethinking entire production processes and business models. Companies need to squeeze costs so they can reach more customers, and accept thin profit margins to gain volume."

Indians pride themselves on their national tradition of *jugaad*, which roughly translated means "making do with whatever you have and never giving up", and it is amazing how this spirit is revolutionizing everything from training illiterate women to be solar engineers, as in the case of Barefoot College, founded by Volans advisory board member Bunker Roy, through to radically cutting the cost of eye and heart surgery – as in, respectively, the cases of Aravind Eye Care in Madurai and the Narayana Hrudayalaya Hospital in Bangalore.

But some of the most striking examples of frugal innovation are now beginning to come out of China. One has been the battery company turned into electric car-maker BYD, among the 50 top innovators we spotlighted in our 02009 report *The Phoenix Economy*.

As *The Economist* reported: "BYD has radically reduced the price of expensive lithium-ion batteries by using less costly raw materials and learning how to make them at ambient temperatures rather than in expensively heated 'dry rooms'. This has reduced their price from $40 to $12 and made them competitive with less powerful nickel-cadmium batteries."

As the pace of exploration and innovation accelerates, so history suggests that we will see intense bursts of cross-pollination and new forms of hybrid vigor, with totally unpredictable outcomes. The next challenge will be to turn these astonishing inventions and innovations into breakthrough business models and new forms of wealth creation.

Box 6.2

How Zeronauts succeed in stage 2

Successful Zeronauts live in a constant state of experimentation – so stage 2 is ongoing. But ask successful Zeronauts what their golden rules are for experimentation and they are likely to mention the following:

1 Adopt the philosophy advanced by Yoda in The Empire Strikes Back: "Do or do not. There is no try."
2 Be prepared to break all the rules – and to create new ones.
3 At the same time, recognize and embrace the role of failure in successful innovation: study the approaches of Thomas Edison or James Dyson, for example.
4 Learn by doing – and spread your bets. Make lots of little bets.
5 Keep an eye on what other innovators are up to, among other things, through award schemes such as the X Prize, Katerva, or the portfolios of extraordinary innovators developed by the likes of Ashoka, the Schwab Foundation, or the Skoll Foundation, or open-source innovation platforms such as Innocentive.
6 Dig into the thinking of people such as Kevin Kelly – and look into ways of achieving what he calls "increasing returns".[14]
7 Keep in mind the necessary next step, adapting or building an enterprise to take the innovation to market and to scale.

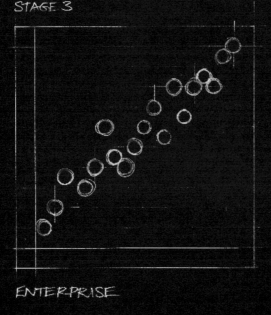

STAGE 3

ENTERPRISE

Figure 6.3 Pathways to Zero: Stage 3

STAGE 3: ENTERPRISE

Ultimately, Zeronautics depends for its impact upon the health and success of enterprise – and upon the availability of entrepreneurial talent. While the benefits of entrepreneurship are all too often invisible to us, every so often you get to appreciate entrepreneurial talent at close quarters, as I did recently while cruising around in two very different vehicles which were both new to the world.

It's a big, disorienting step from Tata's Nano, already mentioned, to the world's fastest electric car, the Tesla Roadster, but it's one I made recently – and both represent stage 3 of the Pathways to Zero model. True, the Nano was in Delhi and the gleaming red Tesla in Vienna, and I was a passenger in the first and the driver in the second; but this was a chance to sample different ends of the spectrum of personal vehicle solutions to what some choose to call sustainable mobility.

The Nano was developed by one of the world's largest incumbent companies, Tata, driven by the entrepreneurial vision of Ratan Tata, whereas the Tesla has been created by a start-up, founded and driven along by Elon Musk. The first offered safer mobility to the masses, the second the current ultimate in electric vehicles for the wealthy.

The Nano is designed and priced to replace the ubiquitous and heavily overcrowded scooters and motorbikes you see everywhere in India – and is extremely energy efficient, though conventionally powered by gasoline. The

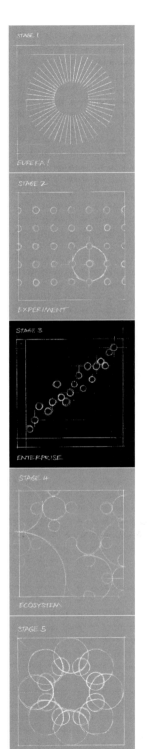

STAGE 1

EUREKA!

STAGE 2

EXPERIMENT

STAGE 3

ENTERPRISE

STAGE 4

ECOSYSTEM

STAGE 5

ECONOMY

Roadster, on the other hand, accelerates faster than most sports cars yet produces no emissions, at least while being driven.

Clearly, TQM can play a critical role in either trajectory. Tesla's goal, for example, is to produce a full range of electric cars, from premium sports cars to mass-market vehicles – relentlessly driving down the cost of electric vehicles. When I took a quick look on the internet, I found Tesla advertising for engineers with quality training, specifying Six Sigma skills and related techniques. Such high-energy start-ups are punching great expanding holes in the boundaries of the possible.

At the same time, however, this is a critical branching point, where decisions have to be made in terms of the balance between public and private forms of transport – and approaches, among them urban design and better use of the internet, that seek to maximize access while minimizing movement.

You could argue that stage 3 is the point in the Pathways to Zero model where the work of the TQM community is most obviously relevant – and potentially has the most to offer in the drive toward a more sustainable future. But a great deal depends on how the process is framed: focus too much on the short term, or on the activities of a single company, or on avoiding failure, and the chances are that the net outcome will not help drive the necessary transformations.

Many TQM practitioners, to be fair, would argue that this has never been the object of the exercise. Undaunted, meanwhile, the number of companies making zero performance claims and publicly setting zero targets continues to grow. One company which has a long-established program is Shell, with its "Goal Zero".[15]

This award-winning program emerged from Shell-sponsored research into safety and behavior at Leiden, Manchester, and Aberdeen universities. It works to change peoples' attitudes and habits so that they behave safely. It provides practical techniques that help people learn to intervene to stop unsafe behavior. Interestingly, too, Shell and the Energy Institute have been sharing the tools from this "Heart and Minds" program with the rest of the industry to help promote safe behavior.

Take-off

Corporate sustainability reporting has been one approach to sharing. Returning from a trip around Asia, I found an unsolicited copy of PepsiCo's 02010 report. It looked no different from scores of others that we are sent and was on the verge of being consigned to the recycling bin.

But then the subtitle caught my eye: *Path to Zero*.

In his foreword, PepsiCo UK and Ireland President Richard Evans talked about nothing – or, more accurately, he focused on zero. Aiming for long-term transformation, he noted that the challenges PepsiCo had set itself for the next decade include "making our operations fossil fuel free, our largest factories achieving zero water intake, sending nothing to landfill across our entire supply chain, and making our product packaging from renewable resources". Further details of the activities of the company's Frito-Lay subsidiary can be found in Chapter 7.

Zero seems to be catching on, and in a growing number of sectors. Then, as I was developing this section, a *Sustainable Life Media* blog popped up from Andrew Winston,[16] author of *Green to Gold* and *Green Recovery*.[17] He seemed to be describing zero's version of the Gold Rush.

Box 6.3

The Zero Rush

"If we're to believe the flurry of press releases", Andrew Winston, contributing to the Sustainable Life Media blog, began, "organizations of all stripes are trying to drastically reduce the waste they send to landfills. In the years since Subaru announced a 'zero waste' facility in 02004, the pace of announcements has risen, and they've come from a broader range of organizations."

Winston had dutifully been keeping a tally of the media releases churned out by leading companies – and concluded that "Across all sectors, waste reduction is big. Recent stories include press releases from GM, P&G, Kraft, Sunny Delight, and Caterpillar. Outside of the private sector", he continued, "zero waste goals are now commonplace with universities (Cal State and ASU, for example), communities, and even countries (Scotland has a detailed plan for getting there). And influential stakeholders such as the investor-backed Ceres have recently made zero waste goals part of the 'roadmap' to sustainability."

Nor is it just a question of media releases and, in some cases, of greenwash – or what we might call "zerowash". Winston reported that "All of this activity seems to be working at the macro level. Total municipal solid waste (MSW) in the US is down recently for the first time, and trash giant Waste Management, seeing the writing on the landfill wall, is transitioning as quickly as possible from just hauling waste to helping companies manage recycling streams."

Intrigued, Winston called some of the companies involved to get a sense of how serious all this was – and what was driving the trend. In terms of drivers, the answer was clear. "The short answer", he reported, "is cost savings. Paying someone to haul away waste is, well, wasteful." Caterpillar reported that shifting from 6 to 30 waste streams, "thus increasing recycling rates to about 100 percent at two UK facilities is saving $200,000. Sunny Delight saved $2.5 million in three facilities."

Another closely related driver has been efficiency. "Kraft has found its overall operations improved in facilities that achieved zero waste goals." But perhaps most attractive of all, "companies are finding they can make money by managing waste streams better – a lot of money. Since 02007, GM has actually earned $2.5 billion in revenue from recycling."

In essence, Winston argued, "companies can use zero waste programs to drive continuous improvement". Finally, he added, "companies can build brand value by demonstrating responsible stewardship of resources (the number of press releases would suggest that branding execs agree). For example, GM played a minor, but interesting, role in the Gulf Oil spill cleanup. The company recycled used oil booms and used the material in its new Chevy Volt (how fitting is it to squeeze oil out of a material so it can be reused in an electric car?). The manager of GM's waste efforts, John Bradburn, told me that GM collected enough material to provide one part for the first year of production of Volts."

All to the good, but then came the sting. As he worked his way through the press releases and talked to companies, Winston warned: "it becomes clear very quickly that 'zero waste' never actually means zero waste. Organizations are sending no waste to the landfill, a critical distinction. Internally, companies tend to use this far more accurate, but less catchy, phrase. All waste that would normally leave a facility has to head in a few basic directions (besides paying to dump it in a landfill)." The options include: reuse it in-house; sort it into streams that can be recycled (and sold) outside the company; or incinerate it in waste-to-energy (WTE) plants. "And pretty much everyone", Winston notes, "is still burning some leftover waste."

Each company is pretty much making up its own mind on what it wants to call zero waste. For example, PepsiCo environmental executive Tim Carey told Winston that the company "strives to recycle or repurpose every bit of waste", but that there's still a "tiny bit" left over for incineration. "For GM, at its 76 landfill-free facilities, the tiny bit works out to 3 percent of waste."

A few organizations have taken a shot at defining the appropriate use of "zero", but we are still some way from agreement on the relevant metrics. Leading companies, meanwhile, say they are following guidelines from organizations such as the US Environmental Protection

Agency (EPA) and the Zero Waste International Alliance,[18] whose definition of zero waste is as follows: "Businesses and communities that achieve over 90 percent diversion of waste from landfills and incinerators are considered to be successful in achieving Zero Waste, or darn close."

But the real debate, Winston decided, "is not between three and ten percent incineration, but whether WTE [waste to energy] should 'count' as a sustainable option at all?" The answer tends to depend on a number of factors. "Creating energy from waste could be a sustainability win overall, especially if the end product is inert ash instead of hazardous waste. But the pursuit of 'zero waste' as a goal, without focusing on the cost, revenue, operational, and brand benefits, can lead to some strange outcomes. Some companies have announced 'zero waste' facilities with incineration as high as 40 percent."

Perhaps most interestingly of all, Winston spoke to Erin Meezan, vice president of sustainability for Interface. Depending on which way you cut the data, and how you decide to present the results, it turns out that you can end up with very different results – and wildly various public announcements.

You could say, for example, that Interface is just "1 percent shy of zero waste", based on the calculation that the company "buys 400 million pounds of raw material, and only sends 3.4 million pounds to the landfill". But, as Meezan told Winston, "the math is right, but it's an apples and oranges comparison".

Alternatively, you could say that waste to landfill is down 77 percent – on the basis that Interface sent 15 million pounds to a landfill in 01996, and 3.4 million pounds in 02009. Or, again, you could say that total waste disposal is down 19 percent. The company sent a combined 16 million pounds to landfill and to WTE in 01996, compared with 13 million pounds to both in 02009.

Complicated – and clearly a field that is wide open to abuse. But Andrew Winston wasn't put off. "All of that said, I'm still a fan of zero waste goals", he concluded. "The reality is that even without perfect, technically accurate words, [zero targets] do drive performance and give plant managers, division leaders, and other execs something tangible to grab onto. A zero goal operationalizes sustainability and provides a disciplined way of thinking about the business."

Zero reaches Infiniti

Perhaps it's too strong to call this a Gold Rush, but once you start looking for this stuff, it's everywhere, it sometimes seems. When I asked colleagues to serve as my Zero Scouts, they were amazed by how much they found. Me, too. To take a personal example, as I waited in Geneva airport after a meeting with Virgin Unite, I picked up a copy of *Adeyaka: Infiniti Magazine* – and stumbled across an eight-page profile of Andy Palmer, the Nissan senior vice president responsible, among other things, for zero emission mobility.[19]

Nissan are driving electric vehicles (EVs) hard. Palmer was quick to point out, however, that the focus on EVs doesn't mean "the end of other alternative technologies" at Nissan. Rather, the company – and the Infiniti brand, in particular – aims to benefit from "clean diesels, optimised gasoline engines and hybrids. But perhaps the most exciting will be the application of Zero Emission Electric Vehicles for Infiniti".

Electric vehicles are far from new. As Palmer noted, "you could buy them 50 years ago and even 10 years ago. What has changed now is environmental awareness, Li-Ion battery technology, low weight materials, Internet in the car, to name just a few. Also composite materials are important to reduce mass, thus improving performance and economy."

But the key thing to remember in all of this is that even if EVs are zero emission when in motion, they are still very far from achieving an overall zero footprint. Still, as Palmer insists, "the argument that electric cars are not zero-emission vehicles, because they just transfer the CO_2 output to power stations, is complete bullocks." (I think he may have been intentionally misquoted there.)

"In France", he explained, "the Nissan Leaf will have seven percent of the carbon footprint of a conventional car, because they use nuclear power." Equivalent figures in different countries would be 37 percent in the UK, 46 percent in the US, 68 percent in China and 76 percent in India – because of the particular fuel mixes used in generating electricity. Clearly, the overall performance of EVs is going to depend critically on the design and operation of the electricity grids on which they depend for their power.

But there is no doubt, given the will, that companies can radically reduce their footprints. Perhaps quality can even help to speed the process – could the history of quality point to how a new way of operating can be embedded in how companies work, as sustainability needs to be? Daniel Aronson of Deloitte concluded: "The quality revolution was about innovation in the core set of tools and methods that companies used to manage much of what they do. Quality became a central element of strategy, rather than a tactical tool, smashing previous cost versus fitness-for-use barriers and raising the 'table stakes' for all companies. Sustainability needs to do the same, and maybe it can learn from how quality accomplished that."

Not that the pioneers can expect warm thanks in the early days. One of my Zero Scouts sent me a link to a Herman Miller video called *Zero Is Hero*.[20] The voice-over script from the piece is reproduced in Box 6.4. It's hard not to smile at the last line.

Box 6.4

Zero Is Hero

Laughter.

That's what we heard from people, including government officials and investors, when we told them we'd like to get to a zero operational footprint by 02020.

Not a snicker. Not a chuckle.

Laughter.

But you know what? We're doing it.

As of [0]2009, our VOC air emissions were down 93 percent. Process water use: down 77 percent. Hazardous waste: 95 percent. And solid waste is down 88 percent.

We realize we're still a ways from getting to zero.

After all, it's not the first 20 percent of something that's the toughest to cut, it's the last.

But we're the types who think the only way to achieve audacious results is to set audacious goals.

And, while some would say setting a goal like this is asking for failure, we look forward to a time when a big, fat zero will be considered our greatest success.

Herman Miller, Zero Is Hero ad, 02011

Box 6.5

How Zeronauts succeed in stage 3

It often seems that Zeronauts are most likely to get stuck at stage 3. The challenges of founding, funding, growing, and operating new business ventures are such that they can be all consuming – as can the political challenges involved in pushing new innovations through incumbent businesses. Still, ask leading Zeronauts what their golden rules are for building stage 3 enterprises and they are likely to mention the following:

1 If you're a start-up, build in zero from the outset – and if you're an incumbent, begin experiments with relevant business units as a precursor to spreading solutions across the wider organization.
2 Sort out your zero definitions – this can be a bit of a minefield.
3 Tackle efficiencies early on, but move on to opportunities as soon as you can.
4 Decide what balance you are going to strike between protecting intellectual property and developing an open-source approach, with both options increasingly important.
5 Know that you have to be in this for the long haul – as always with innovation, you will need stamina and the capacity to cope with the unexpected.
6 Make sure that your enterprise is located in – or linked to – the most powerful business ecosystems relevant to your intended future opportunity space.
7 If there is no business ecosystem, and you can't move, start to build one – quick.

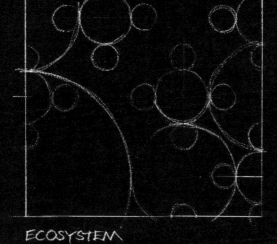

ECOSYSTEM

Figure 6.4 Pathways to Zero: Stage 4

STAGE 4: ECOSYSTEMS

Zeronautics is not just about developing successful experiments and enterprises, but also about the evolution of the necessary clusters of activities – or "ecosystems" – that help to support multiple actors in the drive for transformative change. This is where we begin to move well beyond TQM as currently defined, with stage 4 in our Pathways to Zero model perhaps the most critical step in achieving the scale needed to tip the whole economy to a new state (see Figure 6.4).

The idea that clusters are crucial in developing new industries goes way back, at least to the 01890s, when the economist Alfred Marshall talked about the economics of agglomeration.[21] But the field took a huge leap forward a century later when Professor Michael Porter focused on what he dubbed "business clusters" in his book *The Competitive Advantage of Nations.*[22]

There are thought to be at least four main types: geographical clusters, sectoral clusters (for example, in marine design or photonics), horizontal clusters (where businesses connect, for instance, through resource-sharing networks) and vertical clusters (perhaps organized through a supply chain).

A linked concept that took off several years later is that of the "business ecosystem", the basic definition dating back to the early 01990s, and to a book, *The Death of Competition: Leadership and Strategy in the Age of Business Ecosystems* by James F. Moore.[23] The concept first appeared in the *Harvard Business Review* in 01993. Moore argued that a business ecosystem is:

... an economic community supported by a foundation of interacting organizations and individuals – the organisms of the business world. This economic community produces goods and services of value to customers, who are themselves members of the ecosystem. The member organizations also include suppliers, lead producers, competitors, and other stakeholders. Over time, they co-evolve their capabilities and roles, and tend to align themselves with the directions set by one or more central companies. Those companies holding leadership roles may change over time, but the function of ecosystem leader is valued by the community because it enables members to move toward shared visions to align their investments and to find mutually supportive roles.

The biggest thing, ever

Growing attention has been paid in recent years to reasons why particular clusters and ecosystems have emerged and flourished, or not – and to the ways in which other regions can develop their own versions. One area in which there has been intense recent interest is clean technology.

Having visited a number of cleantech companies in the Silicon Valley area in 02010, among them Better Place and Serious Materials, I have since kept an even closer eye on developments there as an indication of where the rest of the world may be headed, eventually.

Box 6.6

Green launchpad

One journalist who has his finger firmly on the Silicon Valley pulse is Scott Duke Harris. "Silicon Valley earned its name and first great fortune as the cradle of the computer age", he reminded us.[24] "Then it built a launching pad for the Internet age. Now the valley has assumed a leading role in the global competition to develop renewable energy and other clean, green technologies."

He concludes that, despite its ups and downs, cleantech is poised to be the valley's third great wave of innovation - "not just the next big thing, but perhaps the biggest thing ever. Confronting the peril of greenhouse gases and climate change happens to be a multi-trillion-dollar business opportunity."

How big? "Consider that the sum of America's yearly utility bills, one component of the nation's overall energy costs, exceeds $1 trillion", he continued, "or nearly triple the annual global revenues of the semiconductor industry. The solar and wind energy markets, which totaled about $80 billion in 02008, are projected to nearly triple in size in 10 years, employing 2.6 million people worldwide, according to Clean Edge, a cleantech research group."

The nature of the cleantech market may be dramatically different from most New Economy sectors, involving immensely greater investments in infrastructure, for example; but around the valley, former e-commerce and software pioneers are busy trying to electrify the automobile industry, as in the case of Shai Agassi's Better Place, while others, like Serious Materials, are developing energy-efficient glass, drywall, and cement.

"Still others are introducing cutting-edge information technology to the 20th-century electricity grid, working on biofuels and fuel cells, and pioneering new methods to recycle waste, protect air and water quality and enhance agriculture and aquaculture", he reported.

So, he asked, "will Tesla Motors become the Apple of automakers? Will Serious Materials become the Intel of green building materials? Will Silver Springs Networks be the Cisco of the smart grid electricity management technologies - or will that be Cisco itself?"

While venture funding overall dipped in 02009, many governments around the world stepped in to fund cleantech projects. "Governments spent the year earmarking hundreds of billions of dollars for clean technology in pursuit of economic growth", noted Nicholas Parker, then the Cleantech Group's executive chairman.

The Obama administration boosted the cleantech sector with more than $70 billion in economic recovery funds. Tesla Motors, (the ill-fated) Solyndra, MiaSolé, and Nanosolar were among the Silicon Valley cleantech start-ups awarded loan guarantees or tax credits by the Department of Energy.

Not everyone thinks that success is guaranteed, however. "Most of what Silicon Valley is doing is nibbling right now", mused David Victor, former director of Stanford University's Program on Energy and Sustainable Development. "That said, small organisms must start somewhere – and they start with nibbling. Most of the nibblers will die. A few will flourish. Some might come to dominate the energy system and become trillion-dollar players."

Meanwhile, Silicon Valley is far from alone in its cleantech quest. Texas, for example, is emerging as a powerful hub for wind energy, while Germany is a leader in solar and Japan in energy efficiency. China, which ranks alongside the US as the leading producer of greenhouse gases, has also embarked on a massive cleantech initiative to confront its increasingly obvious environmental challenges.

But while others may try to steal its spurs, Silicon Valley is unquestionably well placed for what comes next. Its key advantage is its culture of innovation, noted venture capitalist Vinod Khosla. "This is one of the largest new opportunities that Silicon Valley has seen, but competition from other areas will be extensive", he told Harris. "We [in Silicon Valley] don't have a natural advantage in talent – like chemical engineers, fermentation experts, engine designers, and physicists. But we do have a support culture for entrepreneurship and a culture of risk-taking and risk funding. That gives us a head start."

The competitive landscape

Someone else who has kept a close eye on cleantech worldwide is Shawn Lesser, founder and president of Atlanta-based Sustainable World Capital.[25] "Creating such a cluster is no simple task", he insists. "First, the right circumstances must be present: a thriving technology base, abundant entrepreneurial and management talent, access to capital, and a proactive environmental public policy. It's not easy to create, but once in place, a cleantech cluster can, in theory, create thousands of new jobs and attract billions of investment dollars to a region."

The difficulties haven't deterred a growing number of regions from pursuing their own clusters and ecosystems. So which of them have managed to attract and leverage these key ingredients most effectively? Here is an edited version of Lesser's Top 10 List, moving from Europe through Canada to the US:

1 **Eco World Styria, Austria:** Eco World Styria styles itself as Europe's Green Tech Valley. This small region is home to more than 150 cleantech companies, of which perhaps a dozen are world technology leaders in their field, one of the highest concentrations of leading clean technology companies in Europe. These companies have achieved an average (real) growth rate of 22 percent per year – well above the worldwide cleantech market growth of 18 percent per year. The region created roughly 2000 additional green jobs in 02008 alone. Among the key reasons for the area's phenomenal performance: numerous specialized research centers and a strong tradition of engineering.

2 **Copenhagen Cleantech Cluster, Denmark:** Copenhagen has a goal of becoming the world's first CO_2-neutral capital. Denmark is already one of the world's largest exporters of cleantech. The Copenhagen cluster is made up of 40 players, and aims to reach 200 by 02013. The cluster operates under a $30 million budget financed by the European Union (EU), Region Zealand (Region Sjælland), and the Danish Capital Region. It also has a unique set of partners, including Copenhagen Capacity, Scion DTU, Confederation of Danish Industries (DI), Risø DTU, the University of Copenhagen, and a number of municipalities and large companies, including Dong Energy, Vestas, Haldor Topsøe, Novozymes, Siemens, and Better Place Denmark.

3 **Finnish Cleantech Cluster**, based at the Lahti Science and Business Park: this provides access to over 250 cleantech companies, 60 percent of Finland's cleantech business, and 80 percent of cleantech research in Finland. The original goal was to create some 40 new high-growth companies annually, which has already been reached. The aim is also to increase cleantech venture capital investments to 15 percent of total investments. The cluster has created hundreds of new green jobs. Operations have involved projects in Russia, China, and India, the latter through a strategic collaboration with YES Bank India.

4 **Stockholm's Miljöteknikcenter, Sweden**, which also embraces Uppsala to the north and the renowned Ångströmslab, has created cleantech jobs for some 25,000 employees. The region is also home to an internationally known sustainable city area in Hammarby Sjöstad (south of downtown Stockholm), with another emerging in nearby Norra Djurgårdsstaden. Stockholm was chosen as Environmental Capital of the year 02010 by the European Commission, and is home to cleantech investors Sustainable Technologies Fund, Northzone, Pegroco Invest, and Stora Enso Ventures.

5 **MaRS, based in Toronto, Canada**, is a large-scale, mission-driven innovation center aiming to build Canada's next generation of cleantech companies. Led by Tom Rand, a veteran entrepreneur, policy advocate, and venture capitalist, the cleantech practice at MaRS quickly established itself as the largest cleantech deal-flow engine in the country. The MaRS Advisory Services team has worked with over 250 cleantech companies from across the province.

6 **Ontario Clean Water Initiative, based in Toronto**, is dedicated to developing Ontario as a global center of expertise for safe, clean, affordable, and sustainable water and sanitation solutions. Ontario has considerable water-related assets, from one of the largest bodies of fresh water in the world to a strong regulatory regime, an internationally recognized research community, and a track record in world-class water tech. Over 300 local companies are developing wastewater and water treatment, plus an array of filtration-related products and services. Critically, the province is home to 230 relevant university and college programs that produced over 8200 university graduates related to water sciences in 02007 alone.

7 **The CleanTech Center, based in Syracuse, New York**, is at the heart of a green cluster in Central Upstate New York. With 38 colleges and universities, 138,000 college students, $2 billion in annual funded R&D, and a green landscape that supports clean energy production, New York's "green core" is launching and growing cleantech enterprises. The CleanTech Center is a cutting-edge clean energy incubator that links entrepreneurs, investors, and academic researchers, and is also a clearinghouse of information on the cleantech sector in New York State.

8 **New England Cleaner Energy Council, based in Cambridge Massachusetts:** formed in 02007, the council represents some 150 members, including clean energy companies, venture investors, financial institutions, local universities and colleges, industry associations, area utilities, labor, and large commercial end-users. Its ranks include more than 50 clean energy CEOs, representatives from most of the region's top 10 law firms, and partners from over a dozen of the region's top venture capital firms.

9 **CleanTECH, San Diego, California**, boasts an estimated 650 cleantech companies in the region. It has developed a comprehensive one-stop shop and vibrant ecosystem for cleantech companies to accelerate their growth. Having less than one third the population of Los Angeles, San Diego has installed 60 percent more solar roofs than its neighbor to the north. By mid-02009, San Diego was recognized as the leading solar city in the number 1 solar state, with over 2200 rooftop installations and the most solar capacity in the state.

10 **Environment Business Center (EBC), based in San José, California**, was established in 01994 as a non-profit technology commercialization center to assist early-stage for-profit companies in developing products or services intended to have a positive environmental impact. Since 02003, the EBC has specialized in assisting clean energy and emerging energy efficiency companies, and has also worked with the California Energy Commission and the National Renewable Energy Lab to provide commercialization services to selected applied research grant recipients. By 02010, the EBC was managing the largest private technology commercialization program for clean energy start-ups in the US.

When it comes to the relative strengths of particular clusters, it is worth looking beyond such things as people, technology, and business models to such factors as ownership. In Austin, Texas, for example, some 15,000 residents are employed in the burgeoning green economy. And the municipal utility, Austin Energy, has committed itself to getting 35 percent of its electricity from renewable resources by 02020. As *Time* magazine noted: "Perhaps the single biggest factor behind the greening of Austin is an institution that in most cities stands in the way of clean tech: the utility. Because the city of Austin owns its utility – and because politically progressive Austin residents have shown support for renewable power – Austin Energy has more latitude for experimentation than most of its counterparts around the US."[26]

Another sector where zero targets are being energetically pursued is health care. One of our 50 Zeronauts is Gary Cohen of Health Care Without Harm. He was a travel writer whose life was transformed by an assignment to draft a community guidebook about toxic chemicals. After meeting mothers working to protect their families from toxic dumps and other chemical threats, he devoted his life to environmental health. He was co-director of the US National Toxics Campaign and cofounder of the Military Toxics Project, then helped launch a free clinic serving survivors of the Bhopal disaster in India. Health Care Without Harm, which he founded in 01996, has become a worldwide phenomenon, developing partnerships with major hospital systems and their institutional buyers – using combined purchasing power to drive change. Their Healthier Hospitals Initiative is driven by over 500 hospital groups across the USA, or 10 percent of the sector in the country, and aims to reach 1,500 over the next three years.

Over time, expect to see such clusters and ecosystems burgeoning all around the world, with a growing number of links between them. Some will evolve into the sort of zero zones envisaged in Chapter 4. Already, for example, we see the green city complex of Masdar in Abu Dhabi and emerging clusters in China, plus a Global Cleantech Cluster Association.[27] Another, profiled in Box 6.7, has been the complex business ecosystem that evolved around the London 02012 Olympic and Paralympic Games.

Box 6.7

Which bit of zero didn't you understand?

Way back in 02004, I interviewed David Stubbs, later head of sustainability at the London Organising Committee of the Olympic and Paralympic Games (LOCOG), on the 50th floor of a Canary Wharf skyscraper about the sustainability elements of the proposal they were putting together for the 02012 Olympic Games. Then, in the summer of 02011, David and his colleague Felicity Hartnett, sustainability partnerships manager, guided me around the site, pointing out key challenges and explaining how they had been tackled.[28]

My first question to David was how progress to date measured up to the original vision? "When we won the bid", he replied, "the IOC's [International Olympic Committee's] environment advisor said to me that if we achieved even half of what we had promised it would be way ahead of any previous Games. Well, we are amply past that halfway mark. The point was brought home recently when someone who had been away from the project for a few years visited the Olympic Park and said: 'It looks like the pictures you showed us back in the beginning!'"

Any big surprises along the way? "Not a surprise, but a pleasant outcome", David offered. "And that's how we have been able to turn round the perception that sustainability costs more. We have found that by making our requirements very clear upfront, the market has responded. So we are getting some of our best deals from suppliers who are taking sustainability seriously, and our stance has helped draw in significantly stronger interest from commercial sponsors. This means an effective sustainability approach creates efficiencies, saves costs and helps generate additional revenue."

Anything he wishes he had known at the outset? "If we had known at the time of the bid what we eventually found out in the carbon footprint study", he admitted, "we would have presented our carbon and energy commitments differently. There has been a lot of knee-jerk criticism about the shortfall in on-site renewable energy generation, compared with our original targets. It would have been far better to have set an overall approach to avoiding carbon emissions, rather than specifying particular technologies to be followed. What we have actually achieved through design optimization, material choices and procurement strategies has resulted in a massive saving of embodied carbon emissions compared with our 'business-as-usual reference footprint'. The end result is a much lower carbon Games than if we had stuck to the letter of the original targets."

Knowing how polluted the site was, I was interested in how the ground had been cleaned up. The statistics are amazing: nearly two million tons of contaminated soil were cleaned for reuse on the Olympic Park in the UK's largest-ever soil-washing operation. Six "soil hospitals" successfully cleaned most of the one million cubic meters of soil contaminated with oil, petrol, tar, cyanide, arsenic, and lead.

And what lessons can other sustainability champions learn? "To be effective, sustainability has to permeate across all departments", David recommended. "It cannot reside uniquely in a specialist team producing separate policies and glossy reports. There are two particular avenues where you should concentrate your efforts in large projects: procurement, where you need to stamp your authority on what the organization buys, and how it buys; and, second, workforce training – if you can get sustainability strongly profiled in induction and training modules, you reach the whole organization."

As we walked around the site, with major signs calling for "Zero Harm", Felicity noted that various suppliers had resisted the LOCOG specifications. Told that zero waste was the target, for example, one came back to say that they had got down to just four skips of waste – only to be asked, in effect, "What is it about the zero waste target you don't understand?"

The sheer scale of the Games has meant dramatically greater supply chain leverage. "The numbers we deal with are huge", Felicity noted: "14 million meals to be served, four billion people watching it on TV, 10 million tickets sold. And they are matched by the challenging targets – for example, 100 per cent access via public transport, cycling, and walking; zero waste to landfill; and sustainably sourced meals."

So anything that she wishes she had known at the outset? "If I had a crystal ball that told me which of the many opportunities to inspire change was going to have the biggest impact, I could have just focused on that", she said. "But we didn't have a crystal ball. We did, though, learn a lot from the organizing committee for the previous Vancouver Olympics and from the 2008 Beijing Olympics, and are determined to share whatever we learn with the Rio Committee for 2016. Meanwhile, I will keep on chasing a range of opportunities to drive change in the hope that at least one of them will prove to be the 'big one'."

At their best, such constellations of actors accelerate the right sorts of economic growth, create new jobs, help initiate and scale new innovations, cross-fertilize education in universities and business schools, make life easier for investors, help to build a collective voice in politics, and – ultimately – illustrate the wisdom in the saying: "Alone you can go faster, but together we can go further."

Box 6.8

How Zeronauts succeed in stage 4

As innovators and entrepreneurs get older and more experienced, they often end up representing the field which they have helped to pioneer – in effect, playing the elder statesperson role. The key question here is how they can jump the clock and start the process much earlier on because this side of evolving a new set of solutions is now critical.

Whatever their age, if you ask leading Zeronauts what their golden rules are for success in evolving and operating in stage 4 ecosystems, they are likely to mention the following:

1 Creating a cluster or business ecosystem is a long, hard, and complex task. Take the long view.
2 Successful ecosystems cut across – or embrace – the private, public, and citizen sectors, a characteristic that is going to be even more important in relation to 1-Earth clusters and constellations.

3 You need to sort out early whether you are going for a geographical, sectoral, horizontal, or vertical cluster - or for something else.

4 Collaboration and competition are both going to be important - the key is to work out which mode to use when, and how to build and sustain the levels of trust that are needed to promote meaningful long-term exchanges and partnerships.

5 Links with university, other public-sector, and private-sector R&D are a key part of the formula for success; but the relationship should be multi-way, with investment to develop future generations of researchers and research.

6 Consider the ownership dimension of key assets, something that has been a key factor in the evolution of Austin's cleantech cluster (see p.171).

7 The listing above of existing clusters underscores how much experience there is out there already - and how much there is to learn from other cluster builders.

8 As we will see in the next section, a critical success factor is the ability to learn by doing.

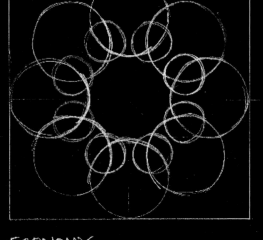

ECONOMY

Figure 6.5 Pathways to Zero: Stage 5

STAGE 5: ECONOMY

Zeronautics is about aligning our technologies and business models with the emerging 1-Earth Paradigm. Once 1-Earth innovation has created new generations of potential solutions, and new enterprises or business units have been formed to drive things forward, the TQM movement can again slot back into place and do what it does best: ensure that the relevant processes are both efficient and effective. Meanwhile, strange as it may seem to those whose job it is to make life easier for their colleagues in business, the time has come to make things tougher for them – much tougher.

The critical question at the interface between stages 4 and 5 is how do you help push industries, supply chains, and entire economies through the Sustainability Barrier? Politicians and policy-makers have too often got used to nurse-maiding industry, nervous that the wrong move will send the golden egg-laying goose elsewhere. The UK's climate change policies, for example, have apparently discouraged international data center firms from investing in the country.[29] But whether they like it or not, we now need governments to make life significantly – and increasingly – uncomfortable for business and industry. A recent example has been the EU's efforts to charge international airlines for their carbon emissions.

Just in case this seems willfully naive or disruptive, a recent study published by Germany's Federal Ministry for the Environment, Nature Conservation, and

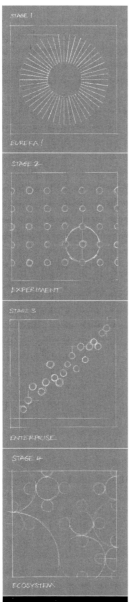

STAGE 1

EUREKA!

STAGE 2

EXPERIMENT

STAGE 3

ENTERPRISE

STAGE 4

ECOSYSTEM

STAGE 5

ECONOMY

Nuclear Safety makes the same point much more powerfully and insistently, using the latest mathematical models. Entitled *A New Growth Path for Europe*, it was undertaken by a group of five organizations, including two universities (Oxford in the UK and the Sorbonne in France), the Potsdam Institute for Climate Impact Research in Germany, and the European Climate Forum.

Learning by doing

The Eurozone's desperate travails at the beginning of the century's second decade left many wondering whether it would survive. Whatever the outcome, anyone who believes that tackling climate change with increasingly tough emission targets inevitably represents a net drag on the economy would have found *New Growth Path* conclusions something of a shock. At a time when the European Union had adopted what it considered to be stretch targets requiring 20 percent greenhouse emission reductions, and when many business leaders were complaining that this was damaging the prospects for future growth, prosperity, and job creation, the new study said nonsense, insisting that "it is time for boldness".

The problem with the 20 percent target is not that it is too aggressive, as we are told, but that it is too weak – though this was clearly not self-evident to the members of the European Parliament who voted down the first proposal to take the EU from 20 to 30 percent.[30] The global financial crisis has shown that existing economic models have serious flaws – and the same is true of existing mathematical models that track the interactions between climate policy and the economy.

Traditional models have a single stable equilibrium, one point where there is a win–win outcome. By contrast, emerging models suggest that multiple growth paths are possible, some of which encourage unexpectedly positive feedback between the emissions, economic, and employment agendas. What we are starting to move toward here is what we might call total system management.

Instead of sticking with 20 percent, the scientists concluded, Europe needs to set truly stretch targets, with "a decisive move to a 30 percent target". If this is done well, the models suggest, by 02020 the rate of European growth could be boosted by up to 0.6 percent a year, European investments could rise from 18 to 22 percent of GDP, GDP itself could grow by up to six percent both in the old (EU15) and new (EU12) member states, and up to six million additional jobs could be created Europe-wide.

There were other counter-intuitive conclusions. For example, the new growth path would benefit *all* major economic sectors – agriculture, energy, industry, construction, and services, with the greatest benefits experienced in construction. Perhaps most surprising of all, the economic opportunities linked to tighter emissions targets would be available whether or not we see a global climate agreement in the wake of 02012's Rio+20 UN summit meeting.

The obvious question: why do the latest models show such different outcomes with tighter emission controls? Answer: they assume that tougher controls trigger greater additional investments, stimulating what they call "learning by doing" across the entire economy, particularly in sectors focusing on such areas as advanced construction materials and renewable energy.

Learning by doing, in turn, increases competitiveness and spurs further economic growth, boosting the expectations of investors – and fueling greater investment.

Consider the alternatives. After the Great Depression of the 01930s, Europe saw a surge of investment as nation-states began the hugely expensive – and horrifically destructive – process of rearmament. While increasing global competition for natural resources might easily trigger another arms race and a vicious downward spiral, sustainable development could trigger a virtuous upward cycle of investment, innovation, and prosperity.

As for solutions, the conclusion is that we need to shift to more energy-efficient construction and to natural gas and renewable energy, rather than coal. Technologies such as photovoltaics, carbon capture and storage, and nuclear power (though this was before the Fukushima disaster in Japan) will make very little additional contribution by 02020, but should also be invested in for the longer term.

Among the macro-economic measures that will help is the use of emission trading revenues to fund carbon reduction efforts in Eastern Europe, the inclusion of low-carbon growth standards in public procurement, and the encouragement of entrepreneurial efforts through tax breaks.

Among micro-economic measures needed are revised building codes requiring greater energy efficiency, standardized smart power grid infrastructures, smart household appliance codes, and the creation of more and better learning networks linking innovative companies.

Changing the system requires bold political vision, sustained government commitment to low-carbon innovation, and clear policy targets and incentives for innovators, entrepreneurs, and investors. But what is very encouraging about the new economic analysis is that it is based on long-established and well-proven lessons from other parts of the economy, including – strikingly – aviation.

Just as our species went from balloons and powered box kites to machines that could break the Sound Barrier and, ultimately, that could reach to the Moon and beyond, so green growth sectors can potentially push our economies onto radically new trajectories.

Chapter 7 now takes a closer look at how zero-based thinking is being used – or might be used – in such disparate fields as population control, the management of pandemics, the fight against poverty, pollution prevention, and the attempts to rein in proliferation of nuclear arms and other weapons of mass destruction. There are many other areas where zero-based thinking can be applied – as indicated in Boxes 8.2 to 8.4 in Chapter 8, but these five give a useful early sense of the potential power of zero.

Box 6.9

How Zeronauts succeed in stage 5

Whether you think of public sanitation, the spread of democracy, the ending of slavery, the provision of public education, or the global adoption of innovations such as the Plimsoll Line, satellite remote sensing, or the internet, we are immersed in evidence that social and economic systems can – and ultimately do – change.

None of these system changes would have happened without extraordinary innovators and entrepreneurs, the "unreasonable people" that Irish playwright George Bernard Shaw saw as the key to transformative change. Given the sort of people they are, the chances are that most Zeronauts will not kick off their shoes and put their feet up when they think they are on the verge of reaching some stage 5 utopia. Instead, they are much more likely to plunge back into the fray in earlier stages – acknowledging that the battle for sustainability is never won.

The best of these people are serial innovators and serial entrepreneurs, and some morph later in life into serial investors. Ask them what their golden rules are for getting to stage 5, where the innovation becomes endemic in the economy, and they are likely to mention the following:

1 As the late, great Steve Jobs put it in a different context, "think different" and aspire to be "insanely great".
2 Forget either/or thinking – focus on both/and.
3 Acknowledge that we have to break out of current time scales that force business to focus on quarterly reporting and politicians to look no further than three to four years ahead.
4 Recognize that creativity loves constraint – and start to constrain those who most need to jump to new mindsets and business models.
5 When pioneers and leaders do the right thing in respect of these new agendas, the greatest rewards often flow to others. Get used to it – or work out how to capture your share of the value you co-create.
6 In the end, this is about politics – and, apart from anything else, it is about new forms of intergenerational politics.

Inevitably, the trends will go sometimes this way and sometimes that, but the underlying trajectory is clear for those with the eyes to see. In its *Vision 2050* study, the World Business Council for Sustainable Development (WBCSD) summarized the challenge as follows: "The transformation ahead represents vast opportunities in a broad range of business segments as the global challenges of growth, urbanization, scarcity and environmental change become the key strategic drivers for business in the coming decade. In natural resources, health and education alone, the broad order of magnitude of some of these could be around $0.5–1.5 trillion per annum in 2020, rising to between $3–10 trillion per annum in 2050 at today's prices, which is around 1.5–4.5 per cent of world GDP in 2050. Opportunities range from developing and maintaining low-carbon, zero-waste cities and infrastructure to improving and managing biocapacity, ecosystems, lifestyles and livelihoods."[31]

7
It's the System that's Stupid

Zeronauts are innovating in an astonishing range of areas, tackling hugely diverse economic, social, environmental, and governance challenges. To give a sense of progress to date, we zero in on five key challenges (the 5Ps): population growth, pandemics, poverty, pollution, and WMD proliferation.

If the first quarter century of the sustainability movement was about getting people to speak the language, and opening up the global C-suite to the need to adapt not just our technologies but also our business models, the next couple of decades will also be about transformative system change. With the 5Cs, we explored areas where the Zero Revolution is beginning to take hold; then with the 5Es we looked at the stages through which a zero-targeted innovation must go to become endemic in the wider economy. Now, with the 5Ps, we look at how all of this is beginning to play out in the real world.

Business, it is clear, cannot do all of this on its own – the financial markets, governments, city administrations, educators, and the general public must all put their shoulder to the wheel. Failing that, it is very likely that we will see some form of environmental collapse well before 02100.

But this is an area where you have to be very careful of the language you use. Several decades ago, I used the term *Armageddon* in an article for the *Guardian* – and a few days later received several extremely irate letters (no email then, or faxes) from Christians challenging my negative usage. Armageddon, they insisted, is to be celebrated as the gateway to a better world for true believers. So once burned, twice shy. I accept that some people may believe the same about the Apocalypse, seeing it as a precursor to the mysteries and wonders of the Last Judgment, but I do not.

Having been educated for several years as a notional Protestant in a Catholic convent school embedded in a Protestant community in Northern Ireland, for me both Armageddon and Apocalypse symbolize nothing but bad news. So I will use the term apocalypse in the second sense suggested in the Wikipedia definition in Box 7.1 as signaling an impending interlinked series of catastrophic events that threaten ultimate system failure.

I was planning to use the phrase "Five Horsemen of the Apocalypse" to cover the looming challenges of population, pandemics, poverty, pollution, and proliferation – but then on flights around Asia I read *Why the West Rules – for Now* and found that its author, Ian Morris, had got there first. For him, the Five Horsemen that stalk our future are famine, epidemics, uncontrolled migration, state failure, and climate change.

Box 7.1

Apocalypse

A•POC•A•LYPSE/ə'päkə lips/Noun

1 The complete final destruction of the world, esp. as described in the biblical Book of Revelation.
2 An event involving destruction or damage on an awesome or catastrophic scale.[1]

There have been many red and amber lights along the way. Paul Gilding, a long-time friend and colleague, recently warned in his book *The Great Disruption* that "It's time to stop just worrying about climate change." Instead, we need to brace for systemic impacts because global crisis is no longer avoidable. "This Great Disruption started in 2008", he argues, "with spiking food and oil prices and dramatic ecological changes, such as the melting ice caps. It is not simply about fossil fuels and carbon footprints. We have come to the end of Economic Growth, Version 1.0, a world economy based on consumption and waste, where we lived beyond the means of our planet's ecosystems and resources."[2]

"This is not science fiction", said Tom Friedman, reviewing Paul's book in *The New York Times*. "This is what happens when our system of growth and the system of nature hit the wall at once. When in Yemen last year, I saw a tanker truck delivering water in the capital, Sana. Why? Because Sana could be the first big city in the world to run out of water, within a decade. This is what happens when one generation in one country lives at 150 percent of sustainable capacity."[3]

So how can each of us better adapt our own compasses in service of a better future for all? The beginnings of an answer were suggested when I recently took the MindTime test, framed as "GPS for the Mind" (see Figure 7.1). Developed by MindTime

Technologies, this aims to help us locate ourselves in terms of the past, present, and future – and of our respective feelings toward certainty, continuity, and possibility.

My own mapping skewed sharply toward the future. With that orientation, it should come as no surprise that each of the following challenges is framed as an opportunity to push toward zero. My intention is to explore how the concept of zero has inspired efforts to tackle – and sometimes eliminate – the relevant scourges. Whichever of the five threats they have chosen to address, the relevant Zeronauts are acutely aware that our challenges often link together in quite unexpected ways, making their resolution more complex.

Efforts to solve one (say, bringing millions of people out of poverty) can trigger a cascade of unintended consequences in other areas (for example, aggravating pollution problems), as China is now acutely aware. And the combination of dense urban populations, intensive animal farms and same-day links between destinations worldwide has created an almost-perfect global incubator for human pandemics, as the story of SARS illustrated so dramatically.

Each of these great challenges poses immense trials for the corporations, citizens, communities, and cities and countries covered in Chapter 4. One leading scientist, Sir Martin Rees, recently pronounced that we have, at best, a 50/50 chance of surviving the twenty-first century.[4] But the defining characteristic of Zeronauts is that they are undeterred by problems that seem insoluble to others. They also point out that solving one of these challenges could well create positive cascades in relation to the others.

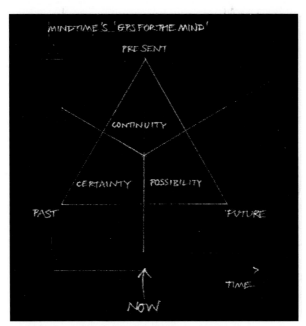

Figure 7.1 MindTime's "GPS for the Mind"

"Pop" was what his students affectionately called the Reverend Thomas Malthus, short for "Population". This was the man who became widely known (and, in some circles, notorious) for his theories about the human population – and its increase or decrease in response to various factors.[6] The six editions of his *An Essay on the Principle of Population* were published between 01798 and 01826, creating a major impact upon people such as Charles Darwin as he thought through the processes of natural selection. And now, two centuries later, Pop seems set for a revival.

Malthus challenged the widespread view in eighteenth-century Europe that the potential to improve society was almost limitless. Rather, he argued, whether we like it or not, two types of checks hold all populations within natural resource limits. First, there are positive checks, which raise the death rate. And, second, there are preventive ones, which lower the birth rate. The positive checks include hunger, disease, and war, while among the preventive checks are abortion, birth control, prostitution, postponement of marriage, and celibacy. His early doomsday scenarios proved over-pessimistic as sewers cleaned up cities, water was filtered and chlorinated, and disease-control technologies such as vaccines spread.[7]

Nonetheless, I find it startling to recall that there were less than three billion people when I was born in 01949, whereas by the time *The Zeronauts* launched there were over seven billion – and, for those who like at least the appearance of certainty, the demographers say that we are headed for 9 billion by the time I might be expected to blow out 100 candles on my birthday cake. Instinctively, this population trend has to be the greatest threat to continuity in terms of our global system, short of World War III – with some arguing that it could well precipitate that. And that's even before we get to the UN's recent forecast that we could even see a doubling to 15 billion by 2100.[8]

The view from inside – and outside – the Vatican

Given the position of the Vatican, it's worth looking under the papal hood on the population issue. Take Pope Benedict XVI, who argued that increased population has been an asset rather than a problem in development.[9] "Poverty is often considered a consequence of demographic change", he said. "For this reason, there are international campaigns afoot to reduce birth-rates, sometimes using methods that respect neither the dignity of the woman, nor the right of parents to choose responsibly how many children to have; graver still, these methods often fail to respect even the right to life", he continued. "The extermination of millions of unborn children, in the name of the fight against poverty, actually constitutes the destruction of the poorest of all human beings."

"For decades", he continued, "the pro-life movement internationally has pointed out that birth control and 'reproductive health' are often pushed in the name of economic prosperity, but that instead they actually repress societies by reducing their population, therefore compromising the ability to utilize resources and achieve self-sufficiency." The possibly slightly paranoid thesis here is that world powers "knowingly use population-control ideology in foreign policy to suppress potential competitors rather than help them."

Benedict went on to assert: "In 1981, around 40 percent of the world's population was below the threshold of absolute poverty, while today that percentage has been reduced by as much as a half, and whole peoples have escaped from poverty despite experiencing substantial demographic growth... This goes to show that resources to solve the problem of poverty do exist, even in the face of an increasing population." (It's interesting, however, that a fair number of the countries doing best in this area are non-Catholic or actively atheist.)

I'm not sure whether authors such as Lester Brown are on the Vatican reading list, but they need to be. I even heard one cardinal argue, a decade or two back, that the world could comfortably accommodate 40 billion people. Presumably as long as most were Catholics? While it is true that we have managed to shoehorn four billion extra people into the biosphere since I was born, the evidence of unsustainable strains on our natural systems should be clear even to popes.

So, what are the possibilities of reining in runaway population growth – and better managing the world's great demographic transitions? Environmentalists have often been accused of choosing to turn a blind eye to the population issue.

But the truth is that population and demography have long been central to both the environmental and sustainability agendas, thanks to the work of people such as Barry Commoner and Paul Ehrlich. One bestseller when I was first at university was *The Population Bomb*, by Paul and Anne Ehrlich.[10]

Population growth was also central to one of the key formulae of the era, developed in discussion between Commoner, Ehrlich, and others: $I = P \times A \times T$. Here, I symbolized total impact upon the system, P stood for human population numbers, whose impact was mediated – and often amplified – by the prevailing levels of affluence (A) and the technologies used to underpin them (T). As the decades went by, so various countries tried to bring the size of their populations under control, most notably India and China – whose experience we investigate later.

For much of their history, interestingly, cities have been an unintentional form of population control – killing varying (but often relatively high) proportions of the people who flowed in from rural areas and smaller settlements. Poor diets, pollution, disease, and wars all took their toll. Then, as conditions improved, there was a growing interest in family planning.

Meanwhile, as concerns about the nature and scale of future environmental change grew, so there has been increasing coverage of the threat of what Lester Brown in 01976 dubbed "environmental refugees". The meme spread widely – though it has now settled back to a lower level. That is likely to change, however, once clearer links are made between climate change and the mass migration of affected people.

Ten billion neighbors

So who, in the midst of all of this, first thought in terms of zeroing population growth, or ZPG? Among Zeronauts in this area, American sociologist and demographer Kingsley Davis is often credited, but George Stolnitz seems to have got there earlier – and himself tracked interest in stationary populations back to the 01690s.[11] A mathematical analysis of population dynamics was offered by Nobelist Sir James Mirrlees.[12]

Then, in the late 01960s, ZPG became a significant political movement in the US and parts of Europe, with strong links to both environmentalism and feminism. Yale University was an epicenter of ZPG activists who believed "that a constantly increasing population is responsible for many of our problems: pollution, violence, loss of values and of individual privacy".[13]

Our system change challenges are going to be aggravated by population pressures, whatever the Vatican may choose to believe. This point was made very clear by the publication of the latest UN population projections to 02100, showing that instead of stabilizing at just above nine billion people sometime around mid-century, the global population is likely to continue growing to 10.1 billion by the end of the twenty-first century.[14] More recently still, UN estimates suggest that world population could grow toward an almost inconceivable 15 billion by 02100.[15]

So, how to look at this? "Every billion more people makes life more difficult for everybody – it's as simple as that", commented Population Council demographer John Bongarts. "Is it the end of the world? No. Can we feed 10 billion people? Probably. But we obviously would be better off with a smaller population."

The director of the UN population division, Hania Zlotnik, has stressed that the time has come for countries around the world to renew their emphasis on family planning. A key focus of development policy in the 01970s and 01980s, such programs became snarled up in ideological battles over abortion, sex education, and the role of women in society. Conservatives, Catholics, and some feminists were among those who managed to slow the process down.

Significantly, the amount of foreign aid going to the supply of contraceptives has scarcely moved over a decade: it was US$238 million in 02009, for example, much of it coming from the US. "The need has grown, but the availability of family planning services has not", said one economist.

The population forecasts are based on the assumption that food and water will be available for the billions of extra mouths, and that potential catastrophes such as climate change, epidemics, or wars will not serve as powerful brakes on population trends. This assumption seems optimistic. "These numbers", as Dr. Zlotnik put it, "are just not sustainable." Indeed, there are those who see the genocide in Rwanda in 01994 as a direct result of overpopulation. Consider, too, the conditions into which hundreds of millions of people are now crowding in the world's sprawling megacities, where the infrastructures now taken for granted in the developed world are often conspicuous by their absence.

Much has been made of the demographic transition, the idea that as wealth grows, people have fewer children. One proponent is Bill Gates, though he is no Pollyanna. "The more people, the harder it is to provide enough food, educate children and sustain the environment", he has noted.[16] "Developing countries cannot possibly break through the vicious cycle of poverty if their populations continue to grow at unsustainable rates." Still, there is good news here. The evidence shows that "over the past 50 years, every nation that has made improvements to its child survival rates has experienced dramatic declines in fertility".

One of the most impressive initiatives I have come across in this area is Thailand's Population and Community Development Association (PDA),[17] which we wrote up in *The Power of Unreasonable People* several years back. Mechai Viravaidya, whom I consider a leading Zeronaut and who has attracted significant funding from the Bill and Melinda Gates Foundation, left government in 01973 and founded the PDA to improve the lives of the rural poor. Seeing family planning as a central challenge, he held condom blowing contests for school children, encouraged taxi cab drivers to hand out condoms to their customers, and founded a restaurant chain called "Cabbages and Condoms" where condoms, rather than mints or fortune cookies, are given to customers together with the bill. I recall the food being good, too.

Does China have enough people?

Fun, but the dark side of population control was spotlighted in the 01970s, when anxiety about the impending population bomb reached a crescendo. In India, Prime Minister Indira Gandhi and her son Sanjay used state-of-emergency powers to force a dramatic increase in sterilizations. As *National Geographic* recalled recently: "Family planning workers were pressured to meet quotas; in a few states, sterilization became a condition of receiving new housing or other government benefits. In some cases, the police simply rounded up poor people and hauled them to sterilization camps."

At the other end of the spectrum, but in the same giant country, there is Kerala, on India's southwestern coast. There, improvements in health and education have dropped the fertility rate to 1.7. The key, according to demographers, is female literacy. At around 90 percent, it's now by far the highest in India. The logic is complex, but it works: girls who go to school start having children later than those who do not, and they are more accepting of contraception. And shifting to smaller family sizes brings other dividends. In Bangladesh, for example, US$62 spent by the government to prevent an unwanted birth is calculated to have saved, on average, US$615 in expenditures on other social services.[18]

One place where the Vatican's pro-birth logic may apply at the moment, paradoxically, is China. "Does China have enough people?" *The Economist* asked recently.[19] The country has long been famous – indeed, infamous – for its draconian measures, particularly its one-child policy, designed to slow the population growth rate. Now, however, there are signs that China may have too low a birth rate to sustain its economic growth. The fertility rate is now just 1.4, far below the replacement rate of 2.1, which (all things being relatively equal) eventually leads to a stabilized population.

As with other countries, among them Japan and a wide range of EU member states, younger people face the prospect of having to support a rapidly aging population. Adding insult to injury, there has been a growing imbalance between genders, with many more boys than girls born. In about 20 to 25 years, it is forecast, there will not be enough brides for almost one fifth of today's boys, with – as *The Economist* put it – "potentially vast destabilizing consequences".

One reason to be nervous about the aging of population is that older people tend to become more conservative – and, at least in democracies, they continue to vote more actively than the young. At the same time, their investments and pensions are generally predicated on the continuation and medium-term success of unsustainable, incumbent companies. Think of BP at the time of the Gulf oil disaster, when that single company accounted for £1 of every £7 of dividend income paid out by the companies in the FTSE 100 index of leading shares.[20]

For the Race to Zero to develop real, sustained traction, we need to get much better at bridging between the interests of the different generations – including those not yet born, as argued in Chapter 8. But first, let's take a look at four other systemic challenges that are tightly coupled with population: pandemics, poverty, pollution, and the proliferation of weapons of mass destruction.

Box 7.2

How Zeronauts tackle population growth

Here are some actions that Zeronauts would add to the C-suite to-do list:

- Get population on the radar screen – it is central to the sustainability agenda.
- Recognize that this isn't just about population, but about wider demographic trends.
- Understand that there will be interference effects between the different parts of the agenda. Take population versus pandemics, for example. According to a recent study, it looks as though the most popular contraceptive for women in Eastern and Southern Africa (a hormone injection given every three months) doubles the risk that the women will become infected with HIV.[21]
- Track the work of key organizations such as Gapminder, which links population trends to many other key factors, including those covered below.
- Understand the links between business and population: industry concentrates people in areas of pollution risk (for example, at Bhopal); but at the same time, when industry suffers – as in Detroit – population numbers can thin out dramatically.
- Take a close look at how your product or service would do in a sustainable, equitable world of 9 to 10 billion people.
- Support your local – or at least your favorite – Zeronauts in this space.

Sometimes there is great controversy and infamy attached to patient zero.

Mary Mallon is a celebrated instance. She was an apparently healthy carrier of the disease typhoid fever. Many people were infected by her and she had to be quarantined to stop her spreading the deadly disease. Dubbed "Typhoid Mary", she came to epitomize the carrier or transmitter of anything undesirable, harmful, or catastrophic."[22]

"Wiping a disease off the face of the planet is an extraordinarily difficult challenge", Bill Gates has said, "but it can be done."[23] Just how big a challenge is illustrated by the efforts to get the disease that has killed more humans than any other, smallpox, back into the bottle. But before we tackle that story, let's pull back a bit and look at the bigger picture.

One way in which early settlements – and, ultimately, cities – killed significant proportions of their populations was through the simple act of concentration. Denser populations were more vulnerable to pandemics. And the worst killer, as we shall see, was smallpox. The difference between an epidemic and a pandemic is that while the first may be widespread, the second jumps to a different level, going national or even global – as the bubonic plague did on several occasions.

Indeed, when I'm in London and not cycling in to work, I generally take the Piccadilly underground line to Holborn. If I sit toward the beginning of the train, or toward the end, the wheels of the coach screech with a particularly shrill intensity as they negotiate a series of bends in the track between South Kensington and Knightsbridge stations. For a number of years I simply winced and wished we could design a better class of Tube trains; but then I discovered why those bends were there. It turns out that the line jinks because the wretched tunnelers boring the original route ran into plague pits from the seventeenth century, in which huge numbers of victims of the bubonic plague had been buried. So the tunnel jinked.

As a child, I devoured books like Daniel Defoe's *A Journal of the Plague Year*, published in 01722 but set in 01665,[24] and *La Peste*, by Albert Camus, which was published in 01947 a couple of years before I was born – and thought to be based on a cholera epidemic that killed huge numbers of people in Oran a century earlier, in 01849, though the novel is set in the 01940s.[25] Generally, though, my mind wasn't on existentialism when I was being inoculated against such diseases as a child. It was on whether or not it would hurt. Often it did.

We traveled a fair amount, so in the end we ended up taking such things for granted. But what was it like being vaccinated for smallpox in the early days? Think of the brave, foolhardy experiment Edward Jenner carried out in 01796. If he were still alive today and attempted the same thing, he would almost certainly end up in prison and be automatically struck off the medical list. The experiment involved him inoculating eight-year-old James Phipps with pus from a milkmaid's cowpox pustule and then, two months later, with a potentially fatal dose of smallpox. Luckily this embryonic vaccine worked – and James proved to be immune to the deadlier disease, smallpox.

History's number one killer

Smallpox has been the biggest scourge of humanity since time immemorial, at least in terms of the numbers of people dying.[26] Ridding the world of smallpox was an immense undertaking, heavily underscoring the immense difficulty of zeroing major pandemics. Since Edward Jenner proved the effectiveness of cowpox in protecting humans from smallpox in 01796, various attempts were made to eliminate the disease. As early as 01803, I was surprised to learn, Spain organized a mission to transport vaccine to its colonies in the Americas and the Philippines, aiming to establishing mass vaccination programs there.[27]

The US Congress passed the Vaccine Act of 01813 to ensure that safe smallpox vaccine would be available to the American public – and by 01897 the disease had largely been eliminated from the country. In Northern Europe, meanwhile, some countries had eliminated smallpox by 01900, and by 01914 the incidence in most industrialized countries had fallen to relatively low levels.

The first hemisphere-wide effort to eradicate smallpox was launched in 01950 by the Pan American Health Organization. It was successful in all American countries, except Argentina, Brazil, Colombia, and Ecuador. Then, in 01958, Professor Viktor Zhdanov, the Soviet deputy minister of health, called on the World Health Assembly to back a global initiative to eradicate smallpox. The proposal was accepted in 01959, at a time when two million people were dying from smallpox every year – though it is worth noting that this was down from 50 million cases a year not that long before.

In order to eradicate smallpox, each and every outbreak had to be stopped in its tracks through a process known as "ring vaccination". This involved the isolation of cases and the vaccination of everyone living nearby. One critical problem the World Health Organization (WHO) faced was the inadequate reporting of smallpox cases, which meant that many cases did not come to the attention of the authorities. On the upside, however, the fact that humans are the only reservoir for smallpox infection, and that carriers who showed no symptoms did not exist, helped immeasurably.

By the end of 01975, smallpox hung on only in the Horn in Africa. Conditions were atrocious in Ethiopia and Somalia, aggravated by civil war, famine, and huge numbers of refugees. Still, an intensive surveillance, containment, and vaccination program was undertaken in these countries in early and mid-01977, under the direction of Australian microbiologist Frank Fenner. As the campaign neared its end, Fenner's team helped to verify eradication. The last naturally occurring case of indigenous smallpox (*Variola minor*) was diagnosed in a hospital cook in Somalia in October 01977. The last naturally occurring case of the more deadly *Variola major* had been detected two years earlier in a two-year-old Bangladeshi girl.

At last, the global eradication of smallpox was certified by a commission of eminent scientists in December 01979, a conclusion subsequently endorsed by the World Health Assembly (WHA) the following year. The first two sentences of the resolution read:

> Having considered the development and results of the global program on smallpox eradication initiated by WHO in 1958 and intensified since 1967 ... [the WHA] declares solemnly that the world and its peoples have won freedom from smallpox, which was a most devastating disease sweeping in epidemic form through many countries since earliest time, leaving death, blindness and disfigurement in its wake and which only a decade ago was rampant in Africa, Asia and South America.

The last outbreak of smallpox involved two cases (one of them sadly fatal) in the UK in 01978. A medical photographer contracted the disease at the University of Birmingham Medical School, following which the scientist responsible for smallpox research at the university committed suicide. In the wake of this deeply worrying accident, all known stocks of smallpox were destroyed or transferred to one of two WHO reference laboratories with top-security facilities: the Centers for Disease Control and Prevention in the US and the State Research Center of Virology and Biotechnology/VECTOR in Russia.

In 01986, the WHO recommended destruction of the remaining virus stocks, and later set the date of destruction for 30 December 01993. This was then postponed to 30 June 01999 due to resistance from the US and Russia. Next, the World Health Assembly agreed in 02002 to permit the temporary retention of the virus stocks for research purposes – despite widespread protests from scientists, particularly among veterans of the WHO Smallpox Eradication Program, that no public health purpose is served by the US and Russia retaining the virus.

Brilliant lessons

So what lessons can we learn from the zeroing of smallpox for our attempts to get rid of other major diseases? I asked a number of people this question, including Larry Brilliant, listed in the Zeronauts Roll of Honor – and who was involved in the final stages of the WHO smallpox eradication process. His has been the most extraordinary life and career. He first came to public attention in 01969, when a group of American Indians from different tribes occupied Alcatraz Island off San Francisco. When they put out a call for a doctor to help one of their number give birth, Brilliant showed up.[28]

Next, because of the intense media coverage, he was cast in a movie called *Medicine Ball Caravan*, where he played a doctor in a tribe of hippies following bands such as the Grateful Dead and (one of my favorites at the time) Jefferson Airplane. Members of the cast were paid with airline tickets to India, which Brilliant amongst others cashed in and rented a bus to drive around Europe. This subsequently turned into a relief convoy to help victims of the 01970 Bhola cyclone in Bangladesh, at the time East Pakistan.

This became something of a pattern in his life, with stints as a volunteer responding to other disasters, including the tsunami disaster in Sri Lanka. Among other things, Brilliant played an active role in the final stages of the WHO smallpox eradication campaign, worked on polio eradication, helped to found the prototypical social network The Well, and cofounded the Seva Foundation (which has helped to restore sight to over two million blind people). Then, when he was awarded the Technology Entertainment and Design (TED) Prize in 02006, granting him "One Wish to Change the World", some of the lessons of the anti-smallpox campaign surfaced. His wish was "To build a powerful new early warning system to protect our world from some of its worst nightmares". And his wish is in the process of emerging, in the form of InSTEDD, based in Cambodia.[29]

However spectacular the adventures and achievements of Zeronauts such as Jenner, Zhdanov, Fenner, and Brilliant, this is an area where zero may yet prove to be illusory. Even if the world ensures the complete destruction of the remaining official stocks of the virus, there must always be the concern that someone somewhere might have some left – and would be willing to use them either as a means of terrorism or of blackmail.

There has been a long, dark history of smallpox being used in this way. The British, for example, may have considered using it as a biological warfare agent against their enemies during the so-called French and Indian Wars (01754 to 01763). Although it is far from clear that there was official backing for the plan, in the summer of 01763 a local trader, William Trent, wrote: "Out of our regard for them [members of the besieging Delawares], we gave them two Blankets and an Handkerchief out of the Small Pox Hospital. I hope it will have the desired effect."

During World War II, scientists from the UK, US, and Japan were all involved in research into producing a biological weapon from smallpox. Plans for large-scale production were never carried through, however, in part because those involved considered that the weapon would not be very effective as the result of the availability of a vaccine.

Much of the story since has been wreathed in clouds of secrecy. In 01947, for example, the Soviet Union set up a secret smallpox weapons factory in the city of Zagorsk, northeast of Moscow. An outbreak of weaponized smallpox may well have occurred during testing there in the 01970s. In 01992, a defector alleged that the Soviet bioweapons program at Zagorsk had produced a large stockpile – as much as 20 tons – of weaponized smallpox, possibly engineered to resist vaccines, along with the refrigerated warheads needed to deliver the virus in a fit state to do its dirty work.

Ultimately, though, the Russian government announced in 01997 that all of its remaining smallpox samples would be moved to the Vector Institute. Still, with the sudden breakup of the Soviet Union and widespread unemployment among the weapons program's scientists, there were concerns that smallpox and the skills needed to turn it into weapons may have been leaked to other governments or terrorist groups, who could exploit the virus as a means of biological warfare. By no means finally, concern has also been expressed that gene synthesis might even be used to recreate the virus from digital genomes.

The zeroing spotlight shifts

But smallpox, for the moment, has been effectively zeroed. Now other diseases are on the zero hit list, among them polio and malaria. Since 01988, according to the Bill and Melinda Gates Foundation, about 2.5 billion children around the globe have been vaccinated against polio, and the number of polio cases per year has fallen by 99 percent. "Many of the key pieces for polio eradication are in place", they say: "effective vaccines, the leadership of a global partnership, the Global Polio Eradication Initiative (GPEI), political will, dedicated volunteers, and a global mandate to eradicate the disease."

But a last push is needed to eliminate polio, in just a few areas in the world.

Strikingly, northern Nigeria, northern India, and parts of Afghanistan and Pakistan now account for more than 75 percent of global polio cases. "Halting poliovirus transmission in these endemic areas is vital not only for the populations in these areas", the Gates Foundation says, "but so that neighboring polio-free areas do not become re-infected".

Malaria is a much bigger problem; but still there is growing confidence that the devastating disease can be brought under control. Illustrating the interlinked nature of so many of these problems, earlier efforts to eradicate malarial mosquitoes with the persistent insecticide DDT led to huge impacts upon wildlife, the wildfire success of Rachel Carson's 01962 book *Silent Spring*, and the rapid evolution of the modern environmental movement.

But significant progress has been made since then, using updated approaches – and based on hitting the disease from every angle possible.[30] "Between 2000 and 2006", the Gates Foundation reports, "several countries in Africa saw a 50 percent decrease in malaria by using a combined set of effective interventions, including insecticide-treated bed nets and indoor spraying of homes with insecticides to control mosquitoes, and drug treatments to prevent and cure malaria."[31]

Despite such successes, malaria still kills millions of poor people in developing countries and can cripple their economies. It is estimated that the disease causes nearly 1 million deaths per year, and 85 percent of those who die are children under five years of age. "Ninety percent of malaria deaths occur in Africa", the Gates Foundation notes, "where the financial cost of malaria is crippling economic development due to the high cost of medicines and reduced productivity."

Unfortunately, the war against malaria is threatened by the growing weaknesses of current tools. Among other things, mosquitoes are becoming resistant to some insecticides used in bed nets and sprays, and malaria parasites are becoming resistant to some of today's drugs.

Pandemics are eternal

If there is one certainty in all of this, it is that while we may drive some diseases to zero we will never rid ourselves of the pandemic risk. All around us, potential pandemic vectors are mutating and evolving, waiting their chance.

A fair number of the diseases that have plagued our species for thousands of years came with the animals we domesticated, whether for food, transport, or company. Measles and chickenpox are just a couple of the diseases that jumped species as we started to live cheek-by-jowl with animals. And the process is still under way. The precursor of the HIV virus that causes AIDS, for example, is thought to have jumped the species barrier when hunters killed and ate chimpanzees.[32] And SARS, which swept the world in 02003, has been variously attributed to civets kept in restaurants in China prior to slaughter, and to bats.[33]

All pandemics start with one infected person, what medical researchers describe as "Patient Zero". During the early years of the AIDS epidemic, there was a huge controversy about one particular alleged Patient Zero, the basis of a complex transmission scenario compiled by scientists at the US Centers for Disease Control (CDC). This study suggested that Patient Zero had infected multiple partners with HIV, and they, in turn, transmitted it to others and rapidly spread the virus to locations worldwide.

Journalist Randy Shilts, who would himself die of AIDS,[34] wrote about this alleged Patient Zero in his 01987 book *And the Band Played On*, a book I read a few years after it was published – and consider one of the most absorbing science books I have yet come across.

Shilts identified Patient Zero as Gaëtan Dugas, a flight attendant who was sexually promiscuous in several North American cities.[35] For some time, as a result, Dugas was vilified as a spreader of HIV, and seen as the original source of the HIV epidemic among homosexual men. Subsequently, however, the original author of the CDC scenario repudiated the study methodology and challenged the way Shilts had represented his conclusions. Later genetic analysis suggests that HIV probably moved from Africa to Haiti, then entered the US around 01969, probably through a single immigrant.[36]

Whatever the origins of the HIV/AIDS pandemic, however, the fact is that we now live in a world which – with its dense populations, poor sanitation in many countries, and mass transit and air-conditioning systems – could scarcely be better designed as a disease incubator. And few recent diseases have underscored our vulnerability as dramatically as SARS.

Still, the key thing in all of this, as Hans Rosling of Gapminder has argued in the case of swine flu, is to keep a sense of proportion. During the 13 days up to 6 May 02011, he noted, "WHO has confirmed that 25 countries are affected by the swine flu and 31 persons have died from swine flu."[37] WHO data indicate that about 60,000 people died from tuberculosis (TB) during the same period. Yet swine flu dominated the media, while TB hardly made it into the footnotes.

But we should note the acceleration risk here. In the days of the Great Plague in London, diseases traveled, at best (or worst), at the pace of a ship or horse – though plague victims fired into besieged cities went a little faster. These days, unfortunately, diseases can travel almost at the speed of sound, thanks to jet aircraft. And key among the potential causes of epidemic and pandemic risks are poverty and pollution, to which we now turn.

Box 7.3

How Zeronauts tackle pandemics

Here are some pointers that Zeronauts would want on the action list:

- First, ensure that pandemic risk is on the radar screen. Again, track the work of organizations such as the World Health Organization, Gapminder, and the Bill and Melinda Gates Foundation, which link the evolution of pandemics to many other key factors.
- Recognize the links to other issues covered here – among them population, poverty, climate change, and refugee movements.
- Acknowledge the risks associated with the misuse of key treatments, among them antibiotics.[38]
- Study the achievements of companies that played major roles in tackling pandemics such as AIDS, among them the mining company Anglo-American in Southern Africa.
- Expect episodic, large-scale interruptions of business, driven by the shutdown of airlines and mass transit systems. Consider stockpiling relevant drugs. In order to minimize the impact of disrupted transport systems and logistics, invest in online and virtual conferencing systems.
- See what you can do to help those working on prevention and early detection, including InSTEDD. Take a look at Pharma Futures's work on access to medicines.[39]
- Support your local – or at least your favorite – Zeronauts in this space.

For many of us, the poor are out of sight, out of mind. But that may be changing. When our eldest daughter, who had recently joined film director Danny Boyle's team, told us she was busy on the *Slumdog* project some years ago, we raised our eyebrows. It meant nothing. But then *Slumdog Millionaire* burst out of the traps and swept the Oscars. As a result of films such as *City of God* and *Slumdog*, there has since been a boom in slum tourism.

Those who have studied the phenomenon say that, done well, this can bring real benefits to poorer communities. "Residents are eager to engage with visitors", reported Ko Koens who had investigated what was happening in the slums around Cape Town.[40] "When tours incorporate the local people and businesses, there are undeniable benefits. But when the big buses drive in, take photos, and drive out, locals despised it. They're not zoo animals."

Zoo animals or not, population growth trends mean that there are a lot more poor people to visit, if you are minded to do so – though too often they are shunted off into far-flung areas, on the basis of out of sight, out of mind – until the riots flare, as they did in my home city of London in the summer of 02011.

Yes, there have been some spectacularly successful anti-poverty campaigns, among them Make Poverty History – which peaked in 02005.[41] Even the Vatican has got into the act in terms of zeroing poverty, with the Zero Poverty Now campaign launched by Caritas.[42] But there is something deeply systemic about poverty that resists most efforts to create change. True, some of the world's poorest countries have made significant gains; but the least developed countries still lag significantly in efforts to improve living standards.

That was the conclusion of a UN report, *The Millennium Development Goals 2011*,[43] which assessed overall progress toward achieving the global target in respect of extreme poverty.[44] The report showed that various other states, including Burundi, Rwanda, Samoa, and Tanzania, have attained – or are nearing – the goal of universal primary education, a key target. Considerable progress has also been made in Benin, Bhutan, Burkina Faso, Ethiopia, Guinea, Mali, Mozambique, and Niger, where net enrolment ratios in primary school increased by more than 25 percentage points from 01999 to 02009.

Despite significant setbacks caused by the global economic crisis that plunged much of the world into recession at the end of the century's first decade, and the high food and energy prices, the world is still on track to achieve at least some of the UN's 02015 goals, according to the report.

"Despite these declines, current trends suggest that the momentum of growth in the developing world remains strong enough to sustain the progress needed to reach the global poverty-reduction target", the UN concluded. "Based on recently updated projections from the World Bank, the overall poverty rate is still expected to fall below 15 per cent by 2015, indicating that the Millennium Development Goal target can be met."

The number of deaths of children under the age of five declined from 12.4 million in 01990 to 8.1 million in 02009, which means that nearly 12,000 fewer children die each day. Increased funding and intensive control efforts have cut deaths from malaria by 20 percent worldwide – from nearly 985,000 in 02000 to 781,000 in 02009, the report noted.

It also stressed, however, that efforts need to be intensified especially among the most vulnerable members of the global population who continue to be marginalized as a result of sex, age, ethnicity, or disability. Disparities in progress between urban and rural areas also remain significant.

Wide gaps remain in women's access to paid work in at least half of all regions and, following the job losses in 02008 and 02009, the growth in employment during the economic recovery in 02010, especially in the developing world, was lower for women than for men. "The poorest of the world are being left behind. We need to reach out and lift them into our lifeboat", Secretary-General Ban Ki-moon said. "Now is the time for equity, inclusion, sustainability and women's empowerment."

An estimated 1.1 billion people in urban areas and 723 million people in rural areas gained access to improved drinking water between 01990 and 02008. Progress has, however, been uneven, highlighting the large gaps between and within countries. The poorest children made the slowest progress in terms of improved nutrition and survival, and nearly one quarter of children in the developing world were underweight in 02009, with the poorest children most affected.

Advances in sanitation have also often bypassed the poor and those living in rural areas, with more than 2.6 billion people still lacking access to toilets or other forms of improved sanitation. In Southern Asia, for example, sanitation coverage for the poorest 40 percent of households hardly increased between 01995 and 02008.

One bright spot of hope has been the work of Muhammad Yunus and the Grameen Bank he founded – although he was rudely ejected by the Bangladeshi government in 02011. A decade or so ago, well before Pamela Hartigan and I had thought of writing our book on social entrepreneurs, *The Power of Unreasonable People*, Dr. Yunus confided in us that his breed of social entrepreneur has to be "70 percent crazy".[45] Attempting the impossible, given that is the nature of the breed, but also objective and professional where necessary. His announced zeroing plan, a few years later, was to put poverty in a "Poverty Museum".

Around the same time, there was a growing focus on what the late C. K. Prahalad dubbed the "bottom of the pyramid" – and others called "base" of the pyramid or just "BoP".[46] In global terms, this potential market sector embraces the 2.5 billion people who live on less than US$2.50 per day. Having briefly worked alongside Professor Prahalad before his death, on the Nestlé Creating Shared Value advisory board, there was no doubting his intense commitment to finding meaningful, sustainable solutions to global poverty.

A growing number of companies have been experimenting with potential BoP solutions, among them S. C. Johnson, which partnered with youth groups in the Kibera slum of Nairobi. They created a community-based waste management and cleaning company, providing home-cleaning, insect treatment, and waste disposal services for residents of the slum.[47] Others have been backing social enterprises that tackle related problems, such as Jeroo Billimoria's Aflatoun, which teaches poor children in around 80 countries to manage money – even if they have little or none.[48]

Meanwhile, worrying pockets of intense poverty are emerging in developed countries. In the US, for example, poverty has grown fastest in the suburbs, particularly in the so-called Sunbelt states.[49] Inequality has been rising strikingly in some developed countries, including in America and China. This can happen either because the wealthier are getting wealthier, or because the poor are getting poorer – or both.[50]

At the same time, even where growth is happening, the benefits are often very unevenly distributed. Consider India, which has been the fastest growing large economy after China.[51] The rapid economic growth has been concentrated in a small number of states, particularly in the south, and among a fairly tight circle of businesses. While government policy-makers have focused on the headline growth rate, Nobel laureate economist Amartya Sen warned New Delhi that it was "stupid" to aspire to double-digit growth without tackling the chronic undernourishment of tens of millions of Indians. Strikingly, the average calorie intake among the country's poorest people has been stagnant for a decade.

For a while, it was fashionable for politicians in certain parts of the world to argue that a rising economic tide floats all boats. What some have called the "Davos consensus" argued that inequality itself was less important than ensuring that those at the bottom of the wealth pyramid were becoming better off.[52]

British minister Peter Mandelson famously declared that the government of the time was "intensely relaxed" about the millions earned by footballer David Beckham, as long as child poverty fell. Increasingly, however, the focus has shifted to poverty itself – among the drivers, a book called *The Spirit Level*, which argued that countries with greater disparities of income suffer to a significantly greater extent from a range of social problems, including lower life expectancies and higher murder rates.[53]

There are no miracle solutions to poverty. Instead, many of the factors that contribute are structural: in China, for example, the system of *hukou* residency permits serves to limit internal migration to the towns. Elsewhere, as in Brazil, there have been sustained efforts to break the pattern of immense wealth divides that have been such a dramatic feature of Latin American societies. Faster growth has helped to boost the incomes of the poor, while an overhaul of public-sector spending has helped to improve the social safety nets – albeit without raising taxes on the rich. That approach may work in a resource-rich society, but may stutter elsewhere.

Meanwhile, the microfinance movement that Dr. Yunus helped to launch in the 01970s has hit serious problems, with concerns about the risks of pushing credit to ill-educated people, of over-lending, and of borrowers being driven to suicide by aggressive debt-collection agents. The sector's very success has been the source of many of its troubles, with the money to be made sucking in less principled lenders.[54]

In India, for example, capital flows to the sector have been hit by concerns about whether the approach is safe and actually beneficial for the poor.[55] Critics claim that the sector has mistakenly concluded that it is "capable of delivering hyper-growth for the indefinite future", as Lok Capital cofounder Rajiv Lall put it.

In the end, at least in the better-regulated markets, things will no doubt settle down. As capital sluiced into the sector, the focus shifted too much to the interests of investors. The future, as Lall noted, will depend on investors recognizing that they should have more realistic expectations.

"The company does not exist to serve [investor] interests. The company exists to serve clients, and they make money because they do that well." In short, there must be a renewed interest in the welfare of clients, which is where Muhammad Yunus started all those years ago.

And it turns out that he was onto something even bigger about driving poverty toward zero. He focused microcredit on women, reasoning that they would be more likely to pay back the loans than their menfolk. And so it proved, although even here the results have been disputed. But the argument for focusing on women, it seems, runs right through the female age spectrum. If you want to change the world, it is increasingly argued, invest in girls.[56]

The World Food Program has discovered that when girls and women earn income, they reinvest some 90 percent in their families. They buy books, medicine, bed nets. Men, by contrast, spend much less on the family, in the region of 30 to 40 percent. No surprise, perhaps, that Larry Summers, when chief economist at the World Bank, argued that "Investment in girls' education may well be the highest-return investment available in the developing world." Yet less than two cents out of every development dollar go to girls. This is why actors such as the Nike Foundation are now investing in adolescent girls.[57]

The good news is that – before the so-called "Great Reset" went into its second round in 02011 – the percentage of people living in extreme poverty had gone down from around 40 percent 30 years ago to around 20 percent. So the eradication of poverty is potentially within range, if only current economic models were environmentally sustainable. Unfortunately, as the next section concludes, they are very far from sustainable.

Box 7.4

How Zeronauts tackle poverty

Economic growth – and the activities of well-run business – is key to success in alleviating poverty. Great progress has been made, particularly in the light of the original doom-laden Malthusian projections; but too much of the success rests on precarious foundations, given the growing concerns about challenges like that of "peak oil", "peak fish", and "peak water":

- Many companies will argue that poverty is no business of theirs, or that their basic business activities are the best cure. Sensible business leaders, however, will ensure that poverty is on their radar screen. Again, they should track the work of key organizations such as Gapminder, which links poverty to other key factors.
- Recognize the powerful links to the other 4Ps – population, pandemics, pollution, and proliferation.
- Investigate the base-of-the-pyramid opportunities for your products and services – or new ones. But beware of overenthusiasm. Consult those who know this field in depth, including universities and business schools such as Cornell, Michigan, and Oxford – and in the emerging economies themselves.
- Get a better understanding of what companies such as Danone are doing with key social enterprise actors such as the Grameen Bank.
- Find out more about the work of organizations such as the Nike Foundation, Aflatoun, and MyBnk.
- Support your local – or at least your favorite – Zeronauts in this space.

The first time I remember being aware of pollution – though I'm pretty sure I didn't then know what had caused it – was when, away at school, I saw what were called "detergent swans" below a weir on Dorset's River Stour. They turned out to be caused by new generations of cleaning product that contained phosphates and, among other problems, created huge banks of brilliant white foam where there was rapid mixing of water.

At the time, there was a sense that a rising quality of life in consumerist terms would almost inexorably be associated with declines in certain forms of environmental quality. Progress was distinctly zero sum for nature. As the Environmental Revolution spread, however, a growing number of polluting substances came under the spotlight, from DDT through PBBs and PCBs to chlorofluorocarbons (CFCs) – and now GHGs, or greenhouse gases.

In 01978, I was asked to write a short report for the Hudson Institute, founded by Herman Kahn. My conclusion was that the world was headed into a period where pollution concerns would increasingly focus on systemic issues. The four areas I spotlighted were ozone depletion, climate change, toxics, and pollution of the seas and oceans. Herman Kahn, known among other things for his work on nuclear scenarios and the Mutually Assured Destruction (MAD) strategy for nuclear deterrence, wasn't persuaded. His response ran along the lines of: "The problem with you environmentalists is that you find yourself driving toward the Grand Canyon and your instinct is to take your foot off the gas pedal and slam down on the brakes. But maybe what you should be doing is flooring the accelerator – and trying to get across the chasm."

At least that's my version of what he said, but his message was clear – technology would save the day. I need no persuading that hardware is critical in crossing the "Sustainability Chasm", illustrated in Figure 2.3 (see p.42). The history of efforts to rein in various forms of pollution shows that in spades, from the work of Joseph Bazalgette who built London's great sewerage system to those now struggling to work out how to make carbon capture, storage, and reuse an economic prospect. But over time it has been much clearer that there are fundamental system challenges that we need to tackle in the coming decades, whose solution requires changes in the economy's basic operating system. These include rebooting the fields of economics, accounting, and company valuation to take account of the wider impacts of pollution.

You can hear this line of thinking in what some business pioneers are now saying publicly. In her acceptance speech at 02010's Ceres–ACCA North American Awards for Sustainability Reporting, Hannah Jones, Nike's vice president of sustainable business and innovation, may have seemed to some people to be, as some Americans would say, "cussing in church". Nike, she insisted, now believes that "the time is fast approaching when we will jettison the language of sustainability, and simply talk about value creation: NPV [net present value], ROIC [return on invested capital], market share, innovation portfolios and shareholder returns".[58]

"We have long said that things we have taken for free will become the new gold", she explained, "water, waste, carbon. Today, externalized costs are being forcibly internalized into cost structures, economies and incomes. The weather is not waiting to be regulated. We believe we have entered the era of climate adaptation, where we are no longer contemplating the potential, but beginning to grapple with the consequences.

"But", she continued, "here's the thing: to be able to deliver this transparency has required data, which in turn has the potential to trigger innovation. We're discovering how combining different data sets can be a tool for empowerment; social change; new insights; new solutions. What happens when we can mash up the data from these reports? How do we apply Silicon Valley, new-business-model thinking to the data we see emerging from the sustainability world? And in a world where open data is starting to create new businesses, new solutions to intractable problems, how do we reap even great value from the world of reporting? How does reporting actually become the start of an innovation story, not only the crowning of an accountability story?"

Finally, she noted that "When we talk about sustainability without the context of value creation we diminish the potential and the opportunity and the speed with which the transition will happen. How do we turn sustainability into a 'pull' function, not a 'push' function, within a corporation?" The answer, she concluded, "lies in viewing sustainability as a strategic prism through which to view the resiliency, future growth trajectory and value creation potential of a company."

Box 7.5

Going for zero at DuPont

The first person I recall being dubbed a "Hero of Zero" was Paul Tebo of DuPont, way back in 02000.[59] So I chased him down to get his thoughts on DuPont's journey to zero.[60] The zero push was supported from the very top of the company, with Ed Woolard, as DuPont's CEO, noting at a conference I attended in 01991 that in his case "CEO" stood for "chief environmental officer".

"The goal of zero injuries, illnesses, and incidents was consistent with the DuPont culture and accepted easily", Tebo told me. "The goals of zero waste, emissions, and new net energy were harder to integrate into the company culture but have been also been very successful. Compared with 01990, global hazardous waste is now down 40 percent, air carcinogens down well over 95 percent, global greenhouse gas emissions down over 60 percent on a CO_2-equivalent basis, and total energy down about 6 percent – while the company has grown in volume by almost 40 percent."

And the impact upon the traditional bottom line? "The energy efficiency projects have saved DuPont over US$6 billion since 1990", Tebo noted. But, he recalled, "There was a substantial difference between zero in safety and zero in waste, emissions, and new net energy. In safety, most of DuPont runs at zero injuries, illnesses, and incidents all of the time. So it is believable, because it has been achieved for substantial periods at many global sites. For waste, emissions, and zero net new energy, by contrast, the challenge was to show where significant progress had already been made – and then to help the businesses identify pathways to further progress that made economic sense. In essence, we needed to make it believable through examples and show how many of the reductions were good for the bottom line."

To check on progress at the giant chemical company, I talked to Linda Fisher (vice president for safety, health and environment and chief sustainability officer) and Dawn Rittenhouse (director of sustainable development).[61] They stressed that DuPont remains a leader in the safety area, but noted that there had been a weakening of performance in some areas, which was being addressed. They agreed that zero targets are more meaningful in the safety area. They said that there was consistently less push-back on safety than on emissions and waste – where businesses tend to say things like "That's not possible", or, even more forcefully, "That's against the laws of thermodynamics".

Linda also noted that there had been a huge shift during recent years in terms of executives "being aware of the consequences of not being aligned with societal expectations. The global marketplace has made people much more aware of the issues. There is zero tolerance in such areas as ethical standards. The responsibility for many of these issues sits with the businesses, but they are now much more thoughtful about the development and introduction of new products – for example, those that could be persistent in the environment."

The persistence issue, in fact, has been a major headache for the company, with PFOA (perfluorooctanoic acid), used since the 01940s in industrial quantities, turning up in the blood of people around the world – spurring growing interest in finding out whether there is a risk to human health.

One big shift, Dawn observed, is that whereas "DuPont used to push its standards into the market, now there is a growing amount of market pull. We are seeing increasing pressures for emission reductions and greener ingredients throughout the supply chain, coming from retailers like Wal-Mart and customers like the automotive industry. This is all still very much in the experimental stage, with strikingly different demands for information coming from different customers. That can be frustrating, but at the same time it's exciting that the market is waking up. It has been talked about for years, but now it is becoming a reality."

You can see the results on DuPont's website, where the Building Innovations domain says that the company is "using evolutionary science every day to create smarter, safer, more comfortable, sustainable building solutions. We're aiming for zero; zero impact, zero waste, zero harm, and net zero energy use."

Paul Tebo, meanwhile, has moved into retirement – and consulting. "I have spent much of my time since I retired from DuPont talking about how to make 'zero' work within a company", he said. "And as I've talked to senior management about DuPont's journey from environmental laggard to sustainability leader, the interest is strong about how to implement a 'zero' mindset within a large organization. Senior leadership commitment and consistent actions are the key. A lot of senior management like to commit to a 'zero' goal, particularly in safety, but then never 'walk the talk'."

This is a theme I have heard time and again, including from major customers that consume large quantities of chemical industry products. At more or less the same time, Stef Kranendijk, CEO of carpet-makers Desso, based in The Netherlands, came through the office to update us on their efforts to radically shrink Desso's environmental footprint. He was worried, however, that many of the companies they deal with are looking for simplistic solutions. "Their decisions are often strictly driven by a concern with carbon footprints", he said, "about doing 'less bad' rather than doing 'more good'."

The scale of the problem is suggested by the fact that in the UK alone, some 600,000 tons of carpet are thrown out every year. One estimate suggests that, in the developed world, around 2 percent of landfill waste is made up from old carpeting.

The breakthrough, at least for Desso, came in discovering the Cradle to Cradle® approach. This had been launched in 02002 by German chemist Michael Braungart and American architect William McDonough in their book *Cradle to Cradle*.[62] And it's from the Braungart-McDonough partnership that the language about "less bad" and "more good" originates. As often happens in competitive areas, there was little love lost between Ray Anderson of Interface and Bill McDonough, but we are at a period where it makes sense to let 1000 flowers bloom – before we start weeding.

Desso's argument is that all product – including carpets – should be designed from the outset with the intention that they will eventually be recycled, as either "technical" or "biological" nutrients. Interestingly, both Desso and the Braungart–McDonough team have to some degree positioned Cradle to Cradle® in opposition to the zero agenda.

They argue that, while the green lobby talks about "minimizing" human impacts, "zero footprints", "banning" harmful substances, or "reducing" energy use, "a Cradle to Cradle® company says instead that it doesn't matter how much we manufacture, or how much 'waste' we create, because wastes simply become the raw materials or nutrients for further manufacturing, with products being reborn and reborn."

As Stef Kranedijk put it: "The Cradle to Cradle® approach makes planned obsolescence respectable. It encourages consumers to buy products, but to do so from innovative companies that have policies in place to recycle old products, turning waste into new products or into nutrients. The difference between Cradle to Cradle® and traditional recycling is that with C2C the original materials from which the products are made should be pure and the products need to be designed for easy disassembly. In traditional recycling, people often do not analyze so well which ingredients are involved before they start the recycling process."

Whichever way all this shakes out, the key point, as DuPont's Dawn Rittenhouse stressed, is that all of this is at the experimental stage (stage 2 in Chapter 6). Stef Kranendijk was more bullish, however, noting that we are "well beyond the experimental stage, with more and more companies participating, such as Steelcase, Herman Miller, Haworth, Orange Box, chemical giants like Dow Chemical, DSM and Eastman, Van der Lande logistic systems, Shaw, Saint Gobain, Nestlé Waters Inc, Aveda, Procter & Gamble, Alcoa and many others. Desso itself has set itself the objective of making sure that all its products are Cradle to Cradle in 2020. Already today we manufacture 60 percent of our modular carpet tiles with 100 percent recycled material, made from 30 percent post-customer and 70 percent post-industrial waste."

Though he says that Desso will continue its efforts on Eco Efficiency (which is how Braungart and McDonough describe efforts to save energy and reduce CO_2 emissions), he claims Eco Effectiveness (by which they mean designing and manufacturing products of pure materials and for easy disassembly, using renewable energy to the greatest extent possible in all stages of the cycle) is now creating more positive energy within the company and through its supply chain, boosting innovation – and demonstrating, as he concluded, "People, Planet and Profit can go hand in hand."

This message also came through loud and clear when I talked to Al Halvorsen[63] of Frito-Lay, whose job title had morphed from director of energy to director of environmental sustainability. The reason I wanted to talk to him was that, as part of PepsiCo, Frito-Lay has been pushing toward a range of zero-based targets. The Casa Grande plant in Arizona had been leading the charge for the company as a whole with its Near Net Zero Project. As Halvorsen told me: "Casa Grande is a learning lab, aiming not just for five percent changes, not for incremental improvements, but for moving off the energy and water grids entirely. Zero-based approaches spur out-of-the-box thinking and, potentially, step function change."

The Near Net Zero project has resulted in some pretty significant improvements. It has already helped Frito-Lay's manufacturing sites to cut water consumption per pound of product against 01999 numbers, with natural gas use dropping 33 percent and electricity demand by 25 percent. A range of projects are being taken forward as part of the overall campaign, including the use of wooden pallets as boiler fuel, wastewater recycling, and fuel-efficient vehicles, and there are plans for a 36 acre solar power farm next door, part funded by Frito-Lay and part funded by a utility. The annual savings generated, Halvorsen reported, are running at around the US$80 million mark.

From 02007 onwards, a paper-based study was done on what it would take Casa Grande to come completely off the grid – looking at likely costs, paybacks, and impacts. One conclusion: the costs would ramp up dramatically as the company closed in on the final 20 percent of reductions, which would come as no surprise to those who argued against blind pursuit of zero targets in the TQM field. As the lessons are rolled out across the rest of the group, the solutions will be tailored to the geography and circumstances of particular sites. But, once again, Al Halvorsen underscored the motivational power of zero, if used in the right way. His CEO's response had been: "Sounds amazing. Keep going!"

Other companies driving hard into the zero pollution space include Nissan, with its commitment to zero-emission vehicles,[64] its partnership with Shai Agassi's Better Place, and its publicity campaign built around the Planet Zero online game.[65] When I took part in a stakeholder session in the company's boardroom in Tokyo a few years back, I was forcefully struck by the sheer scale of their electric vehicle (EV) ambitions – reflecting a market-wide shift that so badly wrong-footed another of our Zeronauts, the Formula Zero team (see pp.135–41).

The long-term success of companies such as Renault–Nissan in this space will very much reflect the extent to which others drive the necessary changes in our financial systems – a point brought home by the launch of *Unburnable Carbon*, the first output from the Carbon Tracker Initiative. This posed the critical question: are the world's financial markets blowing a carbon bubble? Or, to put it another way, are there more fossil fuels listed on the world's stock exchanges than can be burned in a world committed to limiting global warming to 2°C? The answer, it turns out, is that no less than 80 percent of the carbon assets listed are likely to be unburnable.

It's hardly surprising that those responsible for the bubble don't want to hear the bad news. As a result, the launch of the report, held in London's Canary Wharf, surrounded by the glittering towers of many leading banks, attracted a disproportionate number of people one participant jokingly described to me as "climate change luvvies".[66] In one sense, he was right – certainly I recognized many faces – but it was also striking that those present included people who manage climate and carbon issues for some of the world's best-known financial institutions. And the luvvie-spotter himself was working for Richard Branson's Carbon War Room – and was himself en route to a meeting hosted by the International Maritime Organization at which major new greenhouse gas emission controls would be announced for the world shipping industry.

In fact, some of those who have been in the game for quite a while are now in the process of developing practical initiatives that aim to address the immense scale of the challenges we face. Take Peter Head of Arup, a pioneer in sustainable urban design, who at the time was energetically fundraising for the new Ecological Sequestration Trust – whose ambition is to capture the carbon dioxide from coal-fired power stations in countries such as China and India, feeding the resulting gas streams through algal bioreactors to create an array of oil products, as well as soil improvement products and fertilizers that can be used in intensive horticulture and agriculture operations nearby. (Interest declared: I was acting trust chairman for the launch period.)

To ensure that such ventures have a better chance of success, however, carbon must be properly priced in stock markets and in corporate valuation and accounting processes. But there's a systemic problem here. The Carbon Tracker study concludes that, in contrast to Germany's equivalent, the London Stock

Exchange is hugely exposed to new forms of carbon risk. As one participant at the launch event put it – and he made it clear that he was speaking in a private capacity, rather than as an employee of the major financial institution he was just joining – "London prides itself as a green capital, but is really the fossil fuels capital of the world." Strikingly, 70 percent of the initial public offerings in London in the first six months of 02011 had been for mining companies.

"A century ago London was cashing in on carbon", London Mayor Boris Johnson had asserted earlier in 02011, noting that the City must now "harness the wealth of investment opportunities" generated by the shift to a low-carbon future. Unfortunately, it looks as if the City, like other major financial centers, still has a pretty huge carbon habit. In the process, the City is once again helping to build a largely invisible financial bubble, spreading the risk across the entire financial system and, ultimately, putting the entire country at risk.

Someone who has long been a pioneer is this space is Richard Sandor. I first met him around ten years ago when we were both on the advisory board of the Dow Jones Sustainability Indexes. This was around the time when discussions about creating a global carbon market were really getting under way.

Richard led the development of the emissions-trading industry since its beginnings. As chief economist for the Chicago Board of Trade in the 01970s, he helped to develop the financial futures market, and in the late 01980s and early 01990s he all but invented cap-and-trade programs for sulfur dioxide (SO_2) emissions, the pollutant that causes acid rain. The approach was fairly simple: the government puts a cap on SO_2 and then the market trips in, with companies that can reduce SO_2 cost effectively on their own allowed to sell emissions rights to those that can't.

Going the same route with greenhouse emissions was the logical next step, and from the 01992 Earth Summit on, Richard was at the forefront of those efforts, launching the Chicago and the European Climate Exchanges, where companies could trade carbon.

Watch the adventures of such pioneers day to day, or year to year, and it often seems unlikely that anything dramatic will happen. But the same would have been true if you had been watching the Wright Brothers from a safe distance during the early days. History shows that today's impossibility has a way of becoming tomorrow's seeming inevitability.

When it comes to the pollutants that are so severely impacting upon our global biosphere, we must hope that history is going to repeat itself – but even faster this time and with a greater array of problems being tackled. Watching the Republicans trying to dismantle even fairly basic environmental protections in the US makes this hope seem wishful, but America generally awakes from its temporary bouts of insanity. For example, the Tea Party, which has had such a noxious effect on American politics, is now to a degree counterbalanced by the Occupy Wall Street movement. But one thing is clear in all of this – and despite the Tea Party's antipathy to big government. If we are to clean up, and prevent, pollution at the local, regional, and global scales, we will need more (and more effective) government, not less.

Box 7.6

How Zeronauts tackle pollution

Out of sight, out of mind has been the philosophy driving much of our pollution history. Think of the chlorofluorocarbon (CFC)-induced Antarctic Ozone Hole or the vast "gyres" (circulatory systems) of plastic waste discovered in the Pacific. As such forms of pollution increasingly have system impacts upon the biosphere, so our solutions have to be designed to have similar effects. There is an immense amount that companies can do on this front; but in the end the system conditions have to be set by cities, countries, and international regulators. So action points would include the following:

- First, ensure that pollution is on the organizational radar screen. Track the work of key organizations such as Gapminder, WWF, and Greenpeace, which link pollution to many other key factors.
- Next, investigate the links to the other 4Ps – recognizing that this is a global issue, with China's pollution, for example, now turning up in places such as the Rockies.
- Along the way, we have gone from basic problems such as black smoke and sewage to pollutants with systemic impacts, among them organochlorine insecticides, CFCs and greenhouse gases (GHGs).
- Get to know your organization's environmental footprint – most members of the global C-suite have little clue on this front.
- Check out the new tools that have been evolving to facilitate life-cycle assessment and design – which are increasingly used by market gate-keepers such as Wal-Mart and Marks & Spencer.
- Cleantech is a key part of the answer, together with massive investment in infrastructures, particularly in cities. Explore the field and see how your organization can get a jump on the trends.
- Recognize the critical importance of government regulation and policy. Get a better sense of the cap-and-trade (or equivalent) frameworks and related tax regimes, and find out how you can help to increase the political pressure for the right sort of change.
- Support your local – or at least your favorite – Zeronauts in this space.

ZERO PROLIFERATION!

The Bomb had fallen, or at least it had in my nightmares. The ocean waves crashed to shore, but turned into crackling stained glass as they came. The Cold War was at its height when I was a child in the 01950s, haunting our imaginations and, at least in my case, dreams. In retrospect, most of us were too worried about the nuclear arsenals of the opposing superpowers to fret much about the wider proliferation of such weapons of mass destruction (WMD), but here I see one basic certainty: the coming decades are likely to see WMD proliferation assuming even greater urgency.

For young people today, it's tough to imagine what the Cold War was like for their counterparts half a century ago – but the shadow of nuclear Armageddon was very real. While we were living in Northern Ireland during the late 01950s, for example, my father was sent to Christmas Island to fly fallout-monitoring missions around the early British A-bomb tests. As was the rule at the time, these were conducted in the open air. As a result, there was a great deal of public concern about fallout contaminants such as strontium-90 and caesium-137 getting into the milk we drank.

A linked memory, though I can't now recall whether I heard of it at the time or learned of it much later, was the 01954 horror story of the Japanese tuna fishing vessel *Daigo Fukuryū Maru* being overtaken by the fallout cloud from an American nuclear test on Bikini Atoll – and being covered by what was called "Bikini snow". The crew suffered acute radiation sickness and the boat's chief radioman died seven months later, his last words including, "I pray that I am the last victim of an atomic or hydrogen bomb."[68] That, sadly, seems highly unlikely.

Still, one reason why the Castle Bravo test – 1000 times more powerful than the Hiroshima bomb – lives on in the collective memory was that the release of energy was dramatically greater than expected, among other things igniting a fire on a different island 37 kilometers away and spreading a radioactive plume much further afield than originally predicted. It was a reflection of the nuclear paranoia of the time that the test was allowed to go ahead in adverse weather conditions because of very real fears that delays might give the Russians an edge in the nuclear arms race.

The quest for a global ban

Whatever their intention, such tests also lit other distant fires in the political realm. Growing public concern over the following decade helped to catalyze the process that led to the 01963 Partial Test Ban Treaty – banning nuclear tests in the atmosphere, underwater, or in space. Conspicuously, though, France and China refused to sign, a key reason why the following years saw regular (and increasingly violent) clashes between the French authorities and Greenpeace over nuclear testing in the Pacific.

A much bigger step toward non-proliferation of nuclear weapons came with the signing in 01968 of the Nuclear Non-Proliferation Treaty (NPT).[69] This time around non-nuclear weapon states were banned from possessing, manufacturing, or acquiring nuclear weapons or other nuclear explosive devices. All signatories, significantly, and this included nuclear weapon states, had to commit to the goal of total nuclear disarmament.

Paradoxically, given that Prime Minister Jawaharlal Nehru of India (who in this area would probably qualify as a proto-Zeronaut) had proposed a total ban on all nuclear tests as far back as 01954, India refused to sign the NPT – arguing (perhaps understandably) that it discriminated against non-nuclear states.

The logical next step was to ban all nuclear explosions in all environments, whether for military or civilian purposes. This was the goal of the 01996 Comprehensive Nuclear Test Ban Treaty (CTBT) adopted by the United Nations but which has not yet come into force. And one key reason for that failure is that most nuclear states are desperately uneasy about abandoning their nuclear arsenals in a world where these terrible weapons cannot be dis-invented. As Thomas Schelling memorably put it in 02006: "Short of universal brain surgery, nothing can erase the memory of weapons and how to build them."[70]

The US did sign the treaty, but has yet to take the necessary next step to ratify it, insisting on a long list of caveats. Among other things, the Americans (and again perhaps understandably) want an exhaustive survey of stockpiles of nuclear weapons worldwide; intensive (but for many intrusive) monitoring and intelligence gathering on nuclear activities in other countries; ongoing research that will allow the country to attract, train, and retain the necessary experts needed for keeping a nuclear defense edge; and – ultimately – the ability to resume tests in the event that the treaty is deemed to be failing.

Who can blame those who are keen to cling on to their nuclear weapons at a time when rogue states such as North Korea and not always obviously rational states such as Iran have been racing to develop their own nuclear arsenals? Particularly when politicians such as Iran's President Mahmoud Ahmadinejad have threatened to wipe other states (in his case Israel) off the map?

As we briefly review the case for and against zeroing nuclear weapons, it is worth remembering – and this is a truly extraordinary fact – that not a single nuclear weapon state "has an employee, let alone an inter-agency group, tasked full time with figuring out what would be required to verifiably decommission all its nuclear weapons".[71]

The case for zeroing

The core case for zero is that the spread of nuclear weapons to new states, and then indirectly to terrorist groups, will be made less likely if the US and other nuclear-armed countries are seen to be working toward disarmament – and to be doing so in good faith.[72]

The for-zero lobby notes that those who hark back to the us-versus-them simplicity of the Cold War, and imagine we can work our way back to that sort of nuclear lock-in, misunderstand the painful reality. Either we get rid of nuclear weapons entirely, they argue, or we face a world with many more nuclear-armed states and entities.

But what about the inconvenient truth that what has already been invented cannot be dis-invented, that we cannot stuff the nuclear genie back into the bottle? People such as Scott Sagan note that industrial-scale gas chambers have not been dis-invented, but would not be tolerated today. And that CFCs have likewise not been erased from the collective memory by some form of mass brain surgery, but that we have nonetheless discontinued their use in the interest of the health of the stratospheric ozone layer – and those of us who depend upon its ability to screen out deadly ultraviolet radiation.

Even the most ardent pro-zero advocates, however, recognize that none of this is going to work unless there is the sort of global forensic capability needed to track nuclear materials, particularly those in unfriendly hands – and to identify the source of nuclear materials where they are diverted and used in anger by states and non-state actors, including terrorists. Furthermore, we will need the capacity to rein in the nuclear ambitions of people such as the late Kim Il-sung of North Korea and Mahmoud Ahmadinejad of Iran, something that the world has singularly failed to do, at least to date.

The case against zeroing

Those who oppose zeroing nuclear weapons wonder why the pros want to get rid of the weapons that they see as having provided nearly 70 years of relative peace? They also challenge the assumption that a failure to return to zero means that we will see many more countries embracing nukes. People such as Kenneth Waltz have noted that since the end of World War II, nuclear-armed states have never fought one another. Those who "like peace", he insisted, "should love nuclear weapons".[73]

New nuclear states, he argued, are generally greeted with "dire forebodings". We ask whether the government is stable? Whether the rulers are sensible? Yet, however worrying the answers may be, he observed that "every new nation, however bad its previous reputation, has behaved exactly like all the old ones. The effect of having nuclear weapons overwhelms the character of the states that possess them. Countries with nuclear weapons, no matter how mean and irrational their leaders may seem to be, no matter how unstable their governments appear to be, do not launch major conventional attacks on other countries, let alone nuclear ones."

Nuclear weapons give leaders pause, as the Cuban missile crisis showed in spades. The problem, Waltz insisted, is that "no road leads from a world with a small number of nuclear-weapons states to a world with none".

And what would happen if world leaders somehow "blundered into an agreement to go to zero?" What would a sensible leader do, he wondered? His answer was simple: he or she would *cheat*. "Nuclear weapons are small and light. They are easy to hide and easy to move. Nuclear warheads can be placed in small vans or small boats and sent across borders or into harbors." Who, in such circumstances, is going to want to drop their defenses?

Other forms of proliferation

Similar arguments for and against zeroing are heard elsewhere. Nuclear weapons are far from the only weapons of mass destruction – and similar arguments for and against can be deployed for each of the others. The invasion of Iraq in the so-called second Gulf War was in large part justified by the claim – largely spurious, as it happened – that the late President Saddam Hussein had built an impressive WMD stockpile, something he had worked hard to make the Western powers believe.

Remember the range of weaponry that United Nations Chief Inspector Hans Blix was charged with looking for? They included such things as anthrax and VX nerve agent. I remember being part of US military briefings at the World Economic Forum in Davos ahead of the second Gulf War where the threat of anthrax attacks, in particular, was presented as pretty much guaranteed.

To be honest, I was inclined to believe the claims – for the following reasons. Some three decades ago, I began visiting biotechnology firms around the world, ending up visiting – and, in some cases, working with – well over 100 of them. In 01985 I published a book, *The Gene Factory*, summarizing what I had learned to date.[74] My editor, the formidable Gail Rebuck, helped beat the book into shape – including a concluding section called "Beating ploughshares into swords".

Here I noted that germ warfare, once described as "public health in reverse", already had a long and dishonorable history stretching back at least to the fourteenth century, when the Tartars catapulted plague victims into the besieged Crimean town of Kaffa. Far from beating its swords into plowshares and its spears into pruning hooks, I concluded: "our species has displayed a unique facility for turning everyday tools into deadly weapons of war".

I quoted Robert Harris and Jeremy Paxman's book *A Higher Form of Killing*[75] to the effect that "the chlorine that poisoned our grandfathers [or perhaps we should now say great-grandfathers] at Ypres came from the synthetic dye industry and was available due to our [great] grandmothers' desire for brightly colored dresses. Modern nerve gases were originally designed to help mankind by killing beetles and lice", but in military hands they became "insecticides for people."

Most worrying of all, in respect of the potential for the biotech industry to be abused, I summarized a conversation I had had a few years earlier with one of my favorite science fiction authors, Frank Herbert. Best known as the author of the *Dune* series of novels, he had recently published a book called *The White Plague* – in which a rogue molecular biologist developed a lethal pathogen that sought out and attached itself to the human chromosome in such a way that it killed only females.

Incredible? Not to Herbert. He told me that he had recently rethought his numbers. "After setting a basic cost for a relatively sophisticated lab at around $200,000 to $300,000", he recalled, "I did a little more research. This was after the book was published. I found that if you go into the surplus and used markets, my estimate was very high. I know of a surplus $6000 centrifuge that went for $17.95." So his molecular biologist no longer had to be a multi-millionaire to afford the entry ticket to the genetic arms race.

Recall that the Aum Shinrikyo cult which released deadly Sarin nerve gas on the Tokyo subway in 01995 had originally tried to track down stray nuclear weapons in a fragmenting Russia. Luckily it failed. Even so, the attack killed 12 commuters, seriously injuring 54 and affecting almost 1000 more. But just think how much worse it might have been if they had been able to get their hands on a dirty bomb, let alone a full-blown A-bomb.

Clearly, even if the nuclear genie is stuffed back in its bottle and somehow kept there, there are other bottles – and other genies – to be taken into consideration as we seek to go to zero on WMDs.

Zeronaut targets proliferation

No doubt Jeff Skoll has heard much on the proliferation challenge, from all sides. But as a New Economy billionaire, having been founding president of eBay during its heyday, he not only believes that zeroing is possible but is putting some of his money where his mouth is.

I first came across him as the founder of the Skoll Foundation for Social Entrepreneurship and, to declare an interest, the foundation awarded me $1 million in 02006 to explore ways to build bridges between social innovators and mainstream business. In retrospect, the work thus funded, both at SustainAbility and later at Volans, played a critical part in spurring my progression into the world of the Zeronauts.

In addition to his role as a film producer at Participant Media, Skoll launched the Skoll Global Threats Fund in 02009 – designed to tackle "global threats imperiling humanity by seeking solutions, strengthening alliances, and spurring the actions needed to safeguard the future". The initial focus has been on five global issues that, if unchecked, "could bring the world to its knees: climate change, water scarcity, pandemics, nuclear proliferation and Middle East conflict".[76]

One of the initiatives that the fund has got involved in is the international Global Zero movement, launched late in 02008. This soon included more than 300 political, military, business, civil, and faith leaders, as well as hundreds of thousands of citizens. The aim has been to work for the phased, verified elimination of all nuclear weapons worldwide.

Global Zero members believe that the "only way to eliminate the nuclear threat – including proliferation and nuclear terrorism – is to stop the spread of nuclear weapons, secure all nuclear materials and eliminate all nuclear weapons: global zero".

The *Global Zero Action Plan* has called in its first phase for the US and Russia to cut their arsenals to 1000 total warheads each, all other countries with nuclear weapons to freeze their arsenals, and the international community to conduct an all-out global effort to block the spread of nuclear weapons. These steps would be followed by the first multilateral negotiations in history for stockpile reductions by all nuclear weapons countries.

Early in 02010 the second Global Zero Summit convened 200 leaders from around the world. Presidents Obama and Medvedev and UN Secretary-General Ban Ki-moon sent strong statements of support, including President Obama's declaration that Global Zero "will always have a partner in me and my administration". You wonder, though, what he was really thinking.

In partnership with Jeff Skoll's Academy Award winning team that produced *An Inconvenient Truth*, Global Zero produced *Countdown to Zero*, a chilling documentary which opened in theaters across the US in the summer of 02010. In tandem, Global Zero launched a three-year campaign to bring all nuclear weapons countries together to negotiate cuts in arsenals worldwide for the first time in history. This would require the US and Russia to first agree to further reduce their Cold War stockpiles and the leaders of all nuclear weapons countries to commit to multilateral negotiations in 02014.

The *Global Zero Action Plan* aims to cut all arsenals by 50 percent, followed by final negotiations to eliminate all remaining nuclear weapons by 02030. In terms of process, Global Zero planned to build international and domestic political support for negotiations (initially targeting the 02012 presidential campaigns in the US, France, and Russia) by combining the influence of eminent leaders, media, online and grassroots outreach, cutting-edge policy development, and direct dialogue with governments.

For the moment, and this is a personal view, it is possible to imagine certain types of WMD – weaponized smallpox, for example – being consigned to the dustbin of history. And a sustainable world of 9 billion people by mid-century is likely to be impossible without effective action to drive the proliferation of key types of WMD toward zero. But, ultimately, it will fall to political leaders to decide on a course toward a world free of such weapons, including nuclear bombs.

My bet is that there will always be hold-outs and, therefore, excuses for inaction or partial solutions. Paradoxically, our best chance of getting a WMD-free future is probably our worst nightmare. And that is a nuclear exchange or a terrorist outrage on a currently unimaginable scale. Some people may choose to place their faith in Steven Pinker's analysis, articulated in *The Better Angels of Our Nature*,[77] and suggesting that even the horrific carnage of the twentieth century – when seen from a safe distance – is part of a worldwide trend toward less violence. In the meantime, however, we can help to reduce the risk that nuclear, chemical, and biological weapons will be used in anger and at scale by addressing the system conditions – among them the other four Ps spotlighted here – that threaten to bring our global pot to the boil.

Box 7.7

How Zeronauts tackle proliferation

The Global Zero Action Plan provides a useful framework whose last phase, from 02024 to 02030, envisages the "phased, verified, proportionate dismantlement of all nuclear arsenals to zero total warheads by 02030". But I can't help thinking that we are going to need the present-day equivalent of the Daigo Fukuryū Maru incident, on an altogether larger scale and very likely on multiple fronts, to force our leaders to push the WMD needle to anywhere near zero. Among possible action points that Zeronauts would promote:

- It's all too easy to ignore the threat of proliferation, except perhaps when governments constrain our ability to act through their attempts to cut the risks.
- So, first, ensure that it's on the organizational radar screen. One way to keep all of this live is to track the development of the Global Zero Action Plan and similar initiatives.
- Recognize the links to the other 4Ps – for example, the evolution of modern biotechnology means that we are likely to see the proliferation of novel biological and genetic weapons, including man-made pandemics.
- Understand that even mundane products such as fertilizer and Ryder rental vans can be turned into WMDs, as in Oklahoma City in 01995 or in Oslo in 02011.
- Support improved, more effective exchanges of information – and the tagging and tracking of potentially problematic materials and systems.
- Prepare your own contingency plans for when things, perhaps inevitably, go wrong.
- And, once again, support your local – or at least your favorite – Zeronauts in this space.

IV

BEYOND ZERO

LING

On the other side of zero, infinity.

LING

8

Ambassadors from the Future

In order to move from incremental to transformative change, we must embrace wider framings, deeper insights, higher targets, and longer time scales. We investigate some ways in which leading Zeronauts are pushing change in relevant directions, with cases drawn from a spectrum of human activity – from water profligacy to human genital mutilation. If we learn from these pioneers, the twenty-first century could be our best yet.

An ambassador, they used to say, is a good man sent abroad to lie for his country. We mean something different here. Zeronauts are ambassadors in that they spotlight, represent, and seek to address challenges that are likely to matter to future generations.

But not everyone who buys into the need to think about future generations thinks that zero language is the right way to catalyze the necessary breakthroughs. Careful, Paul Hawken warned me, as we brunched together in San Francisco: zero, he advised, is not aspirational. Who, he wondered, ever dreams of zero?

True, and back to Paul's point, most people, most of the time, want more good things, not less bad things. But Paul's own work, including his book *The Ecology of Commerce*,[1] which helped to trigger an epiphany in on-his-way-to-becoming-a-Zeronaut Ray Anderson, underscores just how many aspects of our modern economies and societies we now need to drive to zero.

Strikingly, Paul went on to describe how he had written the zero targets into the milestone speech Wal-Mart CEO Lee Scott made in the wake of Hurricane Katrina. And then he explained how he had cautioned Ray about adopting Interface's "Mission Zero" branding when nearby Coca-Cola had launched its Coke Zero low calorie diet drink. Ray pondered the issue – and then decided to push ahead. As he told me shortly before his death, "'Zero footprint', expressed as reaching the top of 'Mount Sustainability', has been the most powerfully motivating initiative I have ever seen in 55 years of business." Much of the appeal, though, unquestionably came from Ray himself.

At one level, thinking about how to move toward, even beyond, zero impact is no more than a thought experiment – but it is one that growing numbers of innovators, entrepreneurs, intrapreneurs, investors, and policy-makers must undertake. In some ways you can see zeroing as the price of entry to a more sustainable economy by the middle of the twenty-first century. On this side of the Sustainability Barrier, we face a proliferation of risks that threaten the very foundations of our civilization – whereas on the other side of zero there is a different world, potentially an almost infinite realm of opportunity.

For the most part, meanwhile, we remain trapped – and our leaders even more so – in old ways, traditional mindsets, time-expired behaviors, and obsolete cultures. It is way past time to rethink, reframe, and reimagine. As the original quality champions insisted, focusing on zero outcomes is not about being perfect. Instead, it is about changing our perspectives, the way we frame challenges.

As I explored the zero agenda, I kept coming across other sorts of people with problems that they want to drive to zero – where market solutions seem unlikely to deliver the desired outcomes. Instead, the answers are more likely to be found in human values and cultures. Three of these Ambassadors from the Future are profiled in Boxes 8.2, 8.3, and 8.4, with their target areas spanning water profligacy, hunger and obesity, and the excruciatingly horrible subject of female genital cutting.

One of my favorite Zeronauts is Hunter Lovins, now president of Natural Capital Solutions, and one of the pioneers of the Natural Capitalism movement.

Table 8.1 Incremental versus transformative change

	Status quo		Future quo
Change:	Incremental	>	**Transformative**
Scope:	Narrow	>	**Wide**
Analysis:	Shallow	>	**Deep**
Ambitions:	Low	>	**High**
Time scales:	Short	>	**Long**
Strategy:	Alone	>	**Together**

I asked her to sum up the current situation – and the necessary next steps. Here's her reply, which echoes some of the things Herman Kahn said to me many moons ago (see pp.204–5):

Humankind and with us much of the rest of life as we know it on this planet are headed over a cliff. If you're on a bus headed for a cliff with little desire to go over it, the first step to survival is to slow the bus. The next task is to bring it to a stop. Then you'll have time to decide which alternative route may make more sense.

Some on the bus who have left behind an unpleasant past are looking out the windows, admiring the view and hollering to go faster. Others are discussing alternative maps, and the aspirational advantages of these dreams. Quite understandable; but the fact that the bus is accelerating and the cliff is nearing makes these conversations a luxury we can't afford just now.

Some of us are working on the brakes, and single-mindedly focusing on mechanical systems to apply these brakes in time. We're trying first to buy time, but really the goal is to get to zero. Zero speed and zero distance over the cliff. Our work in no way denigrates the dreams of the others, or the enjoyment of those who rightly remark that their prior locations were suboptimal.

The aspirational ones will have their day, Inshallah. But it is not this day. Job one is survival, which means stopping the bus. It means doing it in time, and it means that those who criticize the teams working on brakes are actually part of the problem.

Once the bus has stopped, we must set a new course. We must manage all organizations (companies, civil society, and governments) to be restorative of all forms of capital, human and natural, as well as manufactured and financial. Doing this well will be the foundation of any future worth living. Other forms of management (i.e. business as usual) are really cheater capitalism, impoverishing the 99 percent to benefit the 1 percent. That's bad capitalism, and should be labeled as such.

Hunter's full response can be found at www.zeronauts.com.

One conclusion seems unavoidable. Any leader wanting to drive the sort of systemic changes spotlighted in the previous chapter needs to improve his or her "future quotient". While finishing off *The Zeronauts*, I was also working on a new Volans report, *The Future Quotient*,[2] with the help of JWT, Atkins, The Dow Chemical Company, MindTime Technologies, and the Shell Foundation. The concept, which had flashed into my mind in the midst of a brainstorm at JWT's Knightsbridge offices in London, was that – just as we have measures of IQ, emotional intelligence, and ecological intelligence – we now need a measurement of our future readiness.

Ideally, the future quotient (FQ) would become a universally accepted measure of our ability to think and act in the context of significantly stretched time horizons, out to and including the interests of future generations. The shift from incremental to truly transformative change, moving from today's status quo to what we might dub the "future quo", requires us to be more ambitious in terms of our scope, analysis, targets, and time scales (see Box 8.1). In the end, anyone willingly possessed of – and willing to apply – a high FQ can act as an ambassador for a better future, whether or not they choose to do so.

Then, as I was trying to work out how to conclude *The Zeronauts*, I was invited to a small gathering at which actor Edward Fox recited from memory the entire second quartet from T. S. Eliot's *Four Quartets*, "East Coker". It was quite literally mind-bending. And that led me to buy and reread this astonishingly powerful sequence of poems, including the last one, "Little Gidding".[3] And there I found this extraordinarily serendipitous line:

> Where is the summer, the unimaginable
> Zero summer?
>
> T. S. Eliot, "Little Gidding", Four Quartets

The poet, standing in the midst of "midwinter spring", "suspended in time", "in windless cold", asks where is "the unimaginable Zero summer?" Written in 01941, in the midst of the fires, rubble, and ashes of German air raids, who now among us really knows what Eliot meant here by "Zero"; but for me the line neatly captured where we are with the first wave of Zeronauts. They are playing against often-impossible odds, thinking the unthinkable, attempting the undoable. They dream of brighter times, but have no way of knowing whether or when they will come.

To get a sense of what the transformation might require of us, try asking a question that I have often toyed with in recent decades. What would future generations want us to do today if they could speak to and advise us? Who and what would they vote for in today's world, what would they invest in? Trying to picture myself as an "Ambassador from the Future" has sometimes helped me to decide where to stand on particular issues. For me, Zeronauts are high-ranking Ambassadors from the Future, representing the interests of people who will be affected by our choices – and yet have little or no say in the process.

As they have done, we need to find new ways to help our own brains, the teams we work with and the organizations we are part of to expand their horizons and sense of possibility. We need to link up with people we would never normally talk to: as Kevin Kelly once memorably put it, a network is a "Possibility Factory".

And that is what we have been aiming to develop with Deloitte Innovation as we have sought partners in the "Zero Hub" – modeled on the stages of a journey into space and back (see Box 0.3, pp.12–13). The idea is that the participants, over a series of intensive sessions, would prepare, "blast off", operate, and observe in a different space, then re-enter reality and prepare to share and apply their newfound insights and newly acquired tools. A parallel initiative Volans has been involved in is Nike's "Race to Zero" (see Box 8.1).

Box 8.1

The Race to Zero

How do you get competitive companies to detoxify their supply chains, fast? One answer: you turn it into a competitive issue. That was what Greenpeace decided to do as it evolved its astonishingly effective "Detox" campaign, designed to spur major brands to bring pressure to bear on suppliers and on the governments that are responsible for regulating the safety, health, environmental, and human rights performance of those suppliers.[4]

"As much as 70 percent of China's rivers, lakes and reservoirs are affected by water pollution", Greenpeace asserted. "During our recent investigations, Greenpeace identified links between a number of major clothing brands - including the sportswear giants Nike and Adidas and the fast-fashion retailer H&M - and textile factories in China that are releasing hazardous chemicals into our rivers."[5]

As the pressure built, a number of brands announced that they would seek to comply with Greenpeace's demands. Even more interestingly, however, a number of them began to explore whether there were ways that they could work together to drive the agenda in politically challenging countries such as China.

And so it was that I came to be one of the moderators – alongside Stephanie Draper from Forum for the Future and Michael Sadowski from SustainAbility – of a meeting at Nike's Hilversum European headquarters in Holland. This attracted over 20 industry participants, plus half a dozen key Greenpeace campaigners. The outcomes included a joint industry Roadmap for zero discharges of toxic chemicals by 2020.[6] Soon after, six brands had declared their support for the Roadmap, including Li-Ning, the most important Chinese competitor in this market.

Normally such industry initiatives are defensive, designed to ward off NGOs or other pressures. In this case, however, the spirit seemed different – with a real enthusiasm to engage the issues, though coupled with a real anxiety about the politics likely to be involved. Still, I confess that when I heard about Li-Ning's participation, some part of my brain wondered whether this might not be a subtle Chinese way of learning about some of the zero-oriented market pressures the giant manufacturing country will face in the coming decade.

As such initiatives evolve, my hope is that we will find better ways to future-proof our organizations, economies, and societies by helping them adapt to oncoming realities, and by helping to shape those realities in ways that favor more sustainable outcomes. I can imagine a day when, just as we now have to give our fingerprints when we pass through immigration in some countries, businesses are "future-printed", and the resulting data used to invest in – or disinvest from – them.

Future-printing will likely involve a growing array of tests and processes designed to measure – and boost – an organization's future quotient.[7] My bet is that among them will be techniques, some of which we introduce in *The Future Quotient*, designed to help decision-takers and policy-makers to expand their minds by going wider, deeper, higher, and longer. Let's look at each of those dimensions in turn.

Going wider

So, first, in times of stress and uncertainty, it is a fundamental human response to hunker down, to close in – human, but (at exactly the moment when we should be opening out our horizons) also potentially extremely dangerous. We need to think and act in a wider frame.

Think of Greenpeace International's decision to appoint South African anti-poverty activist Kumi Naidoo as their new head. Brilliant, as is their new framing of the social impacts of climate change as "climate apartheid".[8] As Green for All founder Van Jones put it: "The environmental movement is global now, and you need someone who can speak to people in Asia, Latin America, Africa. That's easier when you have a former anti-apartheid leader sitting across the table."

Years back, I took part in an Institute of Directors panel session at the Royal Albert Hall in London, in front of some 3000 company directors. At one point the moderator asked where I thought the sustainability agenda began and ended. I said that I could see a growing number of ways to make the agenda intelligible and manageable, but that if you embraced it with too great an enthusiasm it could be a bit like taking LSD – where everything in the universe becomes immediately and immensely significant.

She retorted that it sounded as if I knew what I was talking about, and when I said I did, it brought the house down. But these days, I continued to say, I use different mind-expanding techniques – among them, in recent times, talking to people whom I consider to be among the first wave of Zeronauts, including the sort of people flagged in Box 3.1 (see pp.44–6, and in boxes 8.2–8.4).

Box 8.2

I want to zero | Water profligacy

Leaving Earth gives you a very different perspective on the world and our future, says former Astronaut and Cosmonaut Jerry Linenger.

WHAT: Water is the essence of life. When exploring other planets, the top priority is to probe for water. Does the planet have accessible water? If so, human life can be supported; we can extend our presence beyond planet Earth and onto another heavenly body. Here on the planet, freshwater resources, ever so limited, are also the key to our survivability. We need to recognize, as people of planet Earth, that without clean freshwater access, we will perish.

WHY: Nearly one sixth of the world's population – more than one billion people – do not have access to safe drinking water. This results in over 3.5 million deaths each year.

The root cause of many conflicts today, and the predicted cause of future wars, is water rights issues. From my perch in the heavens aboard the Russian Space station Mir, it was striking to observe just how limited our freshwater resources were, and how human civilization (indicated by proxy with lights of cities glowing at night) clung to water sources – rivers and lakes surrounded by lights, the interior of dry continents dark and abandoned.

WHERE: After spaceflights, perspective change is the greatest gift that I brought back with me to Earth. We are one people, one planet, and we all share a precious and limited resource: water. Can we not all agree that as human beings we should all be united in the goal of protecting, of tending with the greatest of care, and of finding common ground around the issue of fresh water? Perhaps it is the one cause that can truly take us beyond our borders and unite us as humans, as inhabitants of this Earth.

WHO: The farmer in Iowa, the city dweller in Rio de Janeiro, the villager in the outback of Australia, the banker in London, the factory worker in Shanghai. Everyone on the planet, and I mean everyone, depends upon water for their life.

WHEN: Now. Act now to protect the essence of life. Value it beyond diamonds and pearls, beyond ideology, beyond political power. Without it, we all wither away.

HOW: By refusing to be partisan over water issues. It is a cause that should unite us all: corporate leader with environmental activist; drought-stricken farmer in sub-Sahel Africa and slum dweller in Cairo. Everyone needs to bend, to find common solutions, to drop their self-righteous "better than you" posturing.

JERRY LINENGER is a former Astronaut and Cosmonaut and hopes that water can serve as a solvent to dissolve the differences between us here on Earth. See examples of what global water advocates (www.circleofblue.org), corporations (www.thecoca-colacompany.com/citizenship/water_main.html), and local communities (www.gtbay.org) are doing.

Someone I haven't spoken to, but whom I see as very much part of all this, is UN Secretary-General Ban Ki-moon. Addressing the 02011 World Economic Forum summit in Davos, he warned that twentieth-century economic and business models increasingly look suicidal.[9] So perhaps Arnold Toynbee is going to be right after all, with our civilization cutting its own throat? For most of the last century, Ban said, using shockingly blunt language, "economic growth was fuelled by what seemed to be a certain truth: the abundance of natural resources. We mined our way to growth. We burned our way to prosperity. We believed in consumption without consequences."

No doubt more than a few delegates sat stunned in disbelief as he continued: "Those days are gone. In the twenty-first century, supplies are running short and the global thermostat is running high. Climate change is also showing us that the old model is more than obsolete. It has rendered it extremely dangerous. Over time, that model is a recipe for national disaster. It is a global suicide pact."

But he didn't leave it there. "So what do we do in this current challenging situation?" he asked. "How do we create growth in a resource-constrained environment? How do we lift people out of poverty while protecting the planet and ecosystems that support economic growth? How do we regain the balance? All of this requires rethinking."

Switching to a more positive note, he continued: "The sustainable development agenda is the growth agenda for the twenty-first century. To get there, we need your participation, your initiative. We need you to step up. Spark innovation. Lead by action. Invest in energy efficiency and renewable energy for those who need them most – your future customers. Expand clean energy access in developing countries – your markets of tomorrow."

Echoing President Reagan's 01987 speech in Berlin,[10] he concluded: "Embed sustainability principles into your strategies, your operations, your supply chains. To government leaders sitting here and elsewhere around the world, send the right signals to build the green economy. Together, let us tear down the walls. The walls between the development agenda and the climate agenda. Between business, Government and civil society. Between global security and global sustainability. It is good business, good politics and good for society."

Going deeper

Second, in times of stress and uncertainty our thinking goes shallow – just as our breathing does. But not everyone succumbs. Ban Ki-moon was encouraging leaders to go wider in their thinking, to see elements of emergent reality that normally get drowned out in the intense background noise of day-to-day business and governance. But he also implied that we must go much deeper, understanding science and the patterns of history to a much greater degree than we currently achieve.

There is much we can learn from quality management, spotlighted in Chapters 5 and 6, but this next phase of our collective history will be less about system improvement than about system change. If you want to know what this means, try reading *Why the West Rules – for Now*, by Ian Morris, already discussed in the "Civilizations" section of Chapter 4, or any of James Lovelock's books, particularly earlier ones such as *Gaia: The Practical Science of Planetary Medicine*.[11]

Leading Zeronauts – think of Gunter Pauli of ZERI, Karl-Henrik Robèrt of The Natural Step, or Mathis Wackernagel and Susan Burns of the Global Footprint Network – would argue that we are headed into an era where we will be increasingly sensitive to the nature and scale of our ecological footprints. That now seems inevitable. As a result, others have been working on new ways of calculating the environmental profit and loss of companies such as Puma (Jochen Zeitz), the new economics of ecosystems and biodiversity (Pavan Sukhdev), or the critical, rapidly evolving science of biomimicry (Janine Benyus).

Box 8.3

I want to zero | Hunger and obesity

The world seems caught between the rock of hunger and the hard place of obesity, both of which need to be zeroed, says Ellen Gustafson.

WHAT: The global food system, the source of food and nutrition for everyone on the planet, is fundamentally broken. There are one billion people hungry and one billion people overweight, an agricultural system in the West that overproduces a number of commodity crops, and an agricultural system in the developing world that does not adequately feed the population.

WHY: People function best when they are well nourished and have productive livelihoods, and societies are safer and grow better when people are healthier. Our current food system ravages the environment as much as it's ravaging our bodies and has created a slew of negative externalities for our planet. The current mechanisms to fight hunger and promote food security often cause people to move right from hunger to obesity and the associated diseases.

WHERE: Our entire planet. From Mississippi, the US state with the highest obesity rate of over 34 percent and where over 18 percent of households are food insecure, to India, where over 50 percent of children under three are undernourished and where over 30 percent of the population is obese, to the African continent where one third of African women and one quarter of African men are estimated to be overweight, and the World Health Organization predicts that will rise to 41 percent and 30 percent, respectively, in the next ten years, while still over 30 percent of African people are undernourished.

WHO: The one billion hungry, one billion undernourished, and one billion overweight on the Earth, and the rest of us who might be teetering on the brink of either hunger or obesity.

WHEN: The next 30 years. We can start now to work toward a vision of a healthier, more sustainable food system for ourselves and our planet.

HOW: By reframing the conversation around our tables to be about a better food system, not just about "ending hunger" or "fighting obesity". By focusing on efforts that ensure nutritious food for all people, not just calories for the hungry and diets for the overweight, we can focus resources on the systemic changes that need to be made.

ELLEN GUSTAFSON is founder/executive director of the 30 Project (www.30project.org).

Many Zeronauts work in several fields simultaneously. Think of Al Gore, a leading politician who dug deeper into climate science with his linked film and book, both called *An Inconvenient Truth*.[12] In parallel, he has worked to build a grassroots political movement with the Alliance for Climate Protection, and explored the dynamics of sustainable capitalism with Generation Investment Management – the investment fund he founded with David Blood.

Despite such efforts, however, from the perspective of future generations, our current spending on solutions with potential to break through the Sustainability Barrier is ill-matched with the nature and scale of the systemic challenge. Why, for example, do we not have something along the lines of a globally funded Sustainability Skunk Works, mirroring the Lockheed facility of that name that helped the US to establish such a commanding lead in aerospace? Or even a global network of such facilities?

Perhaps counter-intuitively, to break free from the stranglehold of climate-destabilizing fossil fuels we need the equivalent of a new high-energy space race. One way in which future generations will access solar energy will be via giant solar power stations in orbit around Earth. As one of the pioneers, photonics expert Stephen Sweeney, has put it: "The solar power we can capture in space has an efficiency of 70 percent. On earth, it weakens to 15 percent because of cloud cover, atmospheric transmissions, day and night, and seasonal variations."[13] Those involved see this as the Holy Grail of renewable energy. "This will be 24/7 energy with zero pollution that can be transmitted anywhere", said Peter Sage, cofounder of Space Energy, one of the firms now competing to tap solar energy in space.

Meanwhile, the uncomfortable truth is that, instead, we have a kaleidoscope of initiatives, each working on a piece of the puzzle, disarticulated, fragmented, weaker than they need to be. And in parallel, the internet, some argue, is rewiring our brains in unhelpful ways, immersing us in the "shallows of distraction".[14] The UN, meanwhile, despite its secretary-general's brave words, is a shadow of what it would need to be to drive and shape the necessary transformations.

But at least you can say that for every problem spotlighted earlier, there are several fascinating initiatives struggling to evolve solutions. Take the loss of soils flagged by Lester Brown – and then consider the work of Zeronaut Allan Savory, whose motto might be zero desertification.[15]

Savory focuses on reversing land degradation in a manner that makes, rather than costs, money. But, as he willingly admits, his early failures were equally impressive. Serving as a member of parliament during Zimbabwe's civil war, and as leader of the opposition to the ruling party headed by Ian Smith, he was exiled in 01979, emigrating to the US. There he cofounded Holistic Management International with his wife, Jody Butterfield.

In 01992 they formed a second non-profit organization near Victoria Falls, the Africa Centre for Holistic Management, donating a ranch that would serve as a learning site for people all over Africa. Since then thousands of land, livestock, and wildlife managers have been able to demonstrate consistent results following the approach he called holistic management.

But how to reverse the global destruction of soils? Savory argues: "In terrestrial environments there are four processes governing the functioning of life – nutrient cycling, water cycling, biological community dynamics and solar energy flow to life above and below ground. The key to the health of these processes, that really function as one, is governed by the fate of the surface of the soil – whether it is covered or exposed, basically."

He continues: "It helps to think of soil as a living organism covered with skin like a human – we can live with a certain percentage of our skin damaged, but if too high a percentage is, we die. So, too, does soil and thus most life." And the key to recovery? "Full functioning of all ecosystem processes, in areas of the Earth that are perennially humid, both terrestrial and aquatic, always occurs when we apply the tool of rest (no human disturbance of any sort). This is why the environment recovered surrounding abandoned civilizations in humid environments."

As population pressures build, so it becomes increasingly important – but ever harder – to put the ideas of people such as Allan Savory into practice. At the same time, it becomes ever clearer that we have to shift public mindsets and even behaviors to cultural change. Unless our societies can raise their sights and ambitions, mobilizing along the lines outlined by Lester Brown in Chapter 4, our chances of getting beyond 02100 in good order are precariously slim.

Going higher

Our third reflex action in conditions of growing stress and uncertainty is to become more pragmatic. As our confidence shrivels, we set our objectives lower. And all this at a time when history suggests that tomorrow's eventual winners will now be raising their sights and embracing stretch targets – often because they are at the edges of the current system, with little to lose.

For a previous book, *The Power of Unreasonable People*, I turned back to the Irish playwright George Bernard Shaw. His memorable formulation on the dynamics of transformative change is worth repeating here: "The reasonable man adapts himself to the world: the unreasonable one persists in trying to adapt the world to himself. Therefore all progress depends on the unreasonable man."

What Zeronauts such as Ray Anderson, GE CEO Jeff Immelt, or Unilever CEO Paul Polman have been doing often strikes their colleagues and competitors as not just unreasonable, but at times even borderline insane. Time alone will tell who is right, and there will be numerous failures along the way, some of them spectacular – with the rate and scale of failure guaranteed to accelerate as we move into an era of creative disruption and destruction. But without such bold stage 2 experimentation we will never break through the Sustainability Barrier.

Our willingness to embrace the wider Race to Zero will only be one dimension of success in surviving and thriving in these market conditions; but my money is on people who are following in the path blazed by people such as TQM pioneer Phil Crosby and pushing for zero.

Among them I would list Amory Lovins (whose negawatt agenda showed long ago that demand-side management has as much potential to solve our energy problems as new supply options), Larry Brilliant (whose work on smallpox showed how even the direst problems can be soluble), Bill Gates (who has picked up the torch in relation to a growing spectrum of diseases), entrepreneur Richard Branson (who has backed the Carbon War Room), and electric vehicle pioneers Shai Agassi (CEO of Better Place) and Carlos Ghosn (CEO of Renault–Nissan), alongside companies that have formally embraced zero – notably Herman Miller (see p.163).

Box 8.4

I want to zero | Female genital cutting

Culture change is at the heart of breaking the Sustainability Barrier, including improvements in health and well-being. Here's a gender crime that must follow foot-binding into history, says Julia Lalla-Maharajh.

WHAT: Female genital cutting (FGC) affects three million girls, each and every year, in Africa alone. The average age when they undergo the cut is between five to eight years. Over 140 million women live with the devastating impacts. It predates organized religion, having started in Egypt more than 2000 years ago. It happens because it is a way of controlling women. In spite of its severe impacts, there is little response to it from agencies, governments, or communities – because it is taboo.

WHY: It is such a problem because once a girl is cut, her entire life changes. FGC happens without anesthetic, ranging from a small nick in the clitoris, through to extensive removal of all external genitalia, with the wound then sewn up so that when it heals, a hard plug of scar tissue means the body literally forms its own chastity belt. This hard plug then is cut open for intercourse, and also each time a child is born. This leads to constant infections. The number of girls and women who have died from FGC is unknown.

WHERE: It happens in 28 countries across Africa and in parts of the Middle East (Yemen, Oman, the United Arab Emirates, Kurdistan), parts of the Far East (Indonesia and Malaysia) and in diaspora communities around the world.

WHO: Three main groups need to be engaged – primarily the communities who themselves need to choose to abandon cutting their daughters; second, stakeholders, who have the ability to work with communities and who may have the resources and mandate to do this (including governments, donors, agencies, and decision-makers); and, lastly, the general public who can influence those stakeholders.

WHEN: If the requisite resources and communications were in place, we might get to zero FGC within a generation. Foot-binding ended within 12 years. FGC could end within 25 years if there were an adequate strategy that employed the use of social norm theory, game theory, and organized diffusion theory, and if that were implemented widely across different countries by different actors.

HOW: Human rights-based community-led empowerment programs have led to large-scale abandonment of FGC within the last five years in West Africa, starting in Senegal. Using the theories mentioned above and, crucially, allowing a community to explore FGC – then choose to abandon – has had success now in over 5300 communities. Once FGC is declared ended, it is not practiced again.

JULIA LALLA-MAHARAJH, founder and CEO, Orchid Project (www.orchidproject.org).

There may seem to be precariously weak links between water conservation, hunger and obesity, and female genital cutting, but all will require profound social transformations. Getting to zero in each case involves Herculean efforts, so going beyond zero sounds like a real stretch. And it will be. What I see in fields such as cradle-to-cradle design,[16] as practiced by the likes of Bill McDonough and Michael Braungart, and in the rapidly evolving science of biomimicry[17] is early evidence that in the seriously long-term future we could develop new technologies and lifestyles attuned to the natural order in ways that are currently unimaginable.

Going longer

Fourth, and finally, in times of growing stress and uncertainty our time horizons tend to collapse back into the moment, the short term, to shrink into the present, and even into the apparent certainties of the past. This is a real problem with the sustainability agenda, which is fundamentally about challenges – and solutions – requiring the ability to operate across extended time scales.

"We are on a journey", CEOs like to say as they sign up to the sustainability agenda. What they often mean is that the outlines of the enterprise are vague, the destination unclear, the captain and crew distracted, and the sailing date still to be agreed. But the business leaders among our Zeronauts mean something very different where they use the phrase.

They see an accelerating shift in the center of gravity of the global economy, with new trade routes opening up, new power dynamics, and many traditional centers of wealth and influence at risk of being marooned. They also sense that changing climate patterns will make life much more complicated over time.

I can't remember where I first heard it, but this paraphrased maxim sticks in my mind: "Extraordinary times call for – and call forth – extraordinary leaders." If so, beyond those we identify here, where are they? With several notable exceptions, the centers of leadership – like sailing vessels in the golden era of wind-powered marine trade – seem becalmed, adrift, in the grip of angry mutinies or headed toward treacherous reefs.

This is where the future quotient, already mentioned, potentially fits in. Yes, we already have the intelligence quotient (IQ)[18] and, thanks to Daniel Goleman, both the emotional quotient (EQ) and ecological quotient (Eco-Q).[19] But, while each of these can contribute to assessing the capacity of an individual, a team, or an organization to make sense of, manage, and even improve the future, none of them is designed to provide an overall assessment of future readiness.

Such metrics must – will – become increasingly important. Potentially, a high future quotient could help individuals or groups to identify new risks ahead of the pack and play more effectively into emerging areas of opportunity. Again, as the Canadians say, in ice hockey, it can help players skate to where the puck is going to be, rather than where it currently is.

Too often, though, the trends are headed in the wrong direction. Warning bells have been sounded by, among others, the US National Intelligence Council, in a series of reports, looking out a decade or two into the future.[20]

Among their conclusions: "The whole international system – as constructed following WWII – will be revolutionized. Not only will new players – Brazil, Russia, India, and China – have a seat at the international high table, they will bring new stakes and rules of the game. The unprecedented transfer of wealth roughly from West to East now under way will continue for the foreseeable future. Unprecedented economic growth, coupled with 1.5 billion more people, will put pressure on resources – particularly energy, food, and water – raising the specter of scarcities emerging as demand outstrips supply. The potential for conflict will increase owing partly to political turbulence in parts of the greater Middle East."

By contrast to the situation in China, where long-term planning has been a key part of the impressive and sustained (if not sustainable on current lines) expansion of the economy and of the country's political position, the West appears to have been increasingly hamstrung by an aggravated case of political short-termism and market myopia.

Such things go in cycles, of course, but our governments, financial institutions, and many business leaders appear to be failing even in terms of the old rules of markets – let alone the new rules imposed by new considerations such as energy security, food security, and climate change.

This is a real problem when we need to shift to profoundly different forms of production and consumption, among them what some call "zero till" and "zero kill" forms of agriculture. Among the champions of this approach is Tim Flannery, who argues that "such practices are creating a new agricultural revolution, one based upon coevolution's capacity to increase biological productivity and ecosystem stability".[21] He notes that zero till and reduced till methods have already helped to boost Australia's production of grain and beef. Combined with a shift away from the feeding of grain to cattle in feedlots, a process that wastes 90 percent of the energy in the grain, he is confident that we could feed nine billion people by mid-century.

Such shifts will involve immense commitments and investments, sustained over time. Unfortunately, our already weak ability to make long-term investments is weakening further, according to the World Economic Forum (WEF).[22] It has concluded that, in 02009, long-term institutional asset holders held slightly under half of the world's professionally managed assets – some US$27 trillion out of US$65 trillion. They had been able to invest only 25 percent of their assets because of the economic crisis and increasing regulation.

And then there are concerns around the tools that we use to manage assets over time. Many involve discounting the future. Economics 101 tells us that a *discount rate* is the percentage by which the value of a cash flow in a discounted cash flow (DCF) valuation is reduced for each time period by which it is removed from the present.[23] The estimation of a suitable discount rate is often the most difficult and uncertain part of a DCF exercise. And the challenge is made even more difficult by the fact that the final result is very sensitive to the choice of discount rate – a small change in the selected discount rate can cause a large change in the ultimate value.

For much of the history of modern environmentalism, there has been a sense that the impact of discounting is pernicious when applied to natural systems such as fisheries, forests, or the climate. The concerns are legitimate, though the precise implications often critically depend upon the time scales within which the discounting is done. Consider the three different ways of thinking about the future suggested by the Long Now Foundation, one of our 50 high future quotient stars. They range, as Figure 8.1 shows, from timespans of a few days through roughly a human generation (30 years) out to the millennia over which the evolution of human civilization can be tracked.

We are teetering on the edge of a new era. As T. S. Eliot put it in a different context, we are coming to know this planet of ours for the first time, and in the process beginning to understand that doing things the old way will not serve us well in the future. We have to think – and act – differently:

> We shall not cease from exploration
> And the end of all our exploring
> Will be to arrive where we started
> And know the place for the first time.
>
> T. S. Eliot, "Little Gidding", Four Quartets

In *The Future Quotient*, we identified a dozen sectors that, by their very nature, tend to think longer term and, in some cases, intergenerationally. They include everything from animal breeding and family businesses, through pension funds and reinsurance, to the design and operation of urban infrastructures.

The twelfth sector was government, which not only powerfully shapes markets but also tends to be a massive purchaser in its own right. That is why, in Chapter 4, Martha Johnson, administrator of the US General Services Administration (GSA), is flagged as an emerging example of Zeronautics in the public sector. Her framing of the developing Zero Environmental Footprint initiative within the GSA as part of our generation's version of the Moon missions is precisely the sort of ambitious vision that we now need.

Very few of us will have the opportunity that the Astronauts and Cosmonauts enjoyed, to see our planet from the outside. But with the sort of information available to us through TV, the internet, and other media, we now have a very different understanding of our home planet than previous generations did. This knowledge is part of what is driving the accelerating shift toward a 1-Earth Paradigm. The key question is whether this will translate into the new values, behaviors, and cultures that are needed.

Zeronauts think it will. Meanwhile, one thing to remember about those space explorers is that most of them had a background in engineering, flight, or other supremely practical disciplines. And that was a point that Paul Hawken made in his eulogy for Ray Anderson on 11 August 02011.[24] To be sure, Ray was a dreamer. But, as Paul stressed, "he also dreamed in balance sheets, thermodynamics, and resource flow theory. He dreamed a world yet to come because dreams of a livable future are not coming from our politicians, bankers, and the media." Ultimately, as Paul concluded, "Ray's work was not about making a sustainable business, it was about justice, ethics, and honoring creation. Zero waste was the path to 100 percent respect for living beings."

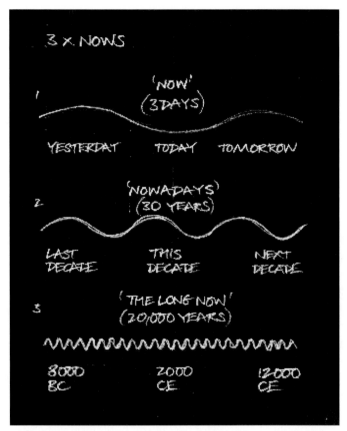

Figure 8.1 The three nows (Long Now Foundation)

Go together

One way that switched-on leaders and their teams are trying to keep pace with – and, in growing numbers of cases, are beginning to support – change agents is through study tours and learning journeys. Such visits can provide new ideas on how to go wider, deeper, higher, and longer. If you are a business, how about taking your C-suite to visit some of the people listed in Box 3.1 (see pp.44–6) – or, perhaps better still, sending your fast track executives?

Another approach is to get involved in initiatives such as the Zero Hub (see Box 0.3, pp.12–13). Our experience with the Race to Zero initiative has shown that mobilizing around zero-based targets can be quite a challenge; but the journey is likely to be more productive if undertaken in the company of others prepared to put their shoulders to the wheel.

These are, indeed, extraordinary times where success is often destined to be short lived, masking looming failures. All leaders worth their salt need their equivalent of the slave who, it is said, would accompany victorious generals on their triumphs through Rome and whisper wise, grounding counsel in their ears. The ethics of zero have scarcely begun to be probed. They need to be.

Perhaps a key part of our future task here will be to create a new breed of sustainability and zero footprint growth "Avatars", online super-advisors distilling the best of everything we know on how to succeed in business, finance, policy-making, and politics on this small blue planet of ours. That is a possibility I have been playing with alongside Jochen Zeitz, who as CEO of Puma pioneered the company's environmental profit-and-loss accounting.

In *The Zeronauts*, I have not yet dug deep into the world of valuation, accounting finance, and investment, though this will be critical in terms of driving the next stage of development and scaling. Instead, I have tried to capture today's mindset challenges as I see them – and to introduce some of the people who are developing potentially breakthrough solutions. But, as Eliot put it toward the end of *Four Quartets*, "Next year's words await another voice", or other voices, and – happily – they are beginning to surface in a variety of sectors.

Something I find immensely encouraging is the way in which so many younger people are keen to move into the relevant sectors. At Volans, we try to support them in a variety of ways as they try to make their way in turbulent times. One pair of Zeronauts spotlighted in our Roll of Honor is the dynamic duo of Pooran Desai and Sue Riddlestone of BioRegional, an incubator of solutions in the field of sustainable urbanism. Visiting such incubators of the future can be a powerful tonic for those of us who spend much of our time thinking about challenges and risks. There are plenty of reasons for pessimism; but I sincerely believe that if we can learn from the Zeronauts and focus our collective efforts on breaking through the Sustainability Barrier, the twenty-first century could well be our best yet:

> What we call the beginning is often the end
> And to make an end is to make a beginning.
> The end is where we start from.
>
> T. S. Eliot, "Little Gidding", Four Quartets

9

The Zero Countdown – and Beyond

So, to cut to the chase, what should your board, C-suite, or senior management group do to manage risks – and seize the opportunities – created by the Zeronaut agenda? Here are some starter questions that you can pose to your team or wider organization.

If you took all the Zeronauts identified in previous chapters and locked them in a room until they came up with an action plan for a given business, economy, or government, they would likely agree on our overall framing: that we need to move from incremental to transformative system change, and that we must connect wider, dig deeper, aim higher, invest longer.

But what sort of narrative line might we hear if we were to take a single Zeronaut and ask them to sit down with a board, C-suite, or cabinet? My sense is that he or she might be well advised to adopt a countdown-to-zero approach. So, here's a working draft of how that might work.

10 Patience is the ability to count down before you blast off

I have no idea where this phrase originated, but – as a Zeronaut such as former Astronaut and Cosmonaut Jerry Linenger would attest – it offers hard-won wisdom. Too often, accelerated countdowns and take-offs end in grief, as in the *Challenger* shuttle disaster of 01986, analyzed to devastating effect (at least for NASA) by Richard Feynman.[1] We have to learn how to see what is hidden in plain view. Three of my favorite books here are by Edward Tufte, who has specialized in the analysis of how critical data are best presented – as in his review of the 02003 *Columbia* shuttle disaster.[2] The key point, as we begin the countdown, is to understand the big picture and likely trajectories before we stab the ignition button.

9 Having taken off as a species, we have landed in the Anthropocene

So, here's the really big picture. Until recently we were told to expect 9 billion people by 02050, with a peak of just over 10 billion – but the UN has now upped the estimates, under certain assumptions, forecasting as many as 15 billion people by 02100. Whatever the actual numbers, welcome to the Anthropocene Era – in which our species is the dominant influence on our planet (see p.xx). The implication: unless we embrace 1-Earth mindsets, behaviors, cultures, and paradigms, we will crash both the biosphere and our civilization. A critical first step will be to see the period to 02020 as our Detox Decade, a period of civilizational rehab (see p.61).

Some initial questions: how would your economic or business models play out in a world of 9 or 10 billion? What would happen if sharply reduced carbon, water, toxic waste, or other footprints became the focus of policy and, ultimately, societal expectations? (or vice versa.) What would a zero impact growth model look like? What would be the risks – and where are the likely opportunities? What sort of time scales might be involved?

8 Get ready to break the Sustainability Barrier

With no particular intention of doing so, we are inflicting a gigantic Ponzi scheme on future generations (see pp.32–3). It is time to break the Sustainability Barrier by embracing the fundamental intergenerational task of winding down the dysfunctional economic and business models of the nineteenth and twentieth centuries – and evolving new ones fit for the twenty-first and twenty-second centuries. One key part of responding to the challenge will involve our finding new ways of cross-generational working and new methods of cross-generational accounting and valuation.

Some initial questions: what are we already doing that maps onto this trajectory? Where in today's world do we already see key actors moving to break the Sustainability Barrier in their markets or geographies? How successful have they been? What are the key constraints they face – and how have they sought to circumvent them? What might we learn?

7 Don't wait for a Sputnik moment

Our politicians – and societies – are most likely to mobilize when there is a clear and present danger, as when the Ozone Hole opened up over our heads during the 01980s. The science suggests that we must cut carbon emissions more than 100-fold (see p.9). Instead of waiting for Sputnik moments, we need to start yesterday.

Some initial questions: what would be a likely Sputnik moment in our markets or geographies? What sort of early warning signals might we expect to see? Have we seen evidence of similar challenges emerging elsewhere? How well prepared are we for black swans, green swans, or even zero swans?

6 Think the unthinkable, do the undoable

Many CEOs say that they have embedded sustainability, but they are usually talking about corporate citizenship, with a few tweaks. In an era where we face the intensifying challenges of peak oil, peak water, peak fish, indeed (as Jeremy Grantham of GMO put it) peak everything, thinking and acting in the old ways could well prove suicidal. Like the late, great Ray Anderson of Interface (see p.144), we must embrace Mission Zero – climbing toward a different peak, that of Mount Sustainability. This means embracing transformational change – going wider, deeper, higher, longer, and, critically, together (see point 2, below).

Some initial questions: what would Mission Zero look like in our organization? How far up Mount Sustainability are we? Should we build out from existing foundations – or start anew? What partnerships – existing or new – will we need to succeed? What's the competition up to on all of this? Are there players on the edges of our world, as currently defined, who could explode into our space with new mindsets, technologies, business models, or branding? How might we benefit from – and contribute to – initiatives such as the Cradle to Cradle community, ZERI, or the Zero Hub?

As I finished the book, news came in that Kraft had achieved "zero waste" at 36 food plants around the world. It's happening.

5 Look at our common future through the lens of zero

The Zeronauts is no more – and no less – than a thought experiment. But it underscores how powerful such thought experiments can be. Take the case of Herman Miller: pursuing zero, it has driven down volatile organic compound (VOC) emissions by 93 percent, hazardous waste by 95 percent, and solid waste by 88 percent (see p.163). Around the world, companies are announcing zero (or net zero) targets. And a growing number have already hit their zero targets in some areas. Some Zeronauts, like Matthew Wright of Beyond Zero Emissions, aim to go beyond, as it says on the box.

Some initial questions: who is already doing this sort of thing in our markets? Why are they doing it – and how are they doing? How might we use such thought experiments in our executive training or in induction processes for new employees? Who among our key stakeholders will be attracted by this – and who might not be? How do we best manage those conversations?

4 Support your local Zeronauts

Most Zeronauts are still considered unreasonable, indeed sometimes crazy, because of their outlandish ambitions. Our first stab at a Zeronaut 50 Roll of Honor (see Box 3.1 on pp.44–6) begins the task of putting faces to this emerging agenda. It spotlights the inventors, innovators, entrepreneurs, intrapreneurs, investors, and managers who are promoting real wealth creation – while driving adverse environmental, social, and economic impacts toward zero. But for this movement to build consistently over decades, zero-based thinking must also become endemic in the thinking and practices of investors, policy-makers, regulators, politicians, and educators. Dig into the science with people like Zeronaut Michael Pawlyn, who helped design Britain's Eden Project.

Some initial questions: who among the Zeronaut 50 do we already know? Who would we want to get to know? Who might we support – and how? What might we learn in the process? How is the process of engagement best handled? Again, what sort of time scales and resources are likely to be involved?

3 Identify, map, and travel the Pathways to Zero

When you don't know where you're going, they say, pretty much any road will take you there. Our five-stage Pathways to Zero model (see Chapter 6) offers a guide for those embarking on the journey toward real system change.

Some initial questions: if you take different areas of the business, where are we on the Pathways to Zero journey? Do we have a clear idea of how we are going to move into higher stages – and, ultimately, toward stage 5? What stage 4 partners would be needed to create the necessary market ecosystem(s)? What would be our role in creating such ecosystems? And what would stage 5 look like for our markets or geographies?

2 Join forces with fellow travelers

There is a growing need for innovators to convene, share notes, and work on new blueprints, frameworks, and solutions. That's why we are co-evolving the Zero Hub with Deloitte Innovation (see pp.12–13). If successful, we envisage a global network of such hubs: what President George W. Bush would probably have dismissed as an Axis of Zero.

Some initial questions: to what extent are our existing alliances, federations, associations, or networks already addressing these issues? Can we believe what they say on this score? What can we do to ensure that they raise their game? Are there new players whom we should engage? Who in our organization is best placed to do this?

Keep an eye out for the work of Jeremy Rifkin, with his focus on what he calls the "Third Industrial Revolution" – based on the emergence of an "energy Internet".

1 Beware of becoming a Zero zealot

Do the analysis. The zero option is but one among a number, and is not always automatically the best way forward. Be thoughtful, self-critical, and disciplined in deciding your approach. The last thing we want to see is a wave of CZOs (chief zero officers). As the almost-inevitable Zero Rush builds, beware zerowashing. There will be a growing temptation to make misleading claims. If market confidence is to be maintained, such claims need to be smacked back, hard.

Some initial questions: where does zero fit into our existing sustainability – and wider – ambitions, targets, and toolkits? Where are we already using zero or net-zero targets? Have we considered doing so, but decided not to; if so, why? Are we – or competitors – already making related claims? If so, how are they being received? If we were to communicate in this space, who would be our key audiences, what would be our core messages, and how would we know if our communications were successful?

0 Use zero to boost your future quotient – then move beyond it

In order to power the necessary transformative, systemic change, we must develop our future quotients (FQs) (see p.228). Take Zeronaut James Hansen, of NASA, who produced a book designed to make us all think of our climatic futures, *Storms of My Grandchildren*.[3] We need FQ, not just intelligence quotient (IQ) or emotional quotient (EQ): and we should think in terms of the future quo, not just the status quo. Zero offers a powerful key to unlocking tomorrow's growth markets. Perhaps we should talk of zeronomics? But to have any chance of making the twenty-first century our best yet, we must also eventually move well beyond zero, designing our technologies, businesses, economies, and civilization so that they are no longer net destructive, but actively restorative. This is what emerging disciplines such as natural capitalism, cradle-to-cradle design, and biomimicry are all about.

Beware of all market research forecasts, but note that Pike Research predicts that the net-zero buildings market alone will reach $1.3 trillion by 2035.[4]

Some initial questions: have we put our team or organization through anything like the future quotient process? If so, with what results? If not, would it be worth trying? Where would be the best place to pilot this? Could it help to reanimate or redirect our corporate social responsibility (CSR), sustainability, innovation, or other initiatives? How would it fit in with existing human resources, strategy, or other mainstream activities? Should we go top down (e.g. board, C-suite) with this – or bottom up? How would we make the best use of the results? Who else is doing this – and how might we learn from (and potentially build on) what they are doing? And what might a Beyond Zero scenario look like?

Whatever our answers to such questions, the time has come to punch through the Sustainability Barrier – and to support and learn from the Zeronauts who are leading the charge. For more on their work, and on the evolving zero agenda, please visit www.zeronauts.com. And please do get in touch: my email address is john@volans.com. Remember what legendary investor Warren Buffett advised: "if you want to go fast, go alone. But if you want to go far, go in company."

Figure 9.1 The Royal Society of Arts stamp to celebrate the Zero Waste initiative, 02004

Glossary

1-Earth: Simplified version of One Planet (q. v.). See explanation on p.40.

1-Earth Paradigm: Paradigms shape how we see and value the world in which we live and work. A 1-Earth Paradigm implies revolutionary changes in governance, economies, business models, technologies, and lifestyles. A stronger version is the Gaian Paradigm (q. v.).

5Cs: The main domains of action spotlighted in Chapter 4: citizens, corporations, cities, countries, and civilizations.

5Es: See Pathways to Zero. The 5Es are Eureka!, experimentation, enterprise, ecosystems, and economy, covered in Chapters 5 and 6.

5Ps: Five great dramas in which early stages of the Zero Impact Growth Economy (q. v.) are visible: population, pandemics, poverty, pollution, and proliferation, all spotlighted in Chapter 7.

biomimicry: One of the early examples of *biomimicry* was the study of birds to enable human flight.[1] Leonardo da Vinci was a keen observer of the anatomy and flight of birds, making numerous notes on his observations, as well as sketches of various "flying machines". The Wright Brothers, who created and flew the first heavier-than-air plane (unless you are Brazilian and are rooting for Alberto Santos-Dumont) in 01903, also drew inspiration from observations of pigeons in flight. The term *biomimicry* appeared as early as 01982. The term was popularized by Janine Benyus in her 01997 book, *Biomimicry: Innovation Inspired by Nature*. She defines biomimicry as a "new science that studies nature's models and then imitates or takes inspiration from these designs and processes to solve human problems".

cleantech: Abbreviation of *clean technology*. There is no standard definition of clean technology, although Clean Edge, a research firm, describes it as "a diverse range of products, services, and processes that harness renewable materials and energy sources, dramatically reduce the use of natural resources, and cut or eliminate emissions and wastes".

CSR: corporate social responsibility.

ecosystem: Used here primarily in the sense of clusters and constellations of actors pushing toward the 1-Earth Paradigm (q. v.) and the Zero Impact Growth Economy (q. v.).

ESG: Stands for environmental, social, and governance – and is a generic term used in capital markets and by investors both to evaluate corporate behavior and to assess the future financial performance of companies.

future-printing: If fingerprints are used today to identify individuals – and particularly those of concern to organizations charged with protecting our security – then, by extension, future-printing aims to identify technologies, business models, corporations, and supply chains that throw an environmental, social, or governance shadow into the future, as a first step toward regulating or excluding them.

future-proofing: To protect the future prospects of a product, technology, company, or economy from threats that could otherwise undermine them.

Gaian Paradigm: Largely interchangeable with 1-Earth Paradigm (q. v.), but with a stronger underpinning from *geophysiology*, first introduced by Professor James Lovelock.

Gen S: The first pan-generational generation, "Generation Sustainability", made up of those operating in the emerging 1-Earth or Gaian Paradigm (q. v.).

net zero: A zero outcome achieved by offsetting positive and negative aspects of the footprint of, for example, a product, technology, building, or organization.

non-zero sum: Term used to describe a situation in which the interacting parties' aggregate gains and losses are either less than or more than zero – although we generally assume that the result is more than zero.

One Planet: Living within the limits of Earth (see p.40).

Pathways to Scale: A five-stage model of change developed by Volans that forms the core of Chapter 6, running from Eureka!, experimentation and enterprise through the formation of ecosystems (q. v.) to the evolution of a 1-Earth Economy. Adapted to Pathways to Zero (see Chapter 6).

peak: As in peak oil, peak water, or peak fish, the notion that the availability of a key natural resource has peaked, or will soon peak, and then head into irreversible decline.

Petri Planet: Petri dishes are shallow, circular, transparent dishes with flat lids, used for the culture of micro-organisms. By extension, the Petri Planet is the world of experimentation from which solutions to breaking the Sustainability Barrier (q. v.) will emerge.

Rubik Earth: The increasingly complex, interlinked challenges facing leaders in the private, public, and citizen sectors as they wrestle to control the trajectories driving us toward unsustainability – and strive to develop solutions and bring them to scale.

SRI: socially responsible investment.

sustainability: A term first used, apparently, by Donella Meadows in 01972. The art of leaving the world no worse – and desirably better – than we found it; alternatively, treating the Earth "as if we intended to stay". Unsustainability is easier to measure, with key drivers being demographics, consumption patterns, and technologies. There are weak and strong forms of sustainability, the former allowing for trading between different forms of capital (e.g. financial, social, and natural), the latter making natural capital sacrosanct. For business, there is the triple bottom line, or TBL (q. v.). Increasingly, there is a sense that progress will involve changing mindsets, behaviors, cultures, and, ultimately, our prevailing paradigm (see Figure 1.1, p.24).

Sustainability Barrier: Like the Sound Barrier during the late 01940s, this represents an immense psychological, technological, and – above all – political challenge. Only if we break through will future generations enjoy anything like a sustainable lifestyle.

TBL: The triple bottom line (also abbreviated as 3BL, and known as "people, planet, profit" or, in less commercial terms, "the three pillars") captures an expanded spectrum of values and criteria for measuring organizational (and societal) success: economic, social, and ecological/environmental. A number of organizations have formal TBL charters, among them the Dow Jones Sustainability Indexes, the Global

Reporting Initiative, Novo Nordisk, and SustainAbility. With the ratification of the United Nations and Local Governments for Sustainability (ICLEI) TBL standard for urban and community accounting in 02007, this also became the dominant approach to public-sector full-cost accounting. First introduced by the author and SustainAbility in 01994/01995.

TTL: The triple top line was first explored by Bill McDonough.[2] The top line, conventionally, refers to the gross sales or revenues of a company, or to a course of action that increases or reduces revenues. A company that increases its revenues is said to be "growing its top line" or "generating top-line growth".

WMD: weapons of mass destruction.

Zero Beat: In newspaper parlance, a beat is the subject area that a reporter is assigned to cover. Beat reporters can cover everything from local crime through a specific sports team to, in this case, the zero impact growth agenda. See, for example, Box 0.2 on pp.9–11.

Zero Economy: The ideal economic end-state of an economic order built around 1-Earth (q. v.), sustainability (q. v.), and Gen S (q. v.) principles.

Zero Hub: The concept of a catalytic venture and/or space designed to attract, train, and help deploy new generations of Zeronauts and, in the process, accelerate the shift toward the Zero Economy (q. v.); the name of a joint venture between Deloitte Innovation and Volans – see pp.12–13.

zero impact growth: Socio-economic value creation connected with a radical reduction in the environmental footprint per unit of growth or wealth creation. Hence, Zero Impact Growth Economy.

Zero Meme: A meme (i.e. an idea or element of social behavior) relating to, for example, zero impact lifestyles, business models, or policies that potentially can spread between people, communities, sectors of the economy, networks, or generations. Evolutionary biologist Richard Dawkins coined the word *meme* as the cultural counterpart of genes, introducing it in his book *The Selfish Gene*.

zero sum: A game in which the sum of the winnings by all the players is zero. In a zero-sum game, a gain by one player must be matched by a loss by another player. Often applied to politics, with zero-sum politics – uncomfortably – the likely twenty-first-century outcome of a failure to embrace and operate within a 1-Earth Paradigm (q. v.). The opposite is non-zero sum (q. v.).

zeroing: The skill of driving a process or system toward a zero-problem outcome, illustrated here in the context of the 5Ps (q. v.) and Boxes 8.2 (see pp.229–30), 8.3 (see pp.232–3), and 8.4 (see pp.236–7).

Zeronaut: 1. An inventor, innovator, entrepreneur, intrapreneur, investor, manager, or educator who promotes wealth creation while driving adverse environmental, social, and economic impacts toward zero. 2. Someone who finds, investigates, and develops breakthrough solutions for the growing tensions between demography, consumerist lifestyles, and sustainability. 3. Political leader or policy-maker who helps to create the regulatory frameworks and incentives needed to drive related "1-Earth" (q. v.) solutions to scale.

Zeronautics: The evolving discipline of conceiving, designing, engineering, and operating technologies, business models, value chains, and economies on 1-Earth principles (see Chapters 5 and 6).

Zeropreneur: Entrepreneur or intrapreneur who pursues zero-based targets.

IN THE END, BEGINNINGS

Notes

Front matter

1   I was struck by the device used by the Long Now Foundation (http://longnow.org/), which adopts a 10,000-year perspective with its Clock of the Long Now – and renders years with a zero added up front, to signal the need to think *much* longer term (see Figure 8.1) – a neat way of underscoring the time scales involved in the pursuit of sustainability. So, at the risk of disconcerting some, this approach is adopted throughout *The Zeronauts* – except in quotations from other sources.

2   Robert Kaplan (01999) *The Nothing that Is: A Natural History of Zero*, Allen Lane/ Penguin Press, London.

3   With thanks to my friend and colleague Zheng Jieying for her help in interpreting *Ling*.

4   For a listing of the books I have authored or co-authored, see p.vi.

5   Andrea Spencer-Cooke (02000) "Hero of Zero", *Tomorrow*, vol 10, no 6, pp.10–16.

6   See 26 July entry, www.johnelkington.com/weblog/2004_07_01_arc.html.

7   Charles Seife (02000) *Zero: The Biography of a Dangerous Idea*, Souvenir Press, London.

8   John Elkington and Pamela Hartigan (02009) *The Power of Unreasonable People: How Social Entrepreneurs Create Markets that Change the World*, Harvard Business School Press, Boston, MA.

9   "A man-made world", *The Economist*, 26 May 02011. See also, www.economist.com/node/18741749.

10   See www.johnelkington.com/journal/journal_entry.asp?id = 250.

11   Serendipity has long been one of my core values, as explained here: www.johnelkington.com/babelfish.htm. For more on the theme, read Chapter 4 of Steven Johnson (02010) *Where Good Ideas Come From: The Natural History of Innovation*, Allen Lane, London.

12   See www.fastcompany.com/social/2008/index.html.

Introduction

1   As explained in the "Ling" panel on p.vii, I have adopted the Long Now Foundation's year numbering scheme as a small indication that we need to think and operate against much more extended time horizons.

2   Email exchange with author, 14 August 02011 (for more, see pp.206).

3   See Zeronaut Roll of Honor (Box 3.1, pp.44–6).
4   Elisabeth Bumiller (02011) "The 'All-Star team' behind the raid", *The International Herald Tribune*, 6 May.
5   See http://en.wikipedia.org/wiki/Zero_growth.
6   The Race to Zero language has been used by a number of pioneers, among them the X Prize Foundation, with its proposed Race to Zero carbon dioxide, and people working in computer virus control and education.
7   Tim Adams (02011) "Profile of Karen Green", *The New Review/The Observer*, 10 April.
8   Michael Braungart and William McDonough (02009) *Cradle to Cradle: Remaking the Way We Make Things*, Vintage Books, London.
9   Email exchange with author, 15 August 02011.
10 Email exchange with author, 21 August 02011.
11 See http://blog.invisiblechildren.com/2010/12/rare-speech-by-viktor-frankl-mans-search-for-meaning/.
12 Email exchange with author, 27 March 02011.
13 See www.factor10-institute.org/index.html.
14 Claude Fussler, email exchange with author, 16 January 02011.
15 BioRegional has trademarked the "One Planet" formulation, with a specific and prescriptive set of rules. Rather than risk breaking them, I am opting for 1-Earth, but very much support the One Planet approach, both in general and as a member of the Council of Ambassadors of WWF-UK, for which I was also involved in producing a 02007 report on *One Planet Business* (see www.sustainability.com/library/one-planet-business).
16 A theme which we explored in our report *The Phoenix Economy: 50 Pioneers in the Business of Social Innovation*, Volans for the Skoll Foundation, 02009.
17 Norimitsu Onishi (02011) "Breach of sea wall shatters town's psyche", *International Herald Tribune*, 2–3 April.
18 *The Phoenix Economy: 50 Pioneers in the Business of Social Innovation*, Volans for the Skoll Foundation, 02009.
19 John Elkington (02010) "A new paradigm for change", *What Matters*, McKinsey & Co., 6 April 02010, http://whatmatters.mckinseydigital.com/social_entrepreneurs/a-new-paradigm-for-change.
20 Tim Jackson (02009) *Prosperity without Growth: Economics for a Finite Planet*, Earthscan, London.
21 Exchange of emails with author, 18 August 02011.
22 See www.scibooks.org/lunarmen.html.
23 See http://en.wikipedia.org/wiki/Homebrew_Computer_Club.

I ZERO: THE NEW BLACK

1 Breaking the Sustainability Barrier

1   Interview with the author, Washington, DC, 17 May 02011.
2   Conversation with author, 5 April 02011.
3   See www.imdb.com/title/tt0086197/.

4   See www.longnow.org/clock.

5   See www.extensor.co.uk/articles/breakthrough_thinking/breakthrough_thinking. html.

6   Gideon Rachman (02010) *Zero-Sum World: Politics, Power and Prosperity after the Crash*, Atlantic Books, London.

7   A key book on this era is Greg Behrman (02007) *The Marshall Plan and the Reconstruction of Post-War Europe*, Aurum Press, London.

8   Robert Wright (02000) *Nonzero: The Logic of Human Destiny*, Pantheon Books, New York.

9   Chairman of the Joint Chiefs of Staff says "Climate change's potential impacts are sobering and far-reaching", Nick Sundt, WWF Climate blog, 11 April 02011, www.wwfblogs.org/climate/content/ video-chairman-joint-chiefs-staff-climate-change-impacts-sobering.

10   *A New Era of Sustainability*, Accenture for the United Nations Development Compact, 02010; see https://microsite.accenture.com/sustainability/research_and_ insights/Pages/A-New-Era-of-Sustainability.aspx.

11   See www.huffingtonpost.com/bill-mckibben/everything-is-negotiable-_b_797679. html.

12   See www.zeri.org.

13   See http://missionzero.org/about.

14   See www.worldchanging.com/archives/011676.html.

15   See http://whatmatters.mckinseydigital.com/social_entrepreneurs/ a-new-paradigm-for-change.

16   When the McKinsey essay was published, Jem Bendell wrote to me to point out the similarities with work by Ken Wilber, http://en.wikipedia.org/wiki/Ken_ Wilber#AQAL:_.22All_Quadrants_All_Levels.22. I was fascinated, but had not – to the best of my knowledge – previously come across Wilber's work.

17   Thomas Kuhn (01962) *The Structure of Scientific Revolutions*, University of Chicago Press, Chicago, IL.

18   See http://en.wikipedia.org/wiki/Spaceship_Earth.

19   See http://dieoff.org/page160.htm.

20   Barbara Ward (01966) *Spaceship Earth*, Columbia University Press, New York, NY.

21   See www.mindtools.com/pages/article/newTMC_87.htm.

22   See www.brandrepublic.com/news/1018827/bmw-zero-emissions-ad-banned/.

23   EcoMotors Chief Don Runkle: "Electric vehicles are not 'zero emissions'", http:// techcrunch.com/2011/05/26/disrupt-transportation-brammo-ecomotors/.

24   See www.guardian.co.uk/sustainable-business/sustainability-with-john-elkington/ armed-forces-military-sustainability.

25   Twitter and email exchange with author, 18 August 02011.

26   Robert Crowe (02011) "The US army has the 'land and demand' for renewable energy", *Renewable Energy World*, 11 August.

27   Juliet Eilperin (02011) "Military spearheads clean-energy drive", *The Washington Post*, 26 September.

2   Houston, We Have A(nother) Problem

1   Clive Cookson (02010) "Transmission mission", *Financial Times*, 24 December.
2   James Lovelock (01979) *Gaia: A New Look at Life on Earth*, Oxford University Press, Oxford.
3   Fiona Harvey (02011) "Honeybees 'entomb' hives to protect against pesticides, say scientists", Guardian.co.uk, 4 April 02011, www.guardian.co.uk/environment/2011/apr/04/honeybees-entomb-hives.
4   Interview by the author, Washington, DC, 17 May 02011.
5   Lester Brown (02010) *Civilization's Foundation Eroding*, Earth Policy Institute media release, 28 September.
6   Dave Eggers (02009) *Zeitoun*, McSweeney's Books, San Francisco, CA.
7   Edward Humes (02011) *Force of Nature: The Unlikely Story of Wal-Mart's Green Revolution*, HarperCollins, New York, NY.
8   Jared Diamond (02005) *Collapse: How Societies Choose to Fail or Succeed*, Viking Press, New York, NY.
9   I first made this argument in *One Planet Business: Creating Value within Planetary Limits*, a joint report by SustainAbility and WWF, 02007.
10   See http://en.wikipedia.org/wiki/Uluburun_shipwreck.
11   Nicolette Jones (02006) *The Plimsoll Sensation: The Great Campaign to Save Lives at Sea*, Little, Brown, London; see also www.booktrustchildrensbooks.org.uk/show/feature/Nicolette-Jones-on-Samuel-Plimsoll.
12   Naomi Oreskes and Erik Conway (02010) *Merchants of Doubt: How a Handful of Scientists Obscured the Truth on Issues from Tobacco Smoke to Global Warming*, Bloomsbury Press, New York, NY.
13   Gina-Marie Cheeseman (02011) "How the Koch brothers fund the climate change denial machine", www.triplepundit.com/2011/03/koch-brothers-funding-climate-change-denial-machine/.
14   See www.footprintnetwork.org/en/index.php/GFN/page/at_a_glance/.
15   See www.gapminder.org.
16   See www.google.com/publicdata/home.
17   Geoffrey Moore (01998) *Crossing the Chasm: Marketing and Selling Technology Products to Mainstream Customers*, Capstone Publishing, Oxford.

3   Enter the Zeronauts

1   Pamela Chen (02011) "Hard at work on high steel above ground zero", *International Herald Tribune*, 10–11 September. See also www.courierpress.com/news/2010/jul/13/skywalkers/.
2   Jerry M. Linenger (02003) *Letters from Mir: An Astronaut's Letters to His Son*, McGraw-Hill, New York, NY.
3   See www.circleofblue.org/waternews/about/; full disclosure, the author is a member of the Circle of Blue advisory board.
4   Email exchange with author, 24 May 02011.
5   "You look back at Earth and … you realize how insignificant we really all are", *FT Weekend Magazine*, *Financial Times*, 2–3 April 02011.

6   Quoted in "The Astronauts of Planet Earth", *FT Weekend Magazine*, Financial Times, 2–3 April 02011.
7   See www.chessandpoker.com/rubiks-cube-solution.html.
8   D. H. Meadows, L. Meadows, J. Randers, and W. W. Behrens (01972) *The Limits to Growth*, Universe Books, New York, NY.
9   I was writing *Sun Traps: The Renewable Energy Forecast*, Pelican Books, London, 01984.
10   See http://en.wikipedia.org/wiki/Denis_Hayes.
11   See www.nrel.gov/features/20100419_earthday.html.
12   Kirk Johnson (02011) "A net-zero energy 'lab' lets the (refracted) sunshine in", *The New York Times*, 27 February.

II   CRACKING THE 1-EARTH CODE

4   Turbulent Teens: Our Detox Decade

1   With thanks to Grateful Dead lyricist John Perry Barlow, whom I enjoyed meeting in the Bahamas many moons ago.
2   See http://wbcsd.typepad.com/stigson/2011/05/transitioning-during-the-turbulent-teens.html.
3   It's probably the *zeitgeist*, but I decided to use the detox analogy before I saw Greenpeace's Detox campaign. The motivations and aims are very similar, albeit my intent is to move way beyond toxics to total resource take. See their campaign at www.greenpeace.org/international/en/campaigns/toxics/water/detox/.
4   See Jared Diamond (02005) *Collapse: How Societies Choose to Fail or Succeed*, Viking Press, New York, NY, and Arnold Toynbee (01934–01961) *A Study of History*, 12 volumes, Oxford University Press, Oxford.
5   The detox idea is lifted from a blog on 8 August 02011 by Umair Haque for the HBR Blog Network, http://blogs.hbr.org/haque/2011/08/a_six-step_extreme_makeover_fo.html.
6   See http://en.wikipedia.org/wiki/Margaret_Mead.
7   See http://moneyland.time.com/2011/08/11/this-is-an-emergency-fund-emergency-64-of-americans-dont-have-1000-in-savings/.
8   Umair Haque (02011) "The great splintering", HBR Blog Network, http://blogs.hbr.org/haque/2011/08/the_great_splintering.html.
9   See www.freakonomics.com/2011/04/13/the-5-billion-carbon-fotprint-of-indoor-marijuana/.
10   See http://blessedunrest.com/.
11   Email exchange with author, 10 August 02011.
12   See www.goodguide.com.
13   "Researchers crack the code for persuading skeptical, cynical consumers to go green", www.businesswire.com/news/home/20110608005462/en/Researchers-Crack-Code-Persuading-Skeptical-Cynical-Consumers.
14   Stephanie Clifford and Andrew Martin (02011) "Green products lose to recession", *The New York Times/The Observer*, 29 May.
15   See www.sustainable.org/.

16 Paul Hawken (02007) *Blessed Unrest: How the Largest Movement in the World Came into Being, and Why No One Saw It Coming*, Viking Press, New York, NY.

17 See www.naturalstep.org.

18 Email exchange between Karl-Henrik Robèrt and author, summer 02011.

19 Schumpeter column (02010) "The business of sharing", *The Economist*, 14 October; see also www.economist.com/node/17249322.

20 Morgan Clendaniel (02011) "Zipcar's impact on how people use cars is enormous", www.fastcompany.com/1768007/zipcars-effects-on-how-people-use-cars-is-enormous.

21 Ben Machell (02010) "The cult of less", *The Times Magazine*, 30 October.

22 See www.cultofless.com.

23 Maurice Chittenden and Philip Beresford (02011) "Zero Towers: Mittal's £30m eco-pile", *Sunday Times*, 20 February.

24 See http://thebreakthrough.org/blog/2010/02/make_a_wish_gates_wants_clean.shtml.

25 Deloitte Touche Tohmatsu and the World Economic Forum (02011) *The Consumption Dilemma: Leverage Points for Accelerating Sustainable Growth*, January.

26 See www.volans.com/lab/projects/ageing/.

27 See www.brainyquote.com/quotes/authors/m/maurice_strong.html.

28 Roger Martin (02011) *Fixing the Game: Bubbles, Crashes, and What Capitalism Can Learn from the NFL*, Harvard Business Review Books, Boston, MA.

29 See http://occupywallst.org/.

30 Eric Lowitt (02011) "Zero-sum competition makes business unsustainable", 8 August, www.guardian.co.uk/sustainable-business/blog/zero-sum-competition-business-unsustainable.

31 Accenture (02010) *A New Era of Sustainability*, Accenture, London.

32 Conversation and email exchange with Georg Kell, UN, New York City, spring, 02011.

33 Sarah Murray (02011) "Response falls short of ecological challenges", *Financial Times Sustainable Business Survey*, 4 October.

34 See http://the-planet-zero.com/.

35 "The Great European Carbon Heist", *Bloomberg Business*, 14–20 March 02011.

36 See http://webarchive.nationalarchives.gov.uk/+/http://www.hm-treasury.gov.uk/independent_reviews/stern_review_economics_climate_change/sternreview_index.cfm.

37 Danny Fortson (02011) "King Coal's carbon-capture dreams go up in smoke", *Sunday Times*, 9 January.

38 Michael Sheridan and Richard Jones (02010) "Toxic fallout of China's solar panel boom", *The Sunday Times*, 3 October.

39 See www.patagonia.com/us/patagonia.go?assetid=3351.

40 See www.patagonia.com/us/patagonia.go?assetid=3351.

41 See www.carbonwarroom.com/battle/shipping.

42 Robert Lea (02011) "A handbrake turn: Car giant switches focus to battery power", *The Times*, 11 January.

43 Erik Kirschbaum (02011) "Trains that run like, and on, the wind", *The New York Times*, 21 August.

44 Sarah Murray (02010) "Companies see benefits of 'friendlier' formulas", *Financial Times Sustainable Business Survey*, 4 October.

45 Ramon Arratia (02010) "Mission Zero challenge: Aggressive zero footprint goals", 15 November, www.interfaceflorcutthefluff.com/mission-zero-challenge-aggressive-zero-footprint-goals.

46 See www.guardian.co.uk/sustainable-business/blog/ray-anderson-dies-interface-john-elkington-tribute.

47 Jeff Chu (02011) "Tilting at windmills", *Fast Company*, February.

48 Clayton M. Christensen, Shuman Talukdar, Richard Alton, and Michael B. Horn (02011) "Picking green tech's winners and losers", *Stanford Social Innovation Review*, spring.

49 See www.justmeans.com/press-releases/Nestl-hits-target-of-zero-waste-at-UK-factory/7451.html.

50 See www.newsweek.com/feature/2010/green-rankings.html.

51 Rod Newing (02011) "Valuing nature can cut business costs", *Financial Times*, 22 March.

52 Boyd Cohen (02011) "Top 10 climate capitalists of the 21st century", www.triplepundit.com/2011/04/top-10-climate-capitalists-21st-century/.

53 "Betting on green", *The Economist Technology Quarterly*, 12 March 02011.

54 See www.daniel-libeskind.com.

55 Edward Glaeser (02011) *Triumph of the City: How Our Greatest Invention Makes Us Richer, Smarter, Greener, Healthier and Happier*, Penguin, Harmondsworth, UK.

56 "Urban life: A tale of many cities", *The Economist*, 12 February 02011.

57 D. H. Meadows, L. Meadows, J. Randers, and W. W. Behrens (01972) *The Limits to Growth*, Universe Books, New York, NY.

58 See www.arcosanti.org.

59 See www.grist.org/sprawl/2011-06-22-the-american-suburbs-are-a-giant-ponzi-scheme.

60 "The city of the future", Siemens, www.siemens.com.

61 "Urban life: A tale of many cities", *The Economist*, 12 February 02011.

62 See www.time.com/time/photogallery/0,29307,1882089,00.html.

63 See http://transitionnetwork.org/.

64 John Pontin (02008/02009) *The Converging World: How One Community's Path to Zero Waste Is Helping Save Our Planet*, Piatkus Books, London.

65 Shanta Barley (02010) "Escape to the city", *New Scientist*, 6 November.

66 Shanta Barley (02010) "Escape to the city", *New Scientist*, 6 November.

67 See www.c40cities.org.

68 Daniel Fisher, with Naazneen Karmali and Gady Epstein (02011) "Siemens: Urban outfitter", *Forbes*, 9 May.

69 Bill Powell (02011) "Taming Shanghai's sprawl", *Time*, 14 February.

70 Mireya Navarro (02011) "Whose life looks greener? Towns compare notes", http://green.blogs.nytimes.com/2011/05/02/whose-life-looks-greener-towns-compare-notes/?partner=rss&emc=rss.

71 *The Sustainable Cities Index 02010: Ranking the 20 Largest British Cities*, Forum for the Future, 02010.

72 Victor Mallet (02011) "Clean air boasts cast cloud over Madrid's mayor", *Financial Times*, 5–6 February.

73 Cited by Edwin Heathcote (02010) "Urban evolution: Adapting the city for the future", *Financial Times*, 7 September.

74 Richard Florida (02009) *Who's Your City? How the Creative Economy Is Making Where to Live the Most Important Decision of Your Life*, Vintage Canada, Toronto, Canada.

75 See www.lanl.gov/news/stories/scientists_predict_characteristics_of_cities.html.

76 See www.guardian.co.uk/sustainable-business/sustainability-with-john-elkington/cities-sustainability-eureka-moment-innovation.

77 See http://sei-international.org/news-and-media/2051.

78 Nicolai Ouroussoff (02010) "Seeking a desert utopia", *The New York Times/The Observer*, 3 October.

79 Greg Lindsay (02010) "The new new urbanism", *Fast Company*, February.

80 John Arlidge (02010) "The greenest cities come in a box", *Sunday Times*, 14 November. Or see www.songdo.com/songdo-international-business-district/news/in-the-news.aspx/d=234/title=The_Greenest_Citites_Come_in_a_Box.

81 See www.volans.com/wp-content/uploads/2009/03/volansventuresltd_phoenixeconomy.pdf.

82 See http://edition.cnn.com/2011/10/14/tech/innovation/living-buildings-carbon/.

83 See www.daniel-libeskind.com/.

84 Stephanie Kirchgaessner (02011) "Obama's green credentials tarnished", *Financial Times*, 19 April.

85 Roger Cohen (02011) "Losing the energy game", *The Observer/New York Times*, 13 March.

86 See, for example, Carne Ross (02011) *The Leaderless Revolution: How Ordinary People Will Take Power and Change Politics in the 21st Century*, Simon & Schuster, London.

87 Oliver Morton (02010) "Cooling the Earth: The world in 2011", *The Economist*.

88 Ramez Naam (02011) "The Moore's law of solar energy: Solar cost per watt is dropping on an exponential curve, and will drop below coal by 2020", *Scientific American*, www.scientificamerican.com/blog/post.cfm?id=smaller-cheaper-faster-does-moores-2011-03-15.

89 Danny Fortson (02011) "Road to recovery: The future's bright", *The Sunday Times*, 27 March 02011.

90 See http://envirocenter.research.yale.edu/programs/environmental-performance-management/environmental-performance-index/; see also http://en.wikipedia.org/wiki/Environmental_Performance_Index#2010.

91 Mathis Wackernagel, email to author, 6 January 02012.

92 "Following the footprints", *The Economist Technology Quarterly*, 4 June 02011.

93 Interview with the author, 16 May 02011.

94 Katherine Richardson et al (02011) "Denmark's road map for fossil fuel independence", *The Solutions Journal*, vol 2, issue 4, July, www.thesolutionsjournal.com/node/954.

95 WWF-UK (02011) *The Energy Report: 100% Renewable Energy by 2050*, WWF-UK, Godalming, UK.

96 See http://environment.about.com/od/renewableenergy/a/oilfreesweden.htm.

97 Richard Waters (02011) "Light dims for Silicon Valley as China shines", *Financial Times*, 29 January.

98 Todd Woody (02010) "Chinese eclipse America's solar future", *The New York Times*, 31 October.

99 Don Durfee and James Pomfret (02011) "China struggles to find a formula for innovation", *The International Herald Tribune*, 6 May.

100 See http://gigaom.com/cleantech/doe-chief-on-why-we-dont-have-a-manhattan-project-for-energy/.

101 See www.b-eye-network.com/view/15269.

102 See www.beyondzeroemissions.org.

103 Shai Agassi (02010) "What China and Israel will teach the world: The world in 2011", *The Economist*.

104 Pilita Clark (02011) "Airbus warns of emissions trade war", *Financial Times*, 6 June.

105 See www.ipanews.com/?p=2516.

106 Jeffrey Sachs (02011) *The Price of Civilization: Reawakening American Virtue and Prosperity*, Random House, New York, NY.

107 See http://en.wikipedia.org/wiki/A_Study_of_History.

108 Ian Morris (02010) *Why the West Rules – for Now: The Patterns of History, and What They Reveal About the Future*, Profile Books, London.

109 See http://en.wikipedia.org/wiki/Arnold_J._Toynbee.

110 See www.johnelkington.com/weblog/2005_04_01_arc.htm.

111 See www.kk.org/outofcontrol.

112 See www.kk.org/newrules.

113 See www.kk.org/thetechnium/archives/2006/03/civilizations_a.php.

114 See www.kk.org/books/what-technology-wants.php.

115 See www.teebweb.org/Home/tabid/924/Default.aspx.

116 See www.guardian.co.uk/environment/damian-carrington-blog/2011/jun/29/green-economy-biodiversity.

117 John Moir (02011) "An economist for nature calculates the need for more protection", *The New York Times*, 8 August. See www.nytimes.com/2011/08/09/science/09profile.html?pagewanted=all.

118 Danny Fortson (02011) "Palm oil giant battles to save the planet and itself", *Sunday Times*, 21 August.

119 Laurence C. Smith (02011) *The New North: The World in 2050*, Profile Books, London.

120 See http://webarchive.nationalarchives.gov.uk/+/http:/www.hm-treasury.gov.uk/sternreview_index.htm.

121 D. H. Meadows, L. Meadows, J. Randers, and W. W. Behrens (01972) *The Limits to Growth*, Universe Books, New York, NY.

122 D. H. Meadows, L. Meadows, J. Randers, and W. W. Behrens (01972) *The Limits to Growth*, Universe Books, New York, NY.

123 World Commission on Environment and Development (01987) *Our Common Future*, Oxford University Press, Oxford, UK.

124 See www.trumanproject.org/about/mission.

125 See www.gci.ch.

126 See www.thisisecocide.com/general/465/.

127 See www.thisisecocide.com.

128 Tom Zeller, Jr. (02011) "Does climate change drive warfare? A new study suggests it does", www.huffingtonpost.com/2011/08/24/ climate-change-conflict-warfare_n_935406.html.

129 See http://en.wikipedia.org/wiki/Sousveillance.

130 See http://blog.gatlininternational.co.uk/2011/04/26/ the-united-states-army's-net-zero-initiative/.

131 See www.thewip.net/contributors/2008/03/ green_hawks_in_the_pentagon_th.html.

132 See http://en.wikipedia.org/wiki/Skunk_Works.

133 See www.centri.net/smartbunker.

134 See www.foia.cia.gov/2020/2020.pdf.

135 S. Gilbert (02004) *Environmental Warfare and US Foreign Policy: The Ultimate Weapon of Mass Destruction*; see also www.globalresearch.ca/articles/GIL401A.html.

136 See www.thisisecocide.com/theproblem.

137 See www.earth-policy.org/book_bytes/2011/wotech13_ss5.

138 Doris Kearns Goodwin (01995) *No Ordinary Time: Franklin and Eleanor Roosevelt – The Home Front in WWII*, Simon & Schuster, New York, NY.

139 Jeremy Grantham (02011) "Time to wake up: Days of abundant resources and falling prices are over forever", *GMO Quarterly Letter*, April; or see www.gmo.com/websitecontent/JGLetter_ResourceLimitations2_2Q11.pdf and www.gmo.com/websitecontent/JGLetter_Pt2_DangerChildrenatPlay_2Q11.pdf.

140 http://www.foreignaffairs.com/articles/137246/ amory-b-lovins/a-farewell-to-fossil-fuels.

III BREAKING THROUGH

5 The Race to Zero

1 http://en.wikipedia.org/wiki/The_Vagina_Monologues.

2 http://www.vday.org/home.

3 See "TH!NKING in the sun", 24 July 02006, www.johnelkington.com/weblog/2006_07_01_arc.html.

4 John Reed (02011) "Pioneering maker of battery-powered cars fails after futile search for finance", *Financial Times*, 23 June.

5 See www.qualitygurus.com/timeline.

6 See http://asq.org/about-asq/awards/hutchens.html.

7 Shelly F. Fust and Lisa L. Walker (02007) *Corporate Sustainability Initiatives: The Next TQM?*, Korn/Ferry International Executive Insight, Los Angeles.

8 Mike Fraser (02010) "Sustainability as a business practice: The new TQM?", *Sustainable Life Media*, 2 December, www.sustainablelifemedia.com/content/ column/strategy/sustainability_as_business_practice_the_new_tqm.

9   Ram Nidumolu, C. K. Prahalad, and M. R. Rangaswami (02009) "Why sustainability is now the key driver of innovation", *Harvard Business Review*, http://hbr.org/2009/09/why-sustainability-is-now-the-key-driver-of-innovation/ar/1.

10 Philip B. Crosby, Sr. (01985) *An Inadequate Process vs Zero Defects*, Philip Crosby Associates II, Inc., 8 February.

11 See www.epa.gov/lean/studies/3m.htm.

12 See http://en.wikipedia.org/wiki/Six_Sigma.

13 See www.businessweek.com/magazine/content/07_24/b4038406.htm.

14 See http://money.cnn.com/2006/07/10/magazines/fortune/rule4.fortune/index.htm.

15 Robert E. Cole (02011) "What really happened to Toyota?", *MIT Sloan Management Review*, summer, pp.29–35.

16 Email exchange with author, 10 August 02011.

17 Meeting between Yasunori Naito, Zhanna Serdyukova, Olivier Vriesendorp, and author, 5 September 02011.

18 Godert van Hardenbroek, interview with author, 17 August 02011.

19 See www.02.org.

6   Zeronautics 101

1   Lexington column (02011) "China in the mind of America", *The Economist*, 22 January.

2   Ray Anderson (02009) *Confessions of a Radical Industrialist: How Interface Proved that You Can Build a Successful Business without Destroying the Planet*, Random House Business Books, New York, NY.

3   Paul Hawken (01994) *The Ecology of Commerce: A Declaration of Sustainability*, HarperCollins, New York, NY.

4   Cited in Bryan Walsh (02011) "Meet Ray Anderson, the green industrialist", *Time*, 26 April.

5   See www.kk.org/thetechnium/archives/2011/03/radical_optimis.php.

6   See www.kk.org/thetechnium/archives/2006/01/speculations_on.php.

7   SustainAbility (02008) *The Social Intrapreneur: A Field Guide for Corporate Changemakers*, Skoll Foundation, London.

8   Daniel Quinn (01992) *Ishmael: An Adventure in Mind and Spirit*, Bantam/Turner Books, New York, NY.

9   Daniel Aronson, email exchange with author, July 02011.

10 Frans Johansson (02004) *The Medici Effect: What Elephants and Epidemics Can Teach Us about Innovation*, Harvard Business School Press, Boston, MA.

11 Peter Sims (02011) *Little Bets: How Breakthrough Ideas Emerge from Small Discoveries*, Free Press, New York, NY.

12 Richard Florida (02010) *The Great Reset: How New Ways of Living and Working Drive Post-Crash Prosperity*, HarperCollins, New York, NY.

13 "First break all the rules: The charms of frugal innovation", *The Economist*, 15 April 02010.

14 See www.kk.org/newrules/newrules-2.html.

15 See www.shell.com/home/content/environment_society/safety/culture/.

16 See www.sustainablebrands.com/content/column/strategy/
   what%20_is_zero_waste_and_why_should_you_care.
17 See www.andrewwinston.com/books.
18 See www.zwia.org.
19 Helmut Werb (02011) "The future is now", *Adeyaka: Infiniti Magazine*, issue 6; see
   also www.adeyaka.com.
20 See www.hermanmiller.com/Videos/826/0.
21 See http://en.wikipedia.org/wiki/Business_cluster.
22 Michael Porter (01990/01998) *The Competitive Advantage of Nations*, Free Press,
   New York, NY.
23 See http://en.wikipedia.org/wiki/Business_ecosystem.
24 See www.mercurynews.com/green-energy/ci_14224228?nclick_check = 1.
25 See www.cleantech.com/news/5640/top-10-cleantech-clusters.
26 Bryan Walsh (02012) "Red state, green city", *Time*, vol 179, no 2, 16 January.
27 See www.gccassoc.org/www.globalcleantech.org/Home.html.
28 See www.guardian.co.uk/sustainable-business/sustainability-with-john-elkington/
   london-olympics-2012-zero-waste.
29 Maija Palmer (02011) "Data centres fear impact of drive to curb carbon", *Financial
   Times*, 29 August 2011; or see www.ft.com/cms/s/0/cc219a30-cf3b-11e0-b6d4–
   00144feabdc0.html#axzz1nOUahyvE.
30 See www.wwf.org.uk/what_we_do/press_centre/index.cfm?5066.
31 See www.wbcsd.org/vision2050.aspx.

7   It's the System that's Stupid

1 See www.google.co.uk/search?client=safari&rls=en&q=apocalypse+%2B+
   definition&ie=UTF-8&oe=UTF-8&redir_esc = &ei = 5GCpTcDbKM-0hAf6ivnXCQ,
   16 April 02011.
2 See http://paulgilding.com/the-great-disruption.
3 Tom Friedman (02011) "The Earth is full", *The New York Times*, 7 June.
4 Martin Rees (02003) *Our Final Century: The 50/50 Threat to Human Survival*, Basic
   Books, New York, NY.
5 See www.garretthardinsociety.org/articles/art_tragedy_of_the_commons.html.
6 See http://en.wikipedia.org/wiki/Thomas_Robert_Malthus.
7 "Seven billion", *National Geographic*, January 02011.
8 See www.forbes.com/sites/timworstall/2011/10/23/
   un-population-predictions-up-to-15-billion-by-2100/.
9 See www.lifesitenews.com/news/archive/ldn/2008/dec/08121202.
10 See http://en.wikipedia.org/wiki/The_Population_Bomb.
11 See http://en.wikipedia.org/wiki/Zero_population_growth.
12 See http://en.wikipedia.org/wiki/James_Mirrlees.
13 "ZPG – a new movement challenges the U.S. to stop growing", *LIFE Magazine*, 27
   April 01970, p.12ff.
14 See www.nytimes.com/2011/05/04/world/04population.html.
15 See www.guardian.co.uk/world/2011/oct/22/population-world-15bn-2100.
16 Bill Gates (02010) "Reduce child deaths and end overpopulation", *The Times*, 23 October.

17 See www.pda.or.th/eng/index.asp.
18 Lester Brown (02011) *Smart Planning for the Global Family*,
    www.earth-policy.org/book_bytes/2011/wotech11_ss2.
19 See www.economist.com/node/18651512.
20 See www.timesonline.co.uk/tol/money/pensions/article7148161.ece.
21 Pam Belluck (02011) "Contraceptive used in Africa may double risk of H.I.V.", *The New York Times*, 3 October.
22 See http://sermons.logos.com/submissions/94397-Pandemics-Patient-Zero-and-a-Theological-Reflection#content=/submissions/94397.
23 Bill Gates (02010) "Reduce child deaths and end overpopulation", *The Times*, 23 October.
24 Daniel Defoe (01722) *A Journal of the Plague Year*, E. Nutt, London; or see http://en.wikipedia.org/wiki/A_Journal_of_the_Plague_Year.
25 Albert Camus (01947) *La Peste*, Librarie Gallimard, Paris; or see http://en.wikipedia.org/wiki/The_Plague.
26 See http://awesome.good.is/transparency/web/1108/deadliest-pandemics/flat.html.
27 See http://en.wikipedia.org/wiki/Smallpox; this section draws on the Wikipedia entry, dated 16 August 02011.
28 See http://en.wikipedia.org/wiki/Larry_Brilliant.
29 See http://instedd.org/.
30 Alun Anderson (02010) "A fight to the death", *The World in 2011*, The Economist Group, London.
31 See www.gatesfoundation.org/topics/Pages/malaria.aspx.
32 See www.avert.org/origin-aids-hiv.htm.
33 See www.sciencedaily.com/releases/2008/02/080219150146.htm.
34 See http://en.wikipedia.org/wiki/Randy_Shilts.
35 See http://en.wikipedia.org/wiki/Gaëtan_Dugas.
36 See http://en.wikipedia.org/wiki/Index_case.
37 See www.gapminder.org/videos/swine-flu-alert-news-death-ratio-tuberculosis/.
38 See www.reactgroup.org.
39 See http://pharmafutures.org/.
40 "Destination slum", *Fast Company*, December 02010/January 02011.
41 See www.makepovertyhistory.org/.
42 See www.caritas.org/newsroom/press_releases/PressRelease27_01_10.html.
43 See www.un.org/millenniumgoals/11_MDG%20Report_EN.pdf.
44 The Millennium Development Goals (MDGs) were agreed at the UN Millennium Summit in September 02000, with eight targets for reducing extreme poverty and hunger, improving health and education, empowering women, and ensuring environmental sustainability by 02015.
45 John Elkington and Pamela Hartigan (02008) *The Power of Unreasonable People: How Social Entrepreneurs Create Markets that Change the World*, Harvard Business School Press, Boston, MA.
46 See http://en.wikipedia.org/wiki/Bottom_of_the_pyramid.
47 See http://en.wikipedia.org/wiki/Bottom_of_the_pyramid.
48 See www.aflatoun.org.
49 "Et in Aracadia ego", *The Economist*, 29 January 02011.

50 "Inequality: Unbottled gini", *The Economist*, 22 January 02011.

51 James Lamont (02010) "India's boom fails to feed the hungry", *Financial Times*, 23 December.

52 "The rich and the rest", *The Economist*, 22 January 02011.

53 Richard G. Wilkinson and Kate Pickett (02009) *The Spirit Level: Why More Equal Societies Almost Always Do Bette*r, Allen Lane, London.

54 "Banyan: Under water", *The Economist*, 11 December 02010.

55 Amy Kazmin (02010) "Small loan, big savings", *Financial Times*, 2 December.

56 "The best investment", *Time*, 14 February 02011.

57 See www.girleffect.org/question.

58 See www.guardian.co.uk/sustainable-business/sustainability-with-john-elkington/forgetting-sustainability-reporting-integrated.

59 Andrea Spencer-Cooke (02000) "Hero of Zero", *Tomorrow magazine*, vol 10, no 6, pp.10–16.

60 Email exchange with author, 14 August 02011.

61 Telephone conversation with author, 5 July 02011.

62 Michael Braungart and William McDonough (02009) *Cradle to Cradle: Remaking the Way We Make Things*, Vintage Books, London.

63 Interview with author, 13 July 02011; see also www.greenbiz.com/video/2011/06/25/al-halvorsen.

64 See www.nissan-zeroemission.com/EN/index.html.

65 See http://the-planet-zero.com/.

66 See www.guardian.co.uk/sustainable-business/sustainability-with-john-elkington/london-markets-doomed-fail-again.

67 See http://globalzero.tumblr.com/post/8473624855/remembering-hiroshima-and-nagasaki.

68 See http://en.wikipedia.org/wiki/Daigo_Fukuryu_Maru.

69 See http://en.wikipedia.org/wiki/Comprehensive_Nuclear-Test-Ban_Treaty.

70 See www.foreignaffairs.com/articles/23393/thomas-c-schelling/the-role-of-deterrence-in-total-disarmament.

71 Scott D. Sagan and Kenneth N. Waltz (02010) "The great debate: Is nuclear zero the best option?", *The National Interest*, September/October, vol 109, Research Library, pp.88–94.

72 My thanks to Soushiant Zanganehpour for his help in researching the cases for and against nuclear proliferation.

73 Scott D. Sagan and Kenneth N. Waltz (02010) "The great debate: Is nuclear zero the best option?", *The National Interest*, September/October, vol 109, Research Library, pp.88–94.

74 John Elkington (01985) *The Gene Factory: Inside the Biotechnology Business*, Century Publishing Company, London.

75 Robert Harris and Jeremy Paxman (01982) *A Higher Form of Killing: The Secret History of Chemical and Biological Warfare*, Hill and Wang, New York, NY.

76 See www.jeffskollgroup.com.

77 Steven Pinker (02011) *The Better Angels of Our Nature*, Allen Lane, London.

IV BEYOND ZERO

8 Ambassadors from the Future

1   Paul Hawken (01993) *The Ecology of Commerce: A Declaration of Sustainability*, HarperCollins, New York, NY.

2   John Elkington, Charmian Love, and Alastair Morton (02011) *The Future Quotient: 50 Pioneers in Seriously Long-Term Innovation*, Volans and JWT, London.

3   T. S. Eliot (01969/02004) "Four Quartets", in *The Complete Poems and Plays*, Faber & Faber, London.

4   See www.greenpeace.org/international/en/campaigns/toxics/water/detox/.

5   See www.greenpeace.org/international/en/campaigns/toxics/water/detox/intro/.

6   See, for example, the responses from adidas (www.adidas-group.com/en/sustainability/assets/statements/aG_Individual%20Roadmap_November%2018_2011.pdf), H&M (http://about.hm.com/gb/corporateresponsibility/environment/actionplantohelpleadourindustrytozerodischarge__Action_plan_zero_discharge.nhtml), Nike (http://nikeinc.com/news/nike-roadmap-toward-zero-discharge-of-hazardous-chemicals), and Puma (http://about.puma.com/wp-content/themes/aboutPUMA_theme/media/pdf/2011/pumaroadmap.pdf).

7   We know that FQ has a particular meaning in the world of SMS or text messaging, but we decided we could live with that.

8   Adam Spangler (02011) "Can this man save the planet?", *The Wall Street Journal*, 25 August.

9   See www.un.org/News/Press/docs//2011/sgsm13372.doc.htm.

10 See http://en.wikipedia.org/wiki/Tear_down_this_wall!

11 James Lovelock (02001) *Gaia: The Practical Science of Planetary Medicine*, Oxford University Press, US (originally published by Gaia Books, 01991).

12 See www.imdb.com/title/tt0497116/.

13 Ben Marlow (02011) "2021: A Space Power Odyssey", *The Sunday Times*, 28 August.

14 Nicholas Carr (02010) *The Shallows: How the Internet Is Changing the Way We Think, Read and Remember*, Atlantic Books, London.

15 See www.savoryinstitute.com/.

16 See www.mcdonough.com/cradle_to_cradle.htm.

17 See http://biomimicryinstitute.org/.

18 See http://en.wikipedia.org/wiki/Emotional_intelligence.

19 See http://danielgoleman.info/topics/ecological-intelligence/.

20 See www.dni.gov/nic/NIC_2025_project.html and www.dni.gov/nic/special_climate2030.html.

21 Tim Flannery (02010) *Here on Earth: A New Beginning*, Allen Lane, London.

22 See www.weforum.org/news/long-term-investment-faces-increasing-constraints.

23 See http://moneyterms.co.uk/discount-rate/.

24 See www.greenbiz.com/blog/2011/08/11/reimagining-world-was-responsibility.

9   The Zero Countdown – and Beyond

1   See http://en.wikipedia.org/wiki/Richard_Feynman.
2   See www.edwardtufte.com/bboard/q-and-a-fetch-msg?msg_id=0001yB.
3   James Hansen (02009) *Storms of My Grandchildren*, Bloomsbury, London.
4   http://cleantechnica.com/2012/02/06/zero-energy-building-market-to-hit-1-3-trillion-by-2035.

Glossary

1   See http://en.wikipedia.org/wiki/Biomimicry.
2   See http://en.wikipedia.org/wiki/Sustainable_business.

Index